Tyranny, Inc.

Tyranny, Inc.

How Private Power Crushed American

Liberty—and What to Do About It

SOHRAB AHMARI

FORUM

BOOKS

Published in the United States by Forum Books,
an imprint of Random House, a division of Penguin Random
House LLC, New York.

FORUM BOOKS and colophon are registered trademarks
of Penguin Random House LLC.

Library of Congress Cataloging-in-Publication Data
Names: Ahmari, Sohrab, author.
Title: Tyranny, Inc. / by Sohrab Ahmari.
Description: First edition. | New York: Forum Books, 2023. |
Includes bibliographical references and index.
Identifiers: LCCN 2023011959 (print) | LCCN 2023011960 (ebook) |
ISBN 9780593443460 (hardcover) | ISBN 9780593443477 (ebook) |
Subjects: LCSH: Business and politics—United States. |
Corporations—Corrupt practices—United States. |
Corporate power—United States. | Working class—United States. |
Middle class—United States. |
Social responsibility of business—United States. |
United States—Economic conditions—21st century.
Classification: LCC JK467 .A42 2023 (print) | LCC JK467 (ebook) |
DDC 322/.309730905—dc23/eng/20230405
LC record available at https://lccn.loc.gov/2023011959
LC ebook record available at https://lccn.loc.gov/2023011960

Printed in the United States of America on acid-free paper

forumconservativebooks.com

2 4 6 8 9 7 5 3 1

First Edition

Book design by Fritz Metsch

To Adrian, Chad, Gladden, and Patrick

To Seraphina, the other light of my life

And to Hany, with gratitude

Ecce merces operariorum, qui messuerunt regiones vestras, quae fraudata est a vobis, clamat.

—JAMES 5:4

Our barbarians come from above.

—HENRY DEMAREST LLOYD

Contents

Introduction

FOR MORE THAN a decade, defenders of democracy have been issuing a stark warning: The world is in the midst of a "democratic recession,"[1] with no sign of a turnaround on the horizon. Beginning in the 1970s, dozens of societies built on coercion gave way to ones based on consent, most notably after the collapse of the Soviet Union. But since 2005, consent has hit a wall, and coercion has made an unwelcome comeback across much of the world. Many regions are backsliding into authoritarianism, kleptocracy, and ideological dictatorship.

Freedom, in short, is suffering a global funk.

This tragedy has many causes, varying from region to region and country by country: the seductive allure of populist demagogues; the perceived failure of liberal democracy to solve ordinary people's problems; the advent of social media as a tool for spreading misinformation. Whatever the causes, the sum effect is that vast multitudes now labor under the yoke of coercion, in some cases having willingly thrown in their lot with elected despots, from Poland to the Philippines, Hungary to Turkey.

This is an agonizing development for Americans especially. As one group of pro-democracy advocates has written, the yearning for a noncoercive society "is the question at the center of every pivotal moment of American history." That yearning, we believe, is shared by all people. History has taught us, moreover, that America's flourishing is closely bound up with the flourishing of similarly noncoercive societies around the world. When Americans stand with those who believe in freedom, "we elevate those things that we hold most dear—an equitable, just, peaceful, prosperous, and healthy planet."[2]

To grasp the severity of the problem, consider three pieces of news from around the world, selected from among a mountain of similar stories.

OUR FIRST STORY takes us to the People's Republic of China, whose Communist regime inarguably poses the gravest threat to human freedom in our time. In the spring of 2020, the height of the COVID-19 pandemic, Zhang Ming, a meatpacker at a massive slaughterhouse on the outskirts of Nanjing, had had enough.

The state-owned company subjects its two thousand or so workers to a digital panopticon, using pervasive closed-circuit cameras and GPS to track their every movement. Managers, who ultimately answer to Communist Party bosses, make no bones about the purpose: to stoke a culture of fear, reminding workers that the government is continually monitoring them. Failing to meet production quotas or "wasting the people's time" results in docked pay, forcing many workers to forgo lunch and even bathroom breaks.

At the outset of the pandemic, Chinese demand for food products skyrocketed. Public authorities identified slaughterhouses as "essential" enterprises, and management began ordering employees to put in ever-longer shifts, without regard for the risk of viral contagion. It was that cavalier attitude that prompted Zhang to take action. One day in April, he led a walkout of his colleagues. Their demand was reasonable: They called simply for the complex to be temporarily closed and more stringently sanitized, because several workers had become sick.

Zhang was terminated from his job that very day. His actions had been "immoral, unacceptable, and arguably illegal," wrote the company's general counsel, Liu Wei, in an internal memo characterizing Zhang as a useful tool in its ongoing plan to tarnish dissident workers. Voicing dissent at a state-owned firm in the People's Republic, never exactly easy, could now be framed as a sanitary threat and a violation of Chinese law.

When foreign reporters caught whiff of the story, the slaughterhouse insisted it had done nothing wrong. Dismissing the notion that many employees were aggrieved by the slaughterhouse's handling of the pandemic, a spokeswoman pointed out that "the vast majority" continue to show up every day and do "heroic work," helping feed the Chinese people amid a once-in-a-century crisis. Zhang, meanwhile, remains unemployed as of this writing. The regime continues to silence internal dissidents and to ferociously resist efforts to organize workers.

THEN THERE IS Russia, where Vladimir Putin maintains a choke hold on a population battered by his unjust foreign wars and a corrupt government dominated by well-connected oligarchs. To lend his misrule a veneer of popular legitimacy, the Russian strongman has turned to the dictator's playbook, mandating popular attendance at pro-regime and pro-war rallies, or else face financial punishment by the state.

In the summer of 2022, for example, while Russia's armed forces were prosecuting a barbarous war against Ukraine, thousands of employees of Gazprom, the state-run energy company, were told that they had to attend Putin's speech at the firm's headquarters in St. Petersburg—or to take the day off without pay. The *Novaya Gazeta,* one of the few reformist outlets still permitted to operate in the country, reported that a Gazprom contractor sent a memo to the company's employees informing them that attendance was "not mandatory." Yet the memo made clear that only employees who arrived at the hours-long event would receive pay: "NO QR SCAN AT THE ENTRANCE, NO PAY."

The purpose of the event was to celebrate "Russia's energy dominance," but Putin seized the opportunity to bash the Ukrainian government and its NATO allies, saying, "The West and its lapdogs in Kiev tout free speech, but try criticizing how the Ukrainians treat our Russian-speaking people over there!" All of this at an event sponsored by the Kremlin and funded by Russian taxpayers.

According to the *Novaya Gazeta*, employees were warned that they needed to maintain decorum during the president's visit. "No yelling, shouting, protesting or anything viewed as resistance will be tolerated at the event," the internal memo read. A Gazprom spokesperson told journalists that the Putin speech was no different from when the company invites famous Russian athletes to share "inspirational messages" with workers. Yet the element of intimidation was unmistakable: Failure to attend meant forgoing overtime wages otherwise built into employees' ordinary workweeks—a penalty that only a handful of workers were prepared to tolerate, given the dire economic conditions in Putin's Russia. Nearly 95 percent attended the speech, per the *Novaya Gazeta*.

FINALLY, THERE IS my native Iran, whose ruling regime has spent the last decade strengthening its arsenal of medieval repression with a vast digital-surveillance apparatus. Consider the fate of Abdollah Pourmoradi, a member of the Basij militia in central Iran, who in the spring of 2019 found himself out of a job and socially ostracized after messages mocking his superiors were found in his personal email account.

As a junior-level database analyst for the militia, Pourmoradi was permitted to access his personal accounts on his Basij device. Little did he know, however, that his commanders had installed keylogger software on his computer that recorded everything he typed. It's an "all-too-common tactic deployed by dictatorships to catch thought crimes and to entrap members of unpopular minorities," a program director for Amnesty International told *USA Today*.

Using this software, the militia commanders acquired Pourmoradi's email password to access his account. Soon, his superiors were viewing, forwarding, and discussing among themselves some of his email messages, including ones in which he mildly ribbed one commander for being overweight and another for regularly missing his prayers, though "he likes to make a big show of his piety in public."

In May that year, Pourmoradi discovered that his commanders had been accessing his email account for several months. When he confronted them about it, they accused him of displaying a pattern of "un-Islamic behavior in his online conduct" and dishonorably discharged him—an outcome that carries great stigma in the Islamic Republic. As the Amnesty official noted, getting fired from the powerful militia can be an "economic death sentence" in Iran, since terminated employees of the state security apparatus are barred from unemployment benefits and frequently struggle to obtain new jobs.

Fake, and All Too Real

As some readers likely gathered by the third story, none of these things took place in foreign lands. All three recount developments in the United States, with the fact patterns lightly altered to shift the backdrops to China, Russia, and Iran. I borrowed the language of my fake-but-real news stories, almost verbatim, from actual reporting about events that transpired in America.

Transposed abroad, these events fit comfortably into Western narratives about foreign dictatorship and domestic liberty: We are used to thinking of repression as something done "over there," by tyrannical systems that lack checks and balances like our own. But when we stop thinking about things in such geographic terms and focus, instead, on *who* is meting out the coercion, we reach a discomfiting new understanding: that coercion is far more widespread in supposedly noncoercive societies than we would like to think— provided we pay attention to *private power* and admit the possibility of *private coercion*.

Let's reexamine each story in turn.

It isn't a government-owned Chinese slaughterhouse that uses a digital panopticon to surveil its workers, punishing them for even minor lapses and forcing many to forgo bathroom breaks.[3] And it

wasn't a Chinese slaughterhouse that terminated a worker for leading a walkout at the height of the pandemic over the employer's
careless attitude toward the coronavirus.

No, that would be Amazon, the e-conglomerate founded by Jeff
Bezos. The real "Zhang Ming" is named Christian Smalls, an ex-
worker at Amazon's JFK8 warehouse facility on New York's Staten
Island.

During the first week of March 2020, according to *The New York
Times*, Smalls "began to notice various colleagues coming to work
seeming unwell: fatigued, lightheaded, nauseous." He went to human
resources, which "told him that the company was following guide-
lines established by the Centers for Disease Control and Prevention
and that there were no confirmed cases of Covid-19 at the warehouse."[4]

Reasonably concerned for his and his family's health, the then-
thirty-one-year-old Smalls took several days off without pay, draw-
ing cash from his paltry retirement fund to make ends meet. A few
weeks later, a colleague caught the novel coronavirus but was told
by HR to keep the news on the quiet. That's when Smalls "made it
his mission to disseminate information about cases of Covid-19 at
the warehouse."[5]

Then he led his walkout—an act for which Amazon fired him.
The e-tailer's general counsel described Smalls, who is African American, as "not smart or articulate," according to internal memos.[6]
This, from the same company that a few months later would elbow
its way to the forefront of corporate America's Black Lives Matter
activism in the wake of George Floyd's killing in Minneapolis.

Since his firing, Smalls has fought to organize the eight thousand
workers at JFK8, despite relentless anti-union activity typical of the
firm, including "confiscating pro-union pamphlets [organizers] left
in the break room" and "surveilling where they congregated on a
sidewalk," according to the *Times*.[7]

As for the story about energy workers required to attend a speech
by Vladimir Putin—that, too, happened in the United States, not the

Russian Federation. Substitute Shell for Gazprom, Donald Trump for Putin, and Monaca, Pennsylvania, for St. Petersburg, and you more or less have the real story. Yes, American workers in the twenty-first century can be forced to attend a presidential speech at the risk of losing regular and overtime pay.[8]

It's part of a broader pattern of compelled political activity at work that implicates both sides of the political spectrum. Many of the more typically progressive diversity, equity, and inclusion ideologies promoted by HR departments, after all, compel workers into taking one side in debates about hot-button topics over which reasonable Americans disagree. American Express, Disney, and CVS Health Corporation, for example, are but a few of the many megacorporations that "train" workers to accept controversial progressive precepts on race and gender, with one Disney diversity consultant going so far as to explicitly denounce Republican elected officials in Florida in a captive-audience setting in 2021.[9]

Finally, the keystroke-tracking story took place not in Iran in 2019 but in Indianapolis in 2009. Its real-life protagonist was Lisa Rene, an employee of the retailer G. F. Fishers. "Without informing company employees," a Brookings Institution report noted, "the firm installed keylogger software on the store's computers which recorded characters typed on the business machines and periodically emailed that information to supervisors."[10]

Using the software, supervisors gained access to Rene's personal email and banking passwords and began spying on her private life. Once Rene figured out what was happening, she confronted her supervisors, who then "falsely documented poor performance by Rene for the purpose of terminating her employment," according to a federal district court's summary of her subsequent legal complaint.[11]

The parties eventually settled the suit. Yet as the Brookings analysis explains, in most instances in the United States, if "the monitoring takes place in office workplaces, on company devices, or over firm networks, there aren't many limits on what organizations can do." Video surveillance, location tracking, web browsing, email, and social media use—all are fair game. Workers must accept such snooping as part of the price of earning a paycheck in twenty-first-century America.[12]

The Invisible, Unnameable System

If China treated workers the way Amazon does, if the Kremlin forced them to attend speeches by Putin, and if the Iranian regime subjected individuals to near-total surveillance, Americans would be outraged. Our State Department would reproach the governments in question, Congress would hold hearings, and Western NGOs would highlight the plight of the victims in glossy fundraising campaigns.

In fact, the West's global democracy-promotion organs do these kinds of things all the time. Groups like the Washington-based Freedom House rank world governments on how "free" or "unfree" they are. Republican and Democratic administrations routinely chide foreign countries over their coercive practices, in areas ranging from elections to family law to business climate. And ordinary people of all political stripes don't hesitate to name the relationship between abusive regimes and their citizenry: tyranny.

Yet here in the United States, another form of tyranny has taken root. We haven't quite given a name to it, much less honed political or legal defenses against it, because it involves private coercion in the workplace and the marketplace. This tyranny subjugates us not as citizens but as employees and consumers, members of the class of people who lack control over most of society's productive and financial assets. It is the structural cause behind much of our daily anxiety: the fear that we are utterly dispensable at work, that we are one illness or other personal mishap away from a potential financial disaster. Yet even to speak of private, economic tyranny *as tyranny* challenges some of our society's most fundamental assumptions.

Tyranny, according to the prevailing view, is the threat posed to freedom by the machinery of the modern state: by presidents, prime ministers, lawmakers, judges, prosecutors, law enforcers, intelligence professionals, military officers, regulators, and myriad other elected and unelected officials. Tyranny, then, can only be a public, governmental thing.

The opposite of this public realm, with its potential for abuse, is the private sector, a zone of freedom. We associate private action with economic dynamism, market competition, individual choice, and general spontaneity. The private is that which we try to protect from the attempted power grabs of would-be strongmen. It is the most noncoercive domain of our generally noncoercive regime. True, individual private actors might do abusive things, but in those rare cases we can trust that the authorities will take steps to combat them.

But what if the prevailing view is mistaken? We come face-to-face with that bleak possibility only occasionally: when we find our political viewpoints censored on the internet, for example, and there is no appealing the algorithm citing "Terms of Service" that are at once more ironclad and more obscure than any federal regulation; or when we receive a surprise $3,750 bill for an X-ray procedure ("I have insurance," we insist, but our protests are dismissed: "Yes, but your plan didn't cover *emergency* procedures, only routine X-rays").

Who enacted these laws and regulations? How come we didn't get any say in the process? Like glitches in the Matrix, moments like these briefly reveal a social program that encodes the economic power of private interests and entities. Some end up spending years of their lives repairing the consequences of a "glitch"; others never recover.

For most of us, however, the breach is soon healed, and we go back to telling ourselves soothing tales about the nature of the system. No, no, we insist, the private realm is deeply divided, and this means it can't become a zone of tyranny. Countless individual actors, all pursuing their own private ends, often at cross-purposes, compete every day in marketplaces of goods, labor, services, and ideas. The very diversity and sheer number of these various entities

ensure that no single one could emerge as a tyrant among them—
that is, until, again for example, we find that the apartment we used
to rent from a mom-and-pop landlord is now owned by a distant
hedge fund, and repairs and amenities are fast deteriorating.

Still, we think, even the mightiest private actors can't coerce us on
pain of jail time or worse. CEOs and tech titans generally don't have
their own police forces or armies. At the end of the day, no one can
force you to do anything without your consent. Or so we tell ourselves. So we have been led to believe, at least since the heyday of
Ronald Reagan, who taught that "the nine most terrifying words in
the English language are: 'I'm from the government, and I'm here to
help.'"[13] Nor has the left been entirely immune to such thinking.
Now that corporations champion culturally liberal causes, some
progressives outdo the most ardent Reaganites in defense of private
enterprise's right to do as it pleases.

We have succumbed to a generational effort, mounted by some of
the world's wealthiest individuals, most powerful corporations, and
their ideologues for hire, to make us forget what used to be taken for
granted: that private actors can imperil freedom just as much as overweening governments; that unchallenged market power can impair
our rights and liberties; that there *are* finally such things as private
tyrannies and private tyrants.

We have lost sight of these simple truths and paid a heavy price,
for private tyranny precisely describes the world we inhabit today: a
system that allows the asset-owning few to subject the asset-less
many to pervasive coercion—coercion that, unlike governmental actions, can't be challenged in court or at the ballot box. In other
words, it's a game of power politics in which one side lacks the
power to play while the other side is structurally set up to win.

It is no longer a potential threat but a lived reality. Many of us
intuit this. *Something* has gone wrong with democracy, yet it is hard
to put our finger on it. Our most profitable companies are very
good at delivering certain types of "experiences": mainly, instanta-
neity of all kinds (be it for food delivery or porn). But the kaleido-

scopic novelty somehow coexists with shockingly decrepit public infrastructure—the public services and facilities that supply the necessities of life and allow us to get around, stay healthy, and live in community. All this, while a relatively narrow elite lords over a class hierarchy whose obscene disparities would have left the plutocrats of the Gilded Age blushing.

Defenders of today's arrangements insist we got here through our democratic choices, by consent. But who consented to all this? "Consent" is the fig leaf covering over the sheer power of private individuals and entities to coerce us as consumers, workers, and citizens. As consumers of digital products and services, we "consent" to Tolstoy-length user agreements that few of us bother to read, that are nonnegotiable, and that limit our rights against the seller. When something goes wrong, we seek help. But the chatbot doesn't quite understand what we need, and there is no human *someone* to appeal to beyond the app. Products that met our needs perfectly well suddenly become inaccessible without an upgrade, and there is no appealing the sudden change.

When we are hired for a job, we "consent" to the employment agreement and thereby give our bosses power to control our lives inside and outside the workplace. The employment contract increasingly subjects our "private" lives to regulation—for example, by opening up our personal devices to surveillance—with termination being the price we must pay for pushing back.

Which one person or party can we blame for all this? Who is the bad guy here? No one in particular. We inhabit supposedly noncoercive democracies that are in reality shot through with coercion. But because the coercion is meted out by myriad self-seeking private actors, it eludes normal democratic mechanisms, making it impossible for us to contest who gets to coerce us, for which purposes, and against what limits.

We can't identify one single villain or group of villains in the tragic story of how we ended up here. Tyranny, Inc., has no figure comparable to Nero or Stalin. That, too, is of the nature of the system. Even so, today's private tyranny does substantially benefit some classes—asset owners and the top managers who service their assets—at the expense of others. To truly understand private tyranny, then, we must do more than discern its existence and scale. We must also unmask the structural, class-based domination that gives purpose to the system.

The book you hold does both. In these pages, we first explore how we lost the ability to spot private tyranny. Next, we embark on a grand tour of our system, making stops at the workplace, the employment contract, the courtroom, the investment fund, the retirement system, the newsroom, and the bankruptcy process. At each stop, we will see how a failure to subject the market to sufficient political control and democratic give-and-take has imperiled the livelihoods of millions of ordinary Americans while damaging our economy and the common good.

We will see, moreover, how the general tendency of Tyranny, Inc., is the domination of working- and middle-class people by the owners of capital, the asset-less by the asset rich. Conflicts between classes are as old as human societies. But our system tends to move these conflicts out of the public and into the private sphere, where, we are told, our expectations of due process, checks and balances, democratic deliberation, and the like don't apply. The more the private swells in size—the more we privatize public services and treat the "investment and business climate" as our sole criterion of the common good—the harder it becomes to challenge Tyranny, Inc.

Our tour isn't comprehensive by any means. While there are many other instances of private tyranny racking Western societies, our focus is on abuses we are less likely to notice, rather than those that appear on the front pages (our opening cases are the exception in this sense). This act of noticing is the first step in resisting private tyranny. When we notice class domination being carried out by supposedly nonpolitical means, we can begin to push back. We can insist that economic activity isn't and shouldn't be divorced from justice, fair play, checks and balances, and other principles we associate with a decent political order.

That, as we will see in the book's final chapters, is how we begin to reverse the tide of private tyranny: by insisting that the market exchanges be subjected to political give-and-take, the power of the asset-rich few met by the countervailing power of the asset-less many. That was how our grandparents brought about the prosperous three decades that followed World War II, and we still, to a degree, benefit from their successes, even as the forces of private tyranny have taken the upper hand in our time.

For younger Americans inheriting a much less prosperous and equitable economy, the stakes couldn't be higher. Tyranny, Inc., has drained the vigor and substance out of democracy, facilitated massive upward transfers of wealth, and left ordinary people feeling isolated and powerless. Tyranny does indeed beset freedom—right here, in the land of the free.

Tyranny, Inc.

I

The Rise of Private Tyranny

IT'S A FAVORITE pastime of Americans, and American conservatives especially, to keep watch for various evildoers scheming to seize the public sphere and rob us of our historic liberties. But it's the private sphere that occupies most of our time on earth. It's where we toil, shop, socialize, and increasingly try to make ourselves heard. We tend to be much less vigilant toward the threats we face in that sphere.

It wasn't ever thus. Our Founding Fathers showed a keen awareness of how class interests might undo our highest ideals about liberty and checks and balances, even if they couldn't foresee the magnitude of the problem today, writing as they were before the Industrial Revolution's consequences had fully unfolded.[1] Once the young republic of yeoman farmers gave way to an industrial powerhouse, it forced generations of American thinkers and statesmen to consider national ideals in light of material reality: What could "liberty" mean when chasmic gaps divided workers and their bosses, grasping small-time entrepreneurs and huge trusts? Would "limited government" necessarily yield a society free from coercion amid such eye-watering inequalities?

Elite recognition of the painful gaps between ideal and reality, combined with pressure exerted by mass movements for labor and civil rights, culminated in a set of reforms in the twentieth century aimed at empowering the economically powerless. These reforms—

chiefly, the New Deal—were sometimes half-formed and haltingly implemented. Even so, they gathered a great deal of prestige and became the subject of bipartisan consensus in the immediate postwar decades.

More recently, and for reasons we will explore in depth much later in this book, these reforms have been undone partially or in full. In many ways, we have returned to the conditions of the pre-reform nineteenth century, characterized by vast disparities in power between the wealthy few and the asset-less many. Accompanying this material regression has been an intellectual one: The critical traditions of economic realism that gave rise to the previous century's reforms have faded from memory and been replaced by today's vacuous political rhetoric.

To wrap our minds around Tyranny, Inc., let alone begin to resist it, we first have to recover a richer understanding of both tyranny and liberty. We also need a more sophisticated account of coercion and of the distinction between public and private. We will find that understanding by turning to a quartet of pathbreaking thinkers, one a medieval Italian jurist, the other three belonging firmly to the American tradition of legal and political thought.

Tyrannies Awful and Monstrous

Picture a monster: a humanoid creature with a shrunken head held aloft on a wobbly neck, and several other, Hydra-like heads growing all over its body, snapping their fangs at each other and periodically biting into the body, gnawing on muscle and sinew and biting into the veins. Like leeches, the extra heads grow fat at the expense of their prey, but without killing the creature—not right away, at any rate. The creature survives, groaning and hobbling under the weight.

A horrific image, isn't it? This monster was how the great medieval Italian jurist Bartolus of Saxoferrato pictured private tyranny. Though he didn't use that term, it is to him that we owe one of the earliest and most prescient accounts of such a system.

It was the early fourteenth century, a time of relentless military skirmishes and palace intrigue among dozens of major and minor principalities throughout Italy. Multiple factional lines divided Italian elites, the most important of which was allegiance to the pope or the Holy Roman emperor in the epoch-defining conflict between the two. Subduing the peninsula proved impossible for pontiff and emperor alike, with the result that these two centers of supreme power often found themselves acting like mere Italian factions. Adding to the chaos, the pope had decamped for Avignon, France, early in the century and became something of a proxy for the French king. True, it was in this era that city-states such as Florence flourished as centers of art and commerce, spurring rapid economic development and urbanization and setting the stage for the Renaissance. But that vibrancy did little to ameliorate the political topsy-turvy that characterized Bartolus's Italy.

What manner of regime was this?

Classical political theory going back to Aristotle had identified six regime types—three good ones and three bad. There could be rule by the many in which the majority seeks the common good, its evil corollary being rule by a selfish and immoral mob. Likewise, a small ruling clique could aim for the good of the whole, or it could oppress the people for its own advantage. Finally, power could be vested in a good king who sees himself duty-bound to serve the common good, or in a single evil man who seeks to enrich himself, the tyrant.[2]

What matters in this for our purposes is the notion that political democracy alone doesn't automatically inoculate us against tyranny. A political system can formally guarantee majority rule and yet still end up oppressing the majority. In discerning whether a particular regime is tyrannical, the classical tradition asks us to pay attention to substance as well as form.

So far, so familiar. But, said Bartolus, "there is a seventh mode of government, *the worst one*, which now exists in the city of Rome" (he meant Italy as a whole). "Throughout the different regions there, there are many tyrants there so strong that one [can]not prevail against the other." The central power is "so weak that it cannot [prevail] against any of the tyrants, nor against anyone adhering to the tyrants, except only so far as they allow it."[3]

Aristotle, Bartolus noted, hadn't brought up this seventh form, "and fittingly so, for it is a monstrous thing."[4] For the ordinary Italian in the fourteenth century, it meant that he was constantly vulnerable to the whims of now this would-be potentate, now that ambitious count, selfish figures who loomed much larger in his life than either the distant emperor or the pope: It was the upstart tyrant who could suddenly shake up settled order, impose new and onerous taxes, or plunge the region into armed conflict. For Bartolus, it was this chaos and instability that made the seventh form of government especially "monstrous."

Bartolus kept his discourse brief, yet he gave us much to work with in attempting to define our own situation seven centuries later. Two points especially stand out.

First, note that private tyranny, as Bartolus described it, doesn't mean the absence of a central, public authority. The monstrous body *does* have a head. But it is a weak head; it exercises *some* directive or purposive role over the whole, but not vigorously enough to tame the extra heads—that is, the private tyrants.

Think back to our opening case: It was state governments that declared some retailers, but not others, "essential," permitting Amazon to demand long hours from workers at a time when COVID-19 mitigation was poorly understood while arbitrarily restricting the operations of many small businesses. As we will see throughout this book, public authorities are part of the operation of private tyrannies—including, crucially, in their refusal to regulate market activity.

Second, and relatedly, the weakness of the central head doesn't necessarily lie in its total incapacity. Under the system of private tyranny, public authority might indeed possess vast powers in *some areas.* That's certainly true of today's U.S. government, with its behemoth scope and tremendous war-making and surveillance technologies. The weakness of the central head has rather to do with its corruptibility and its failure to stand independently for the good of the whole body. What we will encounter throughout this book are potent state authorities prone to capture by narrow, private cliques and class interests at the expense of society as a whole.

What Freedom Means

To summarize so far: Classical political philosophy taught that majority rule, without other characteristics of good government such as justice and independence, isn't enough to forestall tyranny. But there are other concepts that demand greater realism than our discourse usually affords them—above all, liberty.

America's founding enshrined liberty as the highest aspiration of our political community. It's a noble commitment, but one that has also given rise to an enduring myth: that there is such a thing as liberty in general. The Constitution's preamble speaks of "We the People" setting out to "secure the blessings of liberty." But it leaves it up to us to notice that in a modern economy the interests of some segments of "We the People" are opposed to those of other segments.

Too often, we fail to notice this. Instead, we treat liberty as a bundle of abstract rights that attaches to each person from birth. Prior to the Civil War, African Americans were thought to have been born without the bundle. The "right" of slavers and slaveholders completely overrode their victims' right to live free from constant terror and to be compensated for their labor. Later, under Jim Crow, the "right" of white southerners to maintain racial purity and privilege came at the expense of black Americans' access to public facilities, among other fundamental rights. Even today, our tendency to define liberty as an abstract bundle of rights that attaches to some people, usually based on their ability to make autonomous choices, risks leaving out many members of the human family, such as unborn children, those with intellectual disabilities, and the elderly at the twilight of their lives.[5]

In the case of the brazen racial power dynamics of yesteryear, we recognize that liberty is always borne out in the relationship between individuals or groups of people, never a freestanding abstraction. The American philosopher and educator John Dewey crisply articulated this point in an influential essay published in 1935. "If one wants to know what the condition of liberty is at a given time," he wrote, "one has to examine what persons *can* do and what they *cannot* do."[6] That is to say, liberty is ultimately about power: You, as an employee, might be free to tell me, your oppressive employer, to "take this job and shove it." But your ability to make good on this threat—and survive physically afterward—depends on the relative power of employers and employees in a given labor market. Or put another way, your freedom to resist that bully boss or to quit that woefully underpaying job is a function of the power differential between bosses and employees at a given time and place.

The relational nature of liberty flows from this. When one group or class demands greater liberties than it currently possesses, it frequently means a reduction in the power of a different group. The liberty of one always implies restrictions on another's. Consider speech. In theory, an NBC exec and a low-income single mom living in the shadow of Rockefeller Center have equal speech *rights*. In practice, the distribution of speech *power* between the two classes is decidedly unequal: The network-news corporation can broadcast its policy preferences to many millions, while the mom can disseminate hers to 215 friends on Facebook (where, incidentally, another megacorporation has the power to censor her views when they violate ever-shifting norms against "disinformation").

How did today's unequal distribution of liberty come about? At the dawn of the liberal age, in the eighteenth and early nineteenth centuries, Dewey observed, political and intellectual leaders believed that the only things threatening liberty were the remnants of feudal authority: aristocrats with inherited privileges, established churches, and so on. But then came the Industrial Revolution, which gave liberty of action to those particular natural endowments and individuals that fitted into the new economic picture. Above all, the Industrial Revolution gave scope to the abilities involved in acquiring property and to the employment of that wealth in further acquisitions. The employment of these specialized acquisitive abilities has resulted in the monopoly of power in the hands of the few to control the opportunities of the wide masses and to limit their free activities in realizing their natural capacities.[7]

And then a new ideology of "liberty" emerged to legitimate this reality: Western societies, America's especially, came to identify liberty with "unrestrained individualistic action in the economic sphere, under the institutions of capitalistic finance," and this proved "as fatal to the realization of liberty for all as it is fatal to the realization of equality."[8] In theory, anyone was "free" to start a prosperous business; in reality, the manufacturing economy raised huge barriers to entry against newcomers. The fiction took hold that there is no tension between the liberty of employer and that of employee, of hedge fund owner and of fixed-income retiree, of monopolistic tech giant and of individual consumer or small business. But real-life conditions revealed an economy in which asset owners used economic and state power to stack the deck in their favor.

Coercion: Or, the Myth of the Economic Robinson Crusoe

"Coercion" is a common term freighted with great stigma in liberal societies. To be coerced, after all, means to be threatened to do something (or not do something). That is how governments treat criminals and taxpayers and people who double-park their cars. But, we insist, coercion has no place in most other circumstances. Blackmail is illegal for a reason. And the market, by its very nature, is free from such coercion. Because there are a multitude of competing buyers and sellers in any given market, the thinking goes, no one of them can bully others. Everyone is free to walk away and find a better deal elsewhere.

That last point—that market exchange is free from coercion and, indeed, offers the only true alternative to it—is practically dogma among mainstream free-market economists. Milton Friedman, one of the architects of our current economic order, famously made the case in the opening pages of his 1962 bestseller, *Capitalism and Freedom.* "Fundamentally," he declared, "there are only two ways of co-ordinating the economic activities of millions. One is central direction involving the use of coercion—the technique of the army and of the modern totalitarian state. The other is voluntary co-operation of individuals—the technique of the market place."[9]

Friedman pictured society as "a collection of Robinson Crusoes," with each household trading its own surplus with other households to obtain goods and services it needs. Of course, none of the households is obligated to trade. Each has the option to produce "directly for itself" instead, with the result that "no exchange will take place unless both parties do benefit from it." My household can enjoy the apples we grow, but if we want peanuts or soap or meat, we had better trade our extra apples with households that produce these other goods. *Et voilà:* "Co-operation is thereby achieved without coercion."[10]

Note the allusion here to Daniel Defoe's classic novel of shipwreck and island survival. It's a revealing choice of literary metaphor: The precondition for Friedman's free-trading, supposedly noncoercive economy seems to be a rupture with the ordinary course of civilization. A less idealistic observer would point out that *that* indeed was how our flesh-and-blood ancestors experienced the rise of market society: a painful and often literal dislocation of settled ways of life as European peasants and indigenous peoples alike were forced off their lands and herded into modern labor markets, in all their Dickensian cruelty and squalor.[11]

The bigger point is that Friedman's account of his (shipwrecked) utopia is just that: a fantasy. Save perhaps for informal markets in cigarettes and Red Cross rations that emerge in POW camps, the real world presents few "pure," Crusoe-style markets of the kind extolled by Friedman and used to demonstrate free-market theories in Econ 101 textbooks.[12] But even there, coercion is a permanent feature of the transaction, even if this isn't always readily apparent.

This was the great insight of the Columbia University legal scholar Robert Hale, which he articulated four decades before Friedman published *Capitalism and Freedom*. It is to Hale we must turn to get a proper understanding of coercion—and a more realistic appreciation of its true extent in ostensibly noncoercive societies.

In Hale's time, apologists for the existing state of private domination—they styled themselves laissez-faire "individualists" back then—dismissed calls for reform. The 1929 stock market crash and the Depression were still a few years away, yet already there were signs that unrestrained economic power was leading to gross material inequalities and brewing social turmoil. Yet the laissez-faire individualists claimed that any government intervention in the economy would be an intolerable intrusion into a zone otherwise characterized by free choice.

They held that government should stick strictly to raising revenues, controlling the border, enforcing contracts, protecting property, providing basic law and order, regulating monopoly prices, and caring for the "feeble-minded." And nothing else. Americans would suffer "but little coercion from such a government," and "none at all at the hands of other individuals or groups" (in Hale's summary of the individualist view).[13]

Hale didn't buy it. In a highly influential 1923 review of an individualist tract, he set out to show that "the systems advocated by the professed upholders of laissez-faire are in reality permeated with coercive restrictions": above all, the power of those who control most of society's assets to make others do their bidding—or go hungry. Indeed, Hale insisted, coercion as such is inevitable in any kind of society, and it undergirds many of the rights, relationships, and transactions that give rise to the modern economy.[14]

Consider private property rights. These, Hale argued, are about far more than owners' rights to keep intruders off their land or out of their factory. They also permit the owner to "remove the legal duty under which the non-owner labors with respect to the owner's property"—an admittedly legalistic way of saying that the factory owner can tell the worker, "Do what I tell you, or you're fired." That is, the factory owner can force the non-owner—that is, his worker—to obey him on pain of not getting paid. And then how will the worker eat? "There is a law which forbids him to eat any of the food which actually exists in the community—and that law is the law of property."

Workers can sometimes coerce owners, Hale granted, by threatening to quit or work for someone else. But as Hale noted, and as we shall see throughout this book, the worker's supposedly reciprocal power is far more narrow and limited in the actually existing economy than it is in laissez-faire theory.[15]

Private property rights also grant the factory owner coercive power over customers. If the latter want his product, they have to pay the price he demands, much as they are required to pay the government tax if they want tobacco. True, as with workers, customers also enjoy a measure of power to coerce the owner, by threatening to purchase the same product from a different owner, assuming there is a different owner willing to sell.[16] And to be clear, Hale didn't think that every instance of consumer coercion is immoral. His point, rather, was simply to show that there *is* a subtle coercion inherent in all of these relationships.

The factory owner coerces his workers (and sometimes vice versa). The owner coerces his customers (and sometimes they return the favor). The government likewise coerces the customers, insofar as it levies taxes on the factory's products. Why then, asked Hale, are Americans so reluctant to call the first two relationships coercive, but don't hesitate to use the *c*-word with respect to the third?

Two factors are in play. One is that our laws proscribe certain forms of outright coercion between private actors. If you warn a bank teller that her children will be tortured unless she empties the vault and hands you the money, you will soon face the business end of the criminal justice system. But this leads us to discount the coercive nature of many other interactions that are perfectly legal.

The second factor is that these other, legal instances of coercion are so humdrum we dare not concede their true character. Very few people consciously tell themselves upon accepting a job offer, "I am now subjecting myself to my new boss's power to coerce me for much of my waking life." More common is, "This job will pay my bills," or even, "I'm embarking on a new career adventure!"

A disturbing paradox results: Precisely because Americans treat coercion as an aberration, a four-letter word, we fail to notice the coercion that envelops us in the course of our routine economic activities.

The language we use to describe ordinary interactions, Hale pointed out, often obscures the reality of coercion. Take "threat" and "promise." We take it as a coercive *threat* when someone warns us that he will do something bad to us or our property unless we pay him: "You better pay us, if you don't want your car smashed." Yet the obverse—"We will cover the cost of the damage to your vehicle, unless you fail to pay the premium and deductible"—is taken as a *promise.* Yet functionally, threat and promise are more alike than we might otherwise figure.

Peer behind these linguistic tricks and the taboo built around coercion, Hale wrote, and it becomes clear that the "income of each person in the community depends on the relative strength of his power of coercion, offensive and defensive." Indeed, the economic concept of "productivity rests precisely on such private coercion": "It is measured . . . by the extent to which production would fall off if one left and if the marginal laborer were put in his place—by the extent, that is, to which the execution of his threat of withdrawal would damage the employer."[17]

When we notice the prevalence of economic coercion, we are also suddenly confronted with the shocking power imbalance between asset owners and everyone else. The market economy isn't made up of billions of Robinson Crusoes trading their surpluses, cooperating happily without coercion. In reality, a relatively few people hold the power to lend or invest their surplus funds for *interest* (or not), to lease their real property for *rent* (or not), to put their farms or factories to productive use for *profit* (or not). Most others have only the power to sell their labor and subject themselves to the coercion of the owner class—or to withhold labor and risk odds of survival as steep as those faced by the famous literary shipwreck.

This was *the* problem that animated the socialist left going back to the nineteenth century, yet in the decades after the Industrial Revolution the same imbalance vexed conservative leaders like the British prime minister Benjamin Disraeli and President Theodore Roosevelt. Seeing the economy as it really is was in those days a conservative virtue. Hale, no starry-eyed idealist, observed how "this power [of employers over employees] is frequently highly centralized, with the result that the worker is frequently deprived, during working hours and even beyond, of all choice over his own activities":[18] a crisis that was especially troubling at a time when, in the name of "liberty," courts blocked even mild reforms aimed at limiting the hours workers could be forced to toil, for example.

The Friedmans of the world would treat this extreme imbalance in coercive power as a passing phase, a problem that would soon be corrected by more competition. But given its enduring hold on our labor market and on-the-job conditions, I think there is a case for calling it tyranny.

None of Your Business?

The fourth and final concept demanding attention is privacy (and its opposite, publicness). Think back to any notable recent controversy involving the actions of a powerful corporation, and you will find not just conservatives but even liberals insisting, "Well, it's a private company. If you don't like it, don't buy its products." Or, "You don't have to use Twitter's services if you don't like the Terms of Service. It's a private company."

For Elizabeth Anderson, a political philosopher at the University of Michigan, such rhetoric betrays a shamefully impoverished understanding of what private and public mean. As Anderson has written, our discourse treats government "as synonymous with the state, which, by supposed definition, is part of the *public sphere*. The supposed counterpart *private sphere* is the place where, it is imagined, government ends, and hence where individual liberty begins."[19] It follows, according to such thinking, that you can't be tyrannized by your employer or social media platform, because you aren't, properly speaking, *governed* in the workplace, on Twitter, and so on.

In reality, Anderson argues, if something is private, it means you can exclude others from decision-making regarding that thing. Your decisions aren't weighed by voters or balanced out by representatives of other members of your community. Whereas when something is public, it means it is the business of a "well-defined group," such that no one can exclude any member of that group when it comes to decision-making and accountability. These boundaries of privacy and publicness aren't absolute. The affairs of some business club might be public for members of X group (say, female tech executives) but private for nonmembers.[20]

The sharp, absolute division we typically draw between public and private serves to limit our rights, giving rise to what Anderson calls "private government":

A government is private with respect to a subject if it can issue orders, backed by sanctions, to that subject in some domain of that subject's life, and that subject has no say in how that government operates and no standing to demand that [his] interests be taken into account, other than perhaps in narrowly defined circumstances.[21]

All of us are embedded in several, overlapping public spheres of consequence by virtue of citizenship. As citizens, we can expect local, state, and federal governments to grant us varying degrees of information, standing, decision-making power, and accountability. But, says Anderson, there are *other* public spheres of consequence in which we deserve to have greater say than we currently do: namely, as employees. We might add our status as consumers, medical patients, retirees, and members of various online communities.

Anderson acknowledges that in some cases other public spheres might address this powerlessness: Federal employment and consumer-protection laws, for example, are supposed to check the powers of the "private" governments lording over us. But these efforts are themselves often premised on the very same sharp and absolute public-"private" distinction that gave rise to the current state of affairs in the first place—rendering them insufficiently protective of our rights.

To recap: None of the political concepts that anchor American public discourse are as simple as our opinion elites typically assume. Tyranny isn't just a matter of the form of the regime, or what the state chooses to do with its power. Liberty doesn't exist in general, but only in relationship to power. Coercion pervades supposedly noncoercive societies. And private and public are relative, rather than absolute, terms.

To see how these realities intersect to create Tyranny, Inc., we now have to observe that system's workings up close. It is to this task that the bulk of this book is dedicated.

Part I

THE POLITICAL
ECONOMY OF DYSTOPIA

2

The Workplace Trap

T HE BIRTH OF a child is one of life's happiest occasions. But the joys of expecting and childbearing—buttressed by the warm glances of strangers at a protruding belly, by baby showers and gifts and balloons and baby-colored postcards—do little to prepare new parents for the difficult parts: the pangs, the pushing, the sleepless nights, an infant's excruciating illnesses, the awesome responsibility of keeping another human being alive.

For women employed in today's mammoth service industry, the demands of the child are compounded by another: that of the manager deploying "just-in-time" scheduling, sometimes with the aid of computer programs, designed to ensure that the shop or restaurant expends the strictest minimum of labor costs needed to meet customer demand—and not a cent more.

So it was for Alicia Fleming. The Massachusetts resident had spent her entire career working in food service, beginning at Dunkin Donuts when she was still a teenager and later rising to franchise eateries and luxury restaurants. She found this line of work rewarding, and the tips at the higher-end establishments allowed her to make ends meet. That is, until her newborn boy came along when Fleming was thirty-two.

By then, she was working at a large Polynesian-themed restaurant especially popular with Bay Staters on weekends. There, a scheduling system that she could tolerate when she was childless suddenly turned into a veritable crucible of physical, psychological, and financial stress. As she later told *Vox,* her employer was "looking at their bottom dollar, and won't schedule you unless they absolutely need you. And then you don't know until a few days before whether or not you're even going to be asked to work."[1]

The restaurant would inform Fleming of her schedule days before she was supposed to show up for shifts that sometimes ran well into the early-morning hours. The unpredictability and short notices made finding childcare impossible. As *Vox* reported, "as a single parent without close family nearby," she "was often scrambling to find childcare. When she wasn't able to do so on short notice, she'd have to miss a shift." That, in turn, caused her income to fluctuate: "It felt like all the time, I would think about the money I could make [if I could make the shifts], and what that could do for us, and then be really intent on trying to find somebody for child care."[2]

Worn down and struggling to pay for life's necessities, Fleming couldn't quit, lest she and her new baby fall into a financial abyss. At the same time, the shifts she managed to pick up in between her childcare needs weren't enough to pay the bills, either.[3]

It's an all-too-common tragedy. As of 2021, America's twenty-five million food-service and retail workers constituted nearly a tenth of the national population and 16 percent of the employed labor force.[4] And a third of such workers receive less than a week's notice of their upcoming weekly schedule.[5] The resulting loss of control over time threatens their health along with their children's social and mental development.

Since the 1970s, American workers have come to bear ever more of the downsides associated with private enterprise. Living wages, health-care and retirement benefits, and general job security—businesses have peeled away these and other former hallmarks of working-class life in exchange for higher short-term profits and shareholder value. Workers on the lower rungs of the labor market have been especially hard-hit.

The sum effect of these shifts, from the workers' point of view, is often described as "precarity": a sense, both mental and material, that very little about their livelihoods is stable and secure.

In the decades since the 1970s, the bottom half of workers have enjoyed no growth in real wages.[6] That's made it hard for millions of Americans to pay their bills, forcing working families to resort to public welfare benefits—including half of fast-food workers and a quarter of part-time college faculty—at a cost of $153 billion a year to the U.S. taxpayer.[7]

Systematically low wages also leave very little, if anything, for long-term savings and covering exigencies. No wonder 45 percent of American adults would struggle to come up with $400 in cash to pay for an emergency expense, according to the Federal Reserve, with 12 percent of adults not being able to pay for the expense at all— perhaps the single best statistical snapshot of working-class wage precarity in the United States.[8]

But wage precarity isn't the only kind. There is also scheduling precarity of the sort that racked Alicia Fleming. As the University of California scholars Daniel Schneider and Kristen Harknett note in a landmark 2019 study of the phenomenon, scheduling precarity is another way of "maximizing control over labor" while forcing workers to bear the costs associated with fluctuating consumer demand. A more predictable work schedule would mean a fairer distribution of the expenses that come with periods of low demand. Instead, workers are asked to be ever flexible and always on call for moments of high demand, while sometimes having their shifts canceled if demand doesn't materialize.

The regime takes a high toll. Surveying a large sample of U.S. service-industry workers, Schneider and Harknett found that just-in-time scheduling, frequent cancellations, "clopening" shifts (workers scheduled only for the opening and closing of the store), and similar practices have an even more caustic influence on employee well-being than low wages. Workers subjected to unstable scheduling sleep poorly, suffer psychologically, and are generally unhappy.[9]

Partly, all this misery owes to the economic turbulence associated with variable workweeks, but an even more important factor is the work-life tensions they cause, which in turn ripple out to children. As *The New York Times,* summarizing other research by Schneider and Harknett, reported, kids whose parents are subjected to such scheduling are "much more likely to exhibit anxiety, guilt or sadness than children of parents with stable schedules, according to survey results from 4,300 workers with children 15 and younger. They were also more likely to argue, destroy things and have tantrums."[10]

The causal dots aren't hard to connect: "Parents with irregular schedules had less money and time for family meals, playing with children or helping them with their homework. The biggest way parents' work schedules affected their children? Those with unpredictable schedules were more likely to feel stressed, irritable or depressed."[11]

In Fleming's case, the choice between wages, precarious scheduling, and childcare proved unbearable. Yet it wasn't until *a year and a half later,* well into a crucial development phase for her baby, that she was able to secure an administrative job with a more predictable schedule.[12]

Your Signature for Your Life

If you follow the news closely, you will encounter much more horrific stories than Alicia Fleming's: cases of workers killed by their robot "colleagues"; or forced to wear diapers for lack of bathroom breaks; or derailed from seeking treatment for workplace injuries by health providers at company-run clinics.[13] The more high profile of these cases receive *some* media attention, and the abusive or neglectful management practices that give rise to them are frequently found illegal, even if government enforcement is lackluster at best and the penalties light.

I picked Fleming's story, however, because it is so ordinary. Her employer's actions were unfair and ultimately damaging. But they finally weren't life shattering, certainly not such as to prompt her to lodge a complaint with the authorities. Indeed, her employer was acting well within the bounds of the law. Nor was she prepared to quit the job immediately and at any cost. On the contrary, given the material pressures she faced, and the state of the labor market in her area, Fleming decided to stay put and suffer for a good while. There was no other choice that wouldn't have jeopardized her family's income and basic well-being.

Precarity is one way to characterize what Fleming and tens of millions of other wage laborers go through for most of their lives. Another way to think about it is as a naked instance of *coercion:* a consequence of the employer's power to control another human being's use of her time in the pursuit of maximal profits, even if it means making utter chaos of her life.

It is *this* sort of coercion that most people experience, especially those who earn an hourly wage. Which is to say, it's the lot of most Americans. To understand how we ended up with this manifestly unjust workplace situation, we have to travel back to a pivotal moment in the development of America's political economy.

IN SEPTEMBER 1859, the Wisconsin State Agricultural Society invited Abraham Lincoln to address the annual state fair. Lincoln, already a Republican superstar and well on his way to the White House, relished the chance to address farmers, the country's largest voting bloc. In classic Lincolnian style, however, he played down the political nature of his presence and his own ambition, cheekily describing himself as "some sort of politician."[14]

Lincoln's "Address to the Wisconsin State Agricultural Society" wasn't a great piece of oratory—not by the towering standards of the Great Emancipator, at any rate. Yet the speech he delivered that autumn day in Milwaukee stands as perhaps *the* emblematic statement of American political economy. In it, Lincoln gave crystalline expression to the American faith that there is no fundamental, lasting conflict between employers and employees.

He began with a striking observation: that *"labor* is the source from which human wants are mainly supplied."[15] To labor, then, belongs the credit for all material goods. More than a decade earlier, he had articulated this idea in even more sweeping fashion, writing that "inasmuch as most good things are produced by labour, it follows that all such things of right belong to those whose labour has produced them."[16]

An unfamiliar reader might be forgiven for assuming Karl Marx penned these words. But Lincoln was, in fact, advancing a fundamentally liberal conception of labor—one firmly planted in the cheery preindustrial age of artisans, farmers, engineers, and others who toiled for no master. As the twentieth-century historian Richard Hofstadter observed, when Lincoln spoke of the rights of labor in this way, he was really referring to "the right to own." To Lincoln's mind, the "laborer" was the farmer who owned his land or the craftsman who owned his tools. This owner, he believed, had a natural right to the fruit of his toil.[17]

But what about the growing ranks of workers who toiled for masters other than themselves? What was the most just way to organize the labor of such people?

Lincoln didn't believe in enduring class distinctions. He didn't imagine it possible that some people, perhaps the vast share of workers, would end up spending their entire lives working for others in exchange for wages. He couldn't foresee the full implications of the Industrial Revolution that was already well under way: how the age of the machine and economies of scale would largely sweep away the so-called masterless men—independent artisans and farmers—who had thrived in an earlier stage of economic development.

The masterless men carried out their economic relations impersonally, consensually, and at "arm's length." But modern industrial relations changed this pattern. After the Industrial Revolution, employer and employee might have encountered each other at arm's length initially. But once the employee signed on the dotted line on the employment contract, he found himself in an intimate embrace with the employer, who could dominate his body and his use of time for much of his waking life.

Lincoln never fully grasped this. Instead, he subscribed to something like a cycle-of-labor theory of social classes (my term). As he put it in Milwaukee, "There is no such thing as a freeman being fatally fixed for life, in the condition of a laborer." Rather, "the prudent, penniless beginner in the world, labors for wages awhile, saves a surplus with which to buy tools or land for himself; then labors on his own account for another while, and at length hires another new beginner to help him."[18] And this next rookie, in turn, rises to ownership and hires still another. And so on.

For Lincoln, this cycle was "free labor": that "just and generous, and prosperous system, which opens the way for all—gives hope to all, and energy, and progress, and improvement of condition to all." If anyone remained a hired worker for the duration of his life, "it is not the fault of the system, but because of either a dependent nature which prefers it, or improvidence, folly, or singular misfortune."[19]

This Lincolnian political economy could be summed up in a simple syllogism (of sorts): Anyone who labors hard enough can obtain the capital necessary to become an asset owner himself and hire other aspiring owners. And, therefore, any toiler whose ownership aspirations aren't realized in his lifetime must have been unforgivably lazy or especially unlucky or dispossessed by the Almighty himself.

Lincoln used free labor as a battering ram against the southern "Slave Power," whose most zealous ideologues were open about their belief that it was better to *own* the man or woman (of whatever race) than to merely *buy* his labor on the market. But Lincoln's quaint view of industry blinded him to the injustices inherent in his free-labor ideal.

As the legal scholars Joseph Fishkin and William Forbath note, Lincoln placed a strong emphasis on the yeoman as a "composite figure"[20] of capital and labor—who was neither fully employer nor fully employee, but shared characteristics of both. This made it seem that there was no disharmony between their interests. If there are no fundamental, enduring power differentials, it follows that labor and capital could encounter each other on generally friendly terms.

Lincoln sincerely believed that such an ideal would yield an economy befitting a republic of dignified, independent citizen-smallholders, who would use their minds and bodies for the betterment of themselves and of the community. As the heterodox writer Christopher Lasch insisted, Lincoln was calling for broadly shared material security, a little ownership for everyone.[21]

But even granting that defense, Lincolnian free labor nevertheless baked a disdain for wage labor into the American spirit, rendering the wage-earning "freeman" an afterthought. This, just at the pivotal moment when the U.S. economy was turning most workers into permanent wage laborers. The disdain persists to our own day. When Mitt Romney and sundry other GOP figures extol "job creators" above, well, jobholders, they can justly claim to stand in an authentic tradition going back to the greatest Republican of all time.[22]

American industrial relations didn't pan out as Lincoln had hoped. As Hofstadter commented,

> Had he lived to seventy, he would have seen the generation brought up on self-help come into its own, build oppressive business corporations, and begin to close off those treasured opportunities for the little man. Further, he would have seen his own party become the jackal of vested interests, placing the dollar far, far ahead of the man.[23]

History falsified Lincoln's naive dream of a relatively classless society. Social mobility—insofar as it was an original American ideal (it wasn't, as we will see)—has ground to a halt. Comparing the wealth of fathers and sons down the generations, scholars have found that "it would take an average of six generations for family economic advantage to disappear in the United States."[24] And contrary to Lincoln's picture of workers and masters rising harmoniously together, fierce, sometimes violent class struggle exploded in the decades after his assassination, from the Gilded Age until the New Deal. As a result of those struggles, the "little man" would win a measure of protection against his employer, not least a minimum wage and the right to collectively bargain. Later came a modicum of health and safety regulations, and laws against certain forms of harassment and discrimination.

Yet as Alicia Fleming's story, and countless others of the kind, remind us, U.S. workers have lost many of the political gains they made in the twentieth century. We will discuss the reason why later. For now, it suffices to note that, thanks to our system's bias in favor of "job creators" and against wage laborers, legal protections against workplace domination form not so much a blanket as a gauzy bedsheet riddled with holes wide enough to ram an arm through. With precious few exceptions, American labor law currently allows bosses to

- pay poverty wages that leave workers no choice but to join welfare rolls;
- schedule worktime with zero regard for workers' well-being;
- regulate and curtail workers' speech—in and out of the workplace;
- compel workers to attend rallies in favor of management's preferred political candidates;
- mandate attendance at anti-union meetings; and
- make decisions that can dramatically alter and sometimes upend workers' lives, without even a semblance of due process or right to appeal.

The patchy reforms enacted since Lincoln's time faced intense opposition from Lincoln's GOP heirs, and sometimes from Democrats as well. At every turn, the chief watchword of the "jackals" was, and remains, "liberty of contract"—the subject of the next stop on our tour of Tyranny, Inc.

3

Gagged by the Contract

H<small>E</small> S<small>TOOD</small> I<small>N</small> the inner circle of the elect—until one day, he didn't.

Scott Lamb was a rising literary star in the evangelical world. An ordained Baptist pastor, he had written the authorized biography of the former Arkansas governor Mike Huckabee, published in 2015. Next, he co-authored a "spiritual biography" of the forty-fifth president, *The Faith of Donald J. Trump*, that garnered endorsements from the likes of Newt Gingrich and Sean Hannity.

In 2018, the year the Trump book was published, Lamb joined Liberty University in Lynchburg, Virginia, as vice president of special literary projects, tasked with writing books under his own name and helping obtain book deals for other university figures to promote conservative Christian ideas.[1] Like any new employee, he signed the documents Liberty's HR team put in front of him, looking forward to an exciting new career as a senior leader of one of the world's largest Christian colleges.

In the new role, he helped craft messaging for Jerry Falwell Jr., then Liberty's president. At a gala inducting Falwell into the local Business Hall of Fame, Lamb raised hosannas to free enterprise and to the Falwell clan's business acumen. "Economic freedom offers the greatest opportunity for prosperity," he quoted his boss, adding in his own words, "The Falwell family has impacted Lynchburg with prosperity in every area of life."[2]

Lamb's effusions paid off. Liberty promoted him to senior vice president of communications in 2019. He now oversaw the official college portal, the student newspaper, and the Standing for Freedom Center, an in-house think tank promoting a down-home mix of piety and capitalist ideology ("We honor human dignity, individual liberty, limited government, and free markets").[3]

Then things went south. In August 2020, Falwell resigned after he and his wife were embroiled in allegations of sexual impropriety.[4] Given the Falwells' prominent role in Republican politics, the ensuing brouhaha garnered national attention, prompting Liberty's board of trustees to hire outside counsel to probe university practices. A news release boasted that Jerry Prevo, the new president, enjoyed "the full range of his presidential authority to implement any changes necessary to improve the ongoing operations of the university and to enrich the spiritual mission" of the school.[5]

As part of the review process, Lamb like other members of the executive team participated in some twenty-five hours of interviews across eight months. Administrators reassured him that he could speak freely with outside counsel. Following that process, he sat down for a meeting on October 4, 2021, with three senior university leaders, including Prevo. At this meeting, Lamb "expressed dismay over the direction of the university and concern that the university had strayed so far from its original mission," according to a lawsuit he subsequently lodged against Liberty.[6]

That summer, twelve Jane Doe complainants had sued the university, charging that its policies made sexual assaults more likely, with administrators berating and accusing accusers. The lawsuit was a grim sort of vindication for Lamb, who in May had emailed his fellow university leaders about the mounting public impression that Liberty's administration was where sex-abuse allegations went to get buried. His warnings had gone unheeded back then.[7]

At the October 4 meeting, Lamb reiterated his concerns about the university's sex-abuse processes. He also cautioned that Liberty was jeopardizing its tax-exempt status by engaging in political advocacy. In a recording later leaked to the media, Prevo could be heard pressing Lamb about whether the in-house think tank was "getting people elected" and "motivating our conservative people to really get out to vote."[8]

Lamb's claims at the meeting enraged Prevo. The new president demanded that Lamb resign or face termination. The next day, he deputized Liberty's general counsel to offer Lamb a severance package, which he refused. The day after that, the university fired Lamb, effective immediately. That's when he filed a wrongful-termination suit, alleging that Liberty had retaliated against him for speaking out against violations of federal antidiscrimination laws.[9]

His complaint was short and to the point, reflecting the confidence of a man who feels he has justice and ample documentary evidence on his side. What he perhaps didn't expect was how far Liberty would go to stop him from speaking out about allegations of wrongdoing, or how much power the employment documents he had signed granted his former employer.

Not long after Lamb sued, the university filed a "gag order" with the court, reminding the plaintiff that he had "promised not to disclose any confidential information without Liberty approval" when he signed on the dotted line. The sort of information Lamb was bringing to light—including allegations about the mishandling of rape cases and misuse of the university's charitable status—amounted to "protected trade secrets" that Lamb had exposed to "commercial enemies of Liberty" without authorization, the memo argued.[10] At a subsequent hearing, Liberty apparently did secure Lamb's silence, as well as the return of "confidential" material he still held from his time at the university.[11]

Liberty and Prevo have repeatedly denied Lamb's characterizations of these events, in court filings and public statements. Lamb declined to be interviewed for this book, citing the gag order. Even if one takes the most cynical view of his story—that the allegations amount to nothing more than sour grapes, a fired employee's attempt at revenge—Lamb's ordeal is illustrative of the vast coercive

powers the modern employment contract grants bosses over workers, even after they part ways. The reality utterly belies free marketeers' stories about arm's-length transactions and equal bargaining
power.

IN 2019, WHILE Scott Lamb was still happily employed at Liberty,
Ann Lai was fighting a similar conspiracy of silence nearly three
thousand miles away in San Francisco.

The Taiwanese-born, Cleveland-raised Lai had first moved to the
Bay Area in 2013, hoping to make her mark in the fast-moving world
of tech start-ups and venture capital. A math whiz with undergradu-
ate and graduate degrees from Harvard and a patent already under
her belt, she soon found analytics work at an online booking service
for beauty professionals. A VC acquaintance, Justin Caldbeck, helped
make the connection. Not long afterward, he started sending Lai
"unwelcome late-night texts," as an *Elle* magazine profile of Lai put
it (Caldbeck has admitted the messages were "inappropriate" but insists "they were part of a mutual exchange").[12]

In 2014, a research gig opened up at Binary, the new fund started
by Caldbeck and his fellow VC Jonathan Teo. Lai jumped at the
chance, thinking she could gain experience and develop a network
before easily gliding on to a different stint. As for their earlier inter-
action, well, Caldbeck was settling down with a wife, and Lai figured
this would temper his aggressive tendencies. She signed "the boilerplate employment agreement without much thought."[13]

Lai figured wrong, on both counts. Marriage, it turned out, didn't
stop Caldbeck from creating a highly sexualized work environment
at Binary:

> There was the search for a receptionist, during which Cald-
> beck and Teo looked up social media profiles to determine the
> "relative 'hotness'" of applicants. . . . There was the retreat
> where Caldbeck and Teo talked about designing an Uber-
> esque app to match people with sex workers . . . and the

women founders pitching for investments whom the duo labeled as "cute" or too pretty—or who they said should lose weight rather than focus on the plus-size market.[14]

When Lai objected, Caldbeck and Teo nicknamed her "HR" (as in, the human resources department; Caldbeck has denied this claim). Ten months in, Lai threatened to walk but was persuaded to stay. Then another female employee confided to Lai that Caldbeck had started an affair with her, which she was desperate to end (Caldbeck has denied this). She also learned that Caldbeck had "been removed from the board of a start-up, Stitch Fix, after its founder complained of his behavior"—a fact corroborated by the discovery process of a later lawsuit between Caldbeck and Teo.[15]

In 2016, Lai gave notice of her resignation, emailing Caldbeck and Teo that Binary's "hostile work environment" made it impossible for her to continue her work. Ninety minutes later came one of Caldbeck's signature text messages, threatening Lai to keep silent about quitting until "legal feedback is consolidated." And when she posted a note on her Facebook wall about her departure from Binary, vaguely suggesting it had liberated her and restored her sense of ethical integrity, he texted her again: "Implying that you quit because Binary Capital forced you to compromise your ethics is a clear violation of your employment agreement."[16]

It soon became clear that Caldbeck was trying to force Lai out of the VC world. Every time a new opportunity came her way, he would pop up on her phone to let her know he had heard about it. Then the job opportunity would slip through her grasp, according to Lai. When her lawyer sent a cease-and-desist letter to the Binary partners over this pattern of conduct, the firm fired back with a warning of its own: Her employment agreement, Binary warned, barred Lai from criticizing the firm—indeed, from even publicizing the fact that she had quit—on pain of an expensive lawsuit.

Lai's agreement with Binary contained a broad "non-disparagement" clause: "To the maximum extent permitted by applicable law, Employee shall not disparage the Company." The clause prohibited Lai from making "any negative comments regarding a Person's business model, business practices, investment-related decisions, affiliates, equityholders, personnel, agents, integrity, fairness, satisfaction of obligations, or overall performance."[17]

If Lai were to have any hope of telling the truth about what went on inside Binary, she would have to remove the contractual gag. As it happens, unbeknownst to most employees and ignored by most employers, the California Labor Code offers robust protections for workers' speech concerning working conditions, wages, and legal violations by their employers. More recently, the Golden State has enacted laws specifically barring the use of nondisclosure and nondisparagement agreements to silence allegations of workplace harassment and discrimination.

Which is why, after a years-long lawsuit and the near destruction of her career, Lai was able to speak out. Binary settled her lawsuit for an undisclosed sum in 2020. While it was still ongoing, several other women went public with sex-abuse allegations against Caldbeck. At first, he denied the claims categorically, before releasing another statement lamenting how "the dynamic of this industry makes it hard to speak up, but this is the type of action that leads to progress and change, starting with me."[18] The Silicon Valley hotshot finally had a comeuppance, of a kind.

Lochner's *Choke Hold*

Two crucial points stand out when we examine Lamb's and Lai's workplace sagas side by side.

The first is that coercion in the employment agreement has no party or ideology. Liberty University is a bastion of rock-ribbed Christian conservatism, while the Bay Area is the bluest part of a very blue state. Liberty calls on students to "glorify God,"[19] while Binary's Caldbeck has sought "the advancement of women and minorities in leadership," according to a puff piece that appeared, after his #MeToo downfall, on the website of Thrive, the company launched by Arianna Huffington to combat workplace burnout.[20] Yet when it came to their material interests as employers, Liberty and Binary acted identically.

The second point: Lamb and Lai were highly sophisticated job seekers before they signed on the dotted line. Lamb was an experienced journalist and operative in the evangelical world who had already contracted two books with a major publishing house before he bound himself to Liberty's employment terms. Lai had an Ivy League pedigree and a background in the hard sciences. Nevertheless, both ended up gagged—Lamb more severely than Lai—by the legal documents they had to sign to earn a living.

Most workers aren't nearly as sophisticated as Lamb or Lai. Much more common is an hourly worker who doesn't speak English as a first language facing off against a corporate behemoth— say, Walmart, which as of 2018 employed 150 lawyers, a figure that doesn't include the army of outside attorneys it retains to troubleshoot legal problems worldwide.[21] Yet the premise of much U.S. labor law is that such a worker and a Walmart possess equal power in forming and maintaining their relationship.

As we saw in the previous chapter, this assumption of equality between the two parties is deeply rooted in a romantic vision of wage labor, seen as a temporary station on every worker's journey to becoming a capitalist. Translated to legal practice over two centuries, the romantic vision has given rise to the doctrine of liberty of contract. A stock definition of the doctrine is that because the two parties hold equal power to enter or exit the relationship as they please, "their negotiated arrangements are optimal and should not be altered or regulated by external forces."[22]

The Tennessee Supreme Court gave the classic articulation to the doctrine in an 1884 decision holding that a railroad had the right to prohibit its employees from buying whiskey from a vendor near the rail yard. The court reasoned that men must be left, without interference to buy and sell where they please, and to discharge or retain employees at will for good cause or for no cause, or even for bad cause without thereby being guilty of an unlawful act per se. It is a right which an employee may exercise in the same way, to the same extent, for the same cause or want of cause as the employer.[23]

After all, Justice Ingersoll wrote for the majority, the employee likewise has the right to "refuse to work" if his employer engages in conduct "he dislikes." More than that, the employee "may persuade his fellows, and the employer may lose all his hands and be compelled to close his doors."[24] Binding employees to obnoxious demands might be immoral, Ingersoll granted, but it finally can't be deemed illegal: "May I not refuse to trade with any one? May I not forbid my family to trade with any one? May I not dismiss my domestic servant for dealing, or even visiting, where I forbid?" And if the good judge could fire a single servant, "why not a hundred or a thousand of them?"[25]

In so cavalierly upholding the right of employers to coerce employees on pain of joblessness, the Tennessee decision foreshadowed the U.S. Supreme Court's infamous *Lochner* era (1897–1937), when the high court struck down numerous reforms aimed at improving workplace conditions and redressing the power imbalance between labor and capital. The *Lochner* court—named for a 1905 case that overturned a New York law limiting bakers' workweeks to sixty hours[26]—elevated liberty of contract into a constitutional principle as sacred as free speech.

In a pivotal 1908 decision, for example, the Supreme Court declared unconstitutional a federal law that banned employers from requiring workers to renounce union membership as a condition of employment. Justice John Marshall Harlan argued that "the right of the employee to quit the service of the employer, for whatever reason, is the same as the right of the employer, for whatever reason, to dispense with the services of such employee." And any interference with this principle is unjustifiable "in a free land."[27] The *Lochner* court likewise ruled that the federal government couldn't regulate child labor, or tax businesses that employed children, or mandate a pension scheme for railroad workers, among many other decisions invalidating public policy on the ground that it intruded into the private realm of contractual freedom.[28]

But amid the miseries of the Great Depression, pressure exerted by FDR compelled the Supreme Court to recognize the limits of liberty of contract. In one emblematic post-*Lochner* case, the high court declined to overturn a Washington State minimum wage for women, reasoning that workers "are in an unequal position with respect to bargaining power and are thus relatively defenceless against the denial of a living wage." Crucially for our purposes, the court noted that the *private* exploitation of women in the workplace is an eminently *public* problem, since it imperils the well-being of women and, thus, "the vigor of the race" and since inadequate wages force taxpayers to subsidize unscrupulous employers through welfare benefits.[29]

The New Deal tamed the *Lochner* court. In the era's signal achievement, the federal government threw its weight behind collective bargaining. The 1935 National Labor Relations Act, also known as the Wagner Act, granted workers the right to organize and join unions. One of the first things newly empowered unions began pushing for was to require that employers show "just cause" for terminating employees.[30] A law guaranteeing a federal minimum wage and overtime pay soon followed.

Yet union membership precipitously declined following its postwar heyday, to 6 percent of the private-economy labor force in 2022, down from a third of workers in the 1950s.[31] This was neither an accident nor the inevitable outcome of globalization and automation, as a commonplace narrative has it. Rather, the collapse of labor unionism in the United States, especially in the private economy, was the product of a deliberate strategy aimed at de-unionizing the American labor force.

We will explore the union question at great depth later in this book. For now, what matters is that, in many respects, the core concept of liberty of contract remains operative for those workers who aren't union members, tenured professors, high-end executives, or superstar artists and athletes—which is to say, for most of the labor force. As one progressive legal scholar has noted, *"Lochner*-ist premises"—above all, the notion that employee and employer enjoy equal power, because each can freely walk away from the other—continue to decisively shape labor law.[32]

Two consequences flow from this that deserve our special attention. One is the sheer unfairness of the content of most employment agreements. The boilerplate clauses used to silence Lamb and Lai are but one in a long litany of coercive restrictions and exploitative provisions tucked into these documents, measures Americans would never tolerate if they were handed down by their government. The second consequence is the perverse way workers' vulnerability is used to justify contractual injustices. We will tackle each in turn.

Happiest First Day

Congratulations! You have just been offered your dream job in the twenty-first-century U.S. economy—or maybe just the job you need to pay your bills and maintain health insurance.

You should be proud of yourself. This wasn't an easy process. You submitted your résumé, letter of interest, and references. Maybe you also filled out an application online or in print. You went through one or more rounds of phone or in-person interviews. You passed a background check. Depending on your industry, a drug test and an intrusive psychological assessment might have been part of the process as well.

Your new employer made an offer—probably in an email—outlining the basic expectations, as well as the pay and benefits. You immediately wrote back to accept. "Looking eagerly forward," you might have signed your reply. After agreeing to a start date, you began making logistical plans for getting to your new job. Maybe you moved across your city or state, or even across the country, which involved finding housing and a suitable school for your children. Your spouse might have had to find a new job, too. He or she perhaps wasn't pleased about the disruption, but wanted to be supportive.

So, here you are. It's your first day on the job. There is a company tote awaiting you at your new desk, with more swag stashed inside (a pen! a fancy water mug!). Your immediate supervisor reassures you that you won't be doing much substantive work today. No, your first day is mostly dedicated to filling out paperwork and sitting through HR orientations. Along with a couple of new hires from other departments, you head down to the conference room, where an HR specialist hands you a fat pile of papers to sign and initial. You happily oblige.

Wait a minute—what did you just sign?

If your new gig is with any mid- to mega-sized firm, the various employment, acceptable-use, and liability-release clauses you just accepted are quite standard. State laws and the nature of your particular industry may introduce some variations, but generally speaking, it is likely that your signature granted your new boss a broad range of ways to surveil, coerce, and silence you.

Consider the employment agreement for a major, New York Stock Exchange–listed tech company I reviewed for this book. Needless to say, the company in question touts its commitment to "diversity, inclusion, and belonging" on its website while recognizing that "this important work" is never over. When it comes to securing its own material interests, however, the firm takes every advantage of America's *Lochner*-ist legal regime, acting no differently than the monocled tycoons of the original *Lochner* era.

Let's start with the acceptable-use policy, which governs the use of company computers, smartphones, networks, and data. Our company says this policy is intended to preserve the confidentiality of your data. Yet it also grants your new boss the power to minutely surveil what you do, not just on company computers and smart-phones, but also on your personal devices, which the company encourages you to use to access internal systems. The policy's scope extends to "any individual who is granted access to [company] systems in his or her capacity as an employee." Note carefully: The determining factor for applying the policy isn't ownership of a device but access to systems.

The policy goes on to state that personal laptops used for work purposes "are subject to confiscation and inspection." Other companies have extended the power to confiscate and inspect to personal smartphones, including use of third-party apps and browsing histories. Such clauses subject even low-level wage workers to total surveillance if they, say, use QR codes on personal devices to pay for items in the cafeteria or to scan and make deliveries.

Now let's turn to our company's "Employee Video, Photo, and Recording Release and Waiver." This document requires you to consent to the "photographing and videotaping of [yourself] and the recording of [your] voice . . . in connection with [your] work." The contract doesn't specify it, but the provision likely covers your voice and visual presence at trainings, as well as on any calls or Zoom meetings you might make using company devices and/or on company networks. The company, and any entity it sells or licenses this recorded material to, may use or reuse "[your] voice, including, without limitation, [your] speaking and singing voices and any musical compositions created by [you]."

By signing the release, you give away ownership of your "actions, likeness, name, appearance and biographical material (i.e., collectively, 'Likeness') in any and all media now known or hereafter devised, worldwide in perpetuity"—forever—to your employer and to any entity to which it might sell, license, or lease your digital presence. You also agree not to sue the company or those third parties for any reason.

You may wonder why your employer wants to own your likeness, including your singing voice. In an older, more innocent world, use of your likeness might have been limited to company training videos or recruitment brochures. But the document you signed makes clear that your likeness may in addition be used for "trade or commercial purposes." Today, there exists an extensive market for voice and human-likeness data. Your employer might record your voice, for example, while you are making sales calls and then sell or license it to Apple so it can improve its Siri service.

Now let's say your visual likeness is sold and subsequently used by a different entity in doctored pornography, or by a future web service that allows users to create their own virtual porn using a database of human likenesses. The question arises: Would you be able to lodge a civil claim against your employer or the entity that created the video? Not if the court strictly interprets your contract on *Lochner*-ist principles. You enjoyed liberty of contract, remember?

Now let's turn to the "Release, Waiver of Liability, Assumption of Risk and Indemnity Agreement." It's a three-page document composed in dense legalese. The upshot is that you forgo your right to sue if you are injured at company recreational facilities, even if they were ill-maintained. You also can't sue in case of injury at off-site events, such as company ball games—which, the agreement adds, are "entirely voluntary" (but try skipping these to see the effect on the "team player" portion of your annual review). This particular waiver is almost certainly illegal and unlikely to be upheld by a court. But your new employer hopes the broadly drawn language will deter you from pursuing a right of action that the law otherwise grants you.

Finally, a host of clauses whose sum effect is to prevent you from

- publicly speaking out about workplace conditions (except in certain narrow situations);
- encouraging others to leave (even if you aren't recruiting them to a different company);
- soliciting the company's clients for business (even after you leave the job);

- "disparaging" the company, including by disclosing information that is already public; or
- even mentioning your prior employment with the company.

Yes, that last provision would theoretically bar you from listing your former company on your résumé. Many of these clauses would be upheld by courts outside California, which, as we saw in Ann Lai's case, has enacted laws aimed at mitigating the worst of these abuses.[33]

Anyway, congrats, again. Here's to a long and happy career with your new employer. Let's hope nothing ever goes wrong that might require you to seek recourse in a court of law—or even blow off steam on Twitter.

Vulnerability as "Freedom"

The liberty-of-contract framework is farcical. But it is just the kind of farce that appeals to the economic libertarians who disproportionately dominate our judiciary. Newly hired workers, in this telling, carefully review each paragraph and voice their objections before coming to a mutual understanding with their employer over disputed provisions. As your own experience likely tells you, that is almost never how this process takes place. "The only people who read the terms," one employment lawyer told me, "are the authors and later claimants"—that is, workers who try to sue their employers after the documents have been signed.

The full set of documents to be signed, moreover, usually comes after the employee has agreed to the offer. Said the lawyer, "You've quit your last job, you've moved across the country, maybe taken out a mortgage or lease, and the first day, they present you with a non-disparagement [clause]. What are you going to do?" Nearly all people sign.

Over the years, a handful of employees have refused to sign agreements over particular clauses, giving rise to lawsuits in which they subsequently prevailed. But such cases are vanishingly rare. In millions more cases, refusing to sign doesn't even cross new employees' minds. That was true for highly educated employees like Scott Lamb and Ann Lai, as we saw. It's even more true for, say, the factory worker without a high-school degree.

Finally, the liberty-of-contract framework permits employment provisions that can bind the worker long after he leaves the job, such as the "likeness"-recording waiver we reviewed. The company, moreover, may unilaterally change certain terms for the already employed—"as if there is a new contract each day," writes the labor economist Lawrence Mishel.[34]

Which brings us to the second major consequence of *Lochner*'s enduring grip on our labor regime: namely, the downright depraved way it equates the employee's "power" to quit with the boss's right to dismiss him. At-will employment is the norm for workers, most of whom don't even have written contracts (firms take explicit steps to ensure employee handbooks and other documents of the kind don't count as contracts).[35] In all U.S. jurisdictions except Montana and a few cities, the law treats all employment as at will. Unless a collective-bargaining agreement or other explicit contract overturns the presumption, companies have the right to terminate employees at any time, for any or no reason.

Defenders of the present order will point to the at-will rule and the supposed symmetry between the right to quit and the right to fire it creates. Both sides, free marketeers insist, can walk away as they please, which means they enjoy equal power. But this is a false symmetry. An employee's quitting entails far more pain for the employee, who has to go without a paycheck and doesn't qualify for unemployment, than it does for his boss.[36]

The liberty-of-contract framework also assumes full employment, a technical term used by economists to describe a situation in which everyone who wants a job can get one. As Mishel, the labor economist, notes, when there is any slack in the labor market—that is, more workers looking for jobs than are available—employer-employee agreements are less than optimal, and an Alicia Fleming can't be said to be free to contract "without constraint or coercion."[37]

How so? Because when there is slack in the labor market, workers have a harder time finding new jobs and are less likely to quit or switch companies. Employers, meanwhile, are more likely to tighten recruitment standards and have an easier time hiring well-qualified candidates without having to pay them higher wages.

This is frequently the case. The U.S. economy is "rarely at full employment and sometimes never so for large segments of the workforce." Economists disagree about what jobless rate constitutes full employment. Assuming a 5 percent jobless rate for full employ-ment, Mishel has found that in the 188 quarters comprising the years 1973 to 2019, the American economy achieved full employment in only 27 percent; in nearly half of the quarters in that period, it failed to achieve full employment.[38]

Workers can sense which way macroeconomic winds are blow-ing, and they react accordingly. They feel much more insecure when the jobless rate ticks up; that's when you might notice yourself stressing out about whether your boss recognizes your diligence, or working extra hard to make sure he does. Yet the liberty-of-contract framework turns your very vulnerability into a sign of your "free-dom": the freedom to walk away into joblessness and financial mis-ery.

On the next stop on our tour of Tyranny, Inc., we will see just how far courts are prepared to go to uphold that "freedom."

4

The Bosses' Court

"WHAT WOULD DAD do?"

The question rattled David Heller's mind as he sat in a conference room at his lawyer's office and considered the choices facing him. The decision he reached that day in 2017 would etch his name in legal textbooks and transform how courts in North America think about the lopsided agreements between companies and employees, setting a limit on the use of privatized "courts" for resolving disputes.

His father, who died when Heller was nineteen, had practiced criminal law. It was Dad who instilled in him an acute sense of right and wrong and a "take no shit" attitude, he told me. That innate will to fight injustice would assert itself with hurricane force after Heller came to work for Uber, the digital ride-sharing firm that operates in some six hundred cities and dozens of countries worldwide. As of this writing, the company enjoys a market capitalization of $55 billion.

Heller joined the food-delivery service Uber Eats in a city in the Northeast when he was in his mid-thirties, having earlier in life worked in various trades like plumbing. He was burned out from traditional jobs, and starting out as an Uber Eats delivery driver seemed remarkably easy. All he needed was a car and a driver's license, both of which he owned, and to click "I agree" twice on a fourteen-page agreement, which he did.

Uber Eats had only recently launched in Heller's area, and the driver pool was small. That meant he was getting steady work while retaining the flexibility to choose his hours or take time off when he needed it. He was earning about $1,200 to $2,000 a month on average, working four or five days a week. Some weeks, he would cross the $800 threshold, allowing him to pay off debts and even take short vacations. He also picked up small bonuses for signing up his friends as drivers, thus helping Uber to deepen its market penetration—and, as it would soon become clear, to lower its labor costs.

At first, things were good. Heller was proud when his earnings allowed him to trade in his clunker for a used 2013 Nissan Altima SL, complete with moonroof and heated seats—"all done up," he recalled. "I would say at that point, I was emotionally or mentally in the best place I had been for a while."

But one evening, a month after he signed the loan on his new Nissan and about seven months since he had first joined, Heller along with every other driver in the area received an email informing them that their pay would be cut, effective midnight. Henceforth, Uber said, they would be paid less per mile driven and per job. They also noticed they could no longer log on to their apps to accept delivery jobs unless they clicked "I agree" on a document setting out these new terms.

Some drivers reported the new agreement popping up and "taking over" their apps while they were in the middle of making a food delivery, such that they had to accept the new terms before they could resume receiving GPS directions. "It didn't even give them an opportunity to glance at it," Heller said. If they wanted to finish the job, they had to quickly consent to whatever was spelled out in the notification, written in the usual fine-print legalese, of course.

Most drivers soon clicked their assent, "agreeing" to wage cuts that amounted to 20 percent to 50 percent of their incomes (the severity varied depending on how many hours individual drivers normally worked and the amount of work available any given night). Having just taken out a loan on a new car, in the hope of using it to work happily and productively for Uber, Heller was stressed out and angered by the prospect of a much lower wage.

He did not click "I agree." As he told me, "Every fiber of my body knew it was wrong. I almost instantaneously knew I was going to fight this somehow. That was Dad coming out."

Heller and a handful of like-minded drivers launched a protest movement that began small but soon garnered attention from the media and labor activists. Not all drivers were supportive, of course. Those who delivered food using bicycles, for example, weren't as bothered by the cuts, because they didn't have to shoulder the financial burdens associated with maintaining motor vehicles; others simply didn't want to rock the boat. Heller warned them that if they didn't take some form of collective action, Uber would change its wage structure again, to their detriment. Time proved him right, when the rideshare giant implemented several more rounds of cuts over the years that followed.

Eventually, Heller got connected with an employee-side law firm that offered to take on his case. A lawyer laid out the options before him. He could sue Uber as an individual under local unfair-wage laws and receive a tidy payout for himself, if he prevailed. Or he could pursue a class-action lawsuit, to vindicate the rights of "everyone who believes in a fair wage—or even just human decency at this point," as his lawyer put it. Which is how Heller found himself in that conference room, torn between his personal interests and a deeper calling. In the end, Heller picked the bigger battle of a class action.

There was only one problem. Tucked in the fourteen-page document he had initially signed to get the gig was a provision mandating that any dispute be resolved using individual, private mediation and then arbitration proceedings, to be held at the International Chamber of Commerce in Amsterdam. In theory, arbitration of this kind is meant to make it easier for warring commercial parties to make peace without the pains of traditional litigation. In practice, it meant Heller would have had to pay an up-front fee of $14,500 just to begin the process. The figure didn't include the costs of traveling to the Netherlands, lawyers' fees, and any lost wages. Recall, moreover, that in a good month Heller earned $2,000 from Uber, before car and gas expenses were paid. To have this private Dutch court hear his claim, he would have to give up nearly all of a year's salary. The contract Heller agreed to when he first started working for Uber hadn't said a word about these costs.

Uber invoked the arbitration clause as soon as Heller filed his lawsuit. The trial court accepted Uber's argument and put a stop to the litigation. But the appeals court disagreed, holding that the arbitration clause was simply too outrageous to be enforced.

The case made it all the way to the Supreme Court. In 2020, the highest court in the land held that the arbitration clause was unconscionable, allowing one party with much greater power and legal sophistication to effectively deny justice to a weaker, less sophisticated party. "The arbitration clause," an 8–1 majority of justices concluded, "is the only way [Heller] is permitted to vindicate his rights under the contract, but arbitration is out of reach for him and other drivers in his position. His contractual rights are, as a result, *illusory*."[1]

The court decided that Heller and his fellow drivers must be allowed to bring their claims in a public court in their own country, not a privatized one an ocean away. The case is ongoing as of this writing. But merely overcoming the arbitration clause, at the Supreme Court no less, was a great source of pride for Heller. As he told me, "It will be printed in books because it was a precedent— *Uber v. Heller*. There's something to that. I was glad that my first name wasn't part of the case name, that it's just 'Heller.' Because to me, that's a way of honoring my father."

YOU MIGHT WONDER why Heller's story appears in this book. Unlike others we have met so far, the underdog in this case prevailed against Tyranny, Inc., despite the odds. The rule of law worked as it was supposed to. Isn't this outcome worth celebrating? You would, of course, be right. There is only one wrinkle: David Heller lives and works in Toronto, and it was the Supreme Court of *Canada* that held Uber's agreement to be unenforceable.

Here is how such cases play out in the United States.

In 2005, Stephen Morris joined the global accounting giant Ernst & Young at its Los Angeles office. He was hired as a low-level staffer, lacking accreditation as a certified public accountant, or CPA. In his role, he would help examine clients' financial statements to make sure they didn't contain errors or falsehoods. But he did so strictly under the direction of his superiors, typically CPA-licensed partners or senior professionals of the firm. As his subsequent lawsuit against his former employer put it, the prohibition ensured that the firm didn't run afoul of the tangle of governmental and professional-association rules that regulate the audit business.

Morris's status as an unlicensed, low-level staffer mattered for his later dispute with EY, because it meant he wasn't exempt from the overtime requirements set out by California labor laws, as well as the federal Fair Labor Standards Act, or FLSA.

During tax season, the hours were *grinding,* to put it mildly. The job description said that staffers like Morris should expect to clock in at least fifty-five hours a week, well in excess of the statutory forty hours, every January through March.[2] His assigned tasks were clearly low-level ("filing papers, organizing and assembling documents, taking notes of meetings, entering data into spread sheets, schedules, or forms," and so on).[3] Yet despite Morris's nonexempt status, EY denied him overtime pay, regardless of the number of hours he put in.

All this took a toll. As one of his lawyers told me, Morris would regularly "work until midnight or one in the morning, shower, and be back there by seven in the morning. No overtime, no special consideration. Often, no meal breaks. Because there was so much work to be done." And it wasn't just Morris. Many similarly situated low-level staffers "had horror stories about the amount of work they were required to do, and what it took away from their family lives."

At one point in the course of Morris's employment, EY sent

workers an email stating that henceforth they must agree to pursue any disputes with the firm through private arbitration. The agreement explicitly barred workers from vindicating their rights collectively through class-action suits. And they had to consent to these terms as a condition of their continued employment.[4] In other words, if Morris showed up at work the next day, he would forgo his right to sue his employer in a court of law.

As we saw in the previous chapter, some would argue that a worker like Morris was now "free" to renegotiate or walk away. Those who inhabit the real world might understand why Morris had to "consent" to the new terms suddenly dictated by his employer: to be able to put food on the table.

As with Heller's case against Uber, the arbitration clause erected a high barrier to justice once Morris decided, in 2012, to sue EY for illegal nonpayment of overtime under the FLSA and local laws. Only, EY's arbitration process dwarfed Uber's in cost, complexity, and sheer deviousness: a multiphase mechanism, seemingly designed to delay any challenge until the challenger was left exhausted or bankrupt.

In addition to barring all court proceedings, individual or class action, the agreement blocked Morris even from banding together with other workers to make their case collectively before the privatized court, meaning each individual claimant would have to pay his own up-front fee, marshal his own separate evidence before the arbitrator, and so on. Even before he could appear individually before the arbitration forum, Morris first had to pursue months-long mediation in a company-controlled process.[5]

If the process reached arbitration, the private court would follow procedures and rules designed by EY, with any conflicts resolved in favor of the employer's preferences. And while the up-front fees were more reasonable than Uber's, the privatized "trial" needed extensive evidence and expert testimony, costs Morris would have to bear. His lawyers had documentation, unchallenged by EY, showing that arbitrating such claims individually would cost $200,000. This, in order to recover just under $2,000, plus roughly the same amount in damages.[6]

Put another way: The privatized "justice" meted out by Morris's employer was not only unaffordable by a worker in his position; it was irrational from an economic point of view. The only way Morris and workers like him could rationally vindicate their rights was if they could band together in class-action litigation, or at least in class arbitration.

So how did our Supreme Court rule? In one of the cruelest decisions ever issued by the high court, Justice Neil Gorsuch, writing for a 5–4 conservative majority, held that Morris and EY had freely "contracted for arbitration," thus "indicating their intention to use individualized rather than class or collective action." The courts "absolutely" couldn't get in the way of what the parties had freely agreed.[7]

Gorsuch's 2018 opinion in *Epic Systems v. Lewis* (the name of the case refers to a similar dispute that was consolidated and decided jointly with Morris's) was the wicked culmination of a line of decisions going back to the 1980s. These rulings further loosened American law's already-flimsy protections for workers and consumers.

Many were handed down by Federalist Society–certified "originalists," whose philosophy urges judges not to substitute their own preferences for the intentions of lawmakers. Yet when it came to arbitration abuse, as we will see in the paragraphs that follow, they shredded the existing law and invented a new one, ushering in what the scholars Katherine Stone and Alexander Colvin have called a "hidden revolution."[8] The result is a vast parallel court system, where powerful interests get to tailor the rules to their advantage, dominate weaker actors, and ultimately close off access to justice.

In the wake of the hidden revolution, the share of nonunionized companies subjecting their workers to mandatory arbitration agreements exploded to 54 percent as of 2017, up from just 2 percent in 1992.[9] Workers forced into arbitration are much less likely to prevail in their cases than those able to access traditional courts. The employee win rate in arbitration is 21 percent—"59 percent as often as in the federal courts and only 38 percent as often as in state courts."[10]

What happens inside the private arbitration chamber is something of a mystery—by design. For one thing, employers and other commercial interests can impose absolute secrecy. A worker, for example, can be barred from sharing evidence gleaned from the "discovery" process (such as it is) with his fellow workers lodging a similar complaint. In this way, the corporation can force each individual to go it alone through the expensive process.

While the larger private arbitration providers have set out certain protocols and protections, it is ultimately the corporations that get to decide whether to incorporate them—or whether and how to modify and abridge them, as we saw with EY. The arbitrator isn't a judge and doesn't even have to be a trained lawyer. There is no court reporter, no casebook of decisions reasoning why a certain decision was reached. "Due process" is a loose term here.

Even when they do win their cases, workers subject to mandatory arbitration are likely to receive far smaller awards. As Stone and Colvin report, "The average outcome in mandatory arbitration is only 16 percent of that in the federal courts and 7 percent of that in state courts"—a jarring gap that can't easily be explained by typical differences between the arbitration process and traditional litigation.[11]

Given the smaller amounts usually involved, workers have a harder time accessing legal counsel to assist them through the arbitration process. Employers, moreover, often enjoy what legal scholars call "repeat-player advantage": Familiarity with the system allows firms to game it to their advantage. A 2014 study of nearly three thousand employment-arbitration cases found that while "the first time an employer appeared before an arbitrator, the employee had a 17.9 percent chance of winning . . . after 25 cases before the same arbitrator the employee's chance of winning dropped to only 4.5 percent."[12]

The private arbitration chamber is the true court system of Tyranny, Inc. It is the bosses' court.

A New Law Out of Whole Cloth

To understand how all this came to be, we have to briefly examine the origins of arbitration, the 1925 federal law that gave birth to America's modern arbitration regime, and how that law interfaces (or is supposed to interface) with labor rights.

Arbitration—submitting a dispute to a neutral mediator for resolution—dates to the Middle Ages. Whereas on "lawday" parties in dispute went to court seeking *judgment,* on "loveday" they sought *reconciliation* of land disputes, family feuds, and the like, with the church often playing the role of arbitrator. The hallmarks of medieval arbitration were speed, informality, low cost, free choice of arbitrator, and the ability to air out all differences between the parties—in contrast to traditional courts, with their slow and rigidly formal processes, high expense, and narrow choice of judges and subject matter.[13]

Medieval arbitration was extremely popular. Yet the rise of market society, with its commercial complexities and more litigious character, transfigured "loveday" in the image of "lawday." By the nineteenth century, quarreling parties came more and more to expect of arbitration the same formal, adversarial process that went on in the courts. And because these parties needed the government to enforce arbitral awards, courts began to oversee arbitration and to develop a body of arbitration law.[14]

The courts, in short, didn't like it. Judges weren't fond of giving up their domain to what they saw as pseudo-judges and pseudo-litigation. Some fretted about stronger parties using arbitration to take advantage of weaker ones. As a result, merchants who had contractually agreed to settle their disputes using arbitration could pull out of the process at any time before an award was handed down, and courts wouldn't lift a finger to hold them to their promises.[15]

As the economy developed, the U.S. court system sank into a quagmire of commercial litigation. And lawyers' hardball tactics ensured that contending merchants' business relationships would be left in tatters by the time they stepped out of the courtroom. There had to be some way of enforcing arbitration agreements between merchants, to recover the ancient practice's promise of speed, informality, and general goodwill for the modern, capitalist context.

Enter, in the 1920s, Julius Cohen and Charles Bernheimer. Cohen served as general counsel to the New York State Chamber of Commerce. Bernheimer was a cotton merchant and chairman of the chamber's committee on arbitration. The pair believed that arbitration was good for businessmen and good for overburdened courts. What they needed were statutes that would compel the courts to enforce arbitration awards.

They began in New York, where in 1920 the state legislature enacted an arbitration law more or less drafted by Cohen and Bernheimer. But a single state law wasn't enough. They also needed a federal law on the books that made arbitration agreements enforceable in federal court. To get such a law enacted, the New York duo teamed up with William H. H. Piatt of the American Bar Association. Herbert Hoover, who served as secretary of commerce at the time, proved a valuable Washington ally.

These proponents made a good case for what would become the Federal Arbitration Act, or FAA. But they had first to allay lawmakers' concerns over the "inclusion of workers' contracts in the law's scheme," as Hoover noted in a letter.[16] Cohen and company went to great lengths to persuade Congress that the arbitration statute they sought would be limited to transactions between merchants; that it emphatically wouldn't cover the employment context, or otherwise be used to strong-arm weaker parties into giving up their rights in take-it-or-leave-it agreements, where one party has no choice but to "consent" to terms dictated by the other.

Piatt, for example, testified that the proposed FAA was "purely" about "giv[ing] merchants the right or the privilege of sitting down and agreeing with each other. . . . Now that is all there is in this." Pressed by a Montana senator about whether the act would compel a weaker party to agree to arbitrate his disputes with a stronger party in involuntary fashion, Piatt replied, "I would not favor any kind of legislation that would permit the forcing [of] a man to sign that kind of a contract. . . . I think that ought to be protested against, because it is the primary end of this contract that it is a contract between merchants"—that is, between commercial parties of relatively equal power. Likewise, when asked for examples of arbitration cases from his New York experience, Bernheimer cited only disputes between merchants.[17]

To address the concern that the new arbitration law would ensnare employees, rendering them incapable of vindicating their rights in court, Piatt proposed language excluding workers involved in sea shipping or other forms of interstate transport. Hoover suggested adding railroad workers.[18] The final statutory language on workers provided that "nothing herein contained shall apply to contracts of employment of seamen, railroad employees, or any other class of workers engaged in interstate or foreign commerce."[19]

The statutory language explicitly excluded only certain categories of employees (railroad hands, seamen, and the like). But as the Loyola University Chicago arbitration expert Margaret Moses has shown, that's only because at the time, the regulation of most employment contracts was seen as purely a *state* affair. And since the new law was meant to enforce agreements between merchants in *federal* courts, members of Congress didn't consider it necessary to expressly protect any workers except those employed in interstate commerce (railroads, shipping lines, and so on). It was taken for granted that other kinds of employment wouldn't fall under the ambit of the FAA.[20]

The FAA passed in 1925, without a single "nay" vote. In the decade following its enactment, Congress cemented the legislative pillars of the New Deal, not least the right of workers to act collectively to secure interests left unprotected by individual action. As for the possibility that employers would use arbitration to abridge workers' rights, Congress had contemplated that evil outcome in 1925 and taken pains to foreclose it. For decades, the courts honored this clear congressional intent.

THAT IS, UNTIL the 1980s, when the court began to elevate a pro-corporate agenda to high legal principle. This was the "hidden revolution." Its seeds were sown, innocently enough, in a 1967 decision in which the high court discussed the constitutional basis of the FAA. Back in the 1920s, proponents had insisted that the FAA was a *procedural* statute resting on Congress's power to "establish and control inferior Federal Courts," as Cohen had testified.[21] But in the 1967 decision, the court ignored this legislative history and stated that the FAA rests on Congress's power to regulate interstate commerce.[22]

The reasons were arcane, having to do with the question of what federal courts are supposed to do when faced with disputes between parties from different states and involving state law. The bottom line: By suggesting the FAA is a broad, substantive statute implicating Congress's prerogative to oversee the national economy, rather than a merely procedural one telling federal courts what to do, the high court opened the door to the dramatic expansion of the FAA.[23]

We can't cover all of the relevant decisions leading up to the 2018 ruling in which the court told Morris he had to individually arbitrate his dispute with EY. But a few highlights are worth touching on.

First, in 1983, the Supreme Court divined that the FAA had created a "liberal federal policy favoring arbitration agreements."[24] This, despite exactly zero evidence in the legislative history suggesting that Congress considered arbitration a *"superior* method of resolving disputes," as Moses notes.[25] The next year, the court determined—again, against the explicit guidance of the legislative history—that the FAA applies in state courts as much as federal ones, and that it overrides any state law contrary to the statute's aim of promoting arbitration.[26]

Soon, the justices concluded that the FAA goes far beyond contractual quarrels between merchants, requiring arbitration even when the disputes involve other federal statutes: antitrust laws in

1985, the RICO antiracketeering statute in 1987, workplace antidis-crimination laws in 1991.[27] In tandem, the court "repeatedly rebuffed attempts by states to enact legislation that would protect consumers and employees from unfair arbitration agreements," as the scholars Stone and Colvin put it.[28] A Montana law requiring that arbitration clauses appear on the first page of a contract and in reasonable font size was struck down in 1996. And even where the underlying con-tract is found to be illegal, fraudulent, or unconscionable under state law, the Supreme Court insisted, the arbitration clause must remain enforceable.[29]

For some time after the 1980s revolution, however, it remained unclear to what extent the new arbitration regime applied to em-ployees. Recall that the FAA precludes the statute from being applied to "contracts of employment." And as we saw, while the statutory text itself mentions only a few categories of employees (railroad hands and the like), that was only because lawmakers in 1925 didn't consider it necessary to mention other workers whose employment was thought to be regulated solely by state law. Nevertheless, in 2001, the Supreme Court interpreted the exception to apply only to work-ers involved in interstate transportation.[30]

Justice Antonin Scalia was especially zealous for arbitration. In a 2011 decision holding that AT&T could force consumers into indi-vidual arbitration found unconscionable under state law, the arch-"originalist" held that even class arbitration gets in the way of "fundamental attributes of arbitration," by depriving defendants of "multilayered" judicial review.[31]

Scalia exhibited no such consideration for weaker plaintiffs left unable to access any justice at all. When a group of merchants brought suit against American Express under the Sherman Antitrust Act, he insisted that the individual-arbitration clauses be upheld, though the cost of arbitrating far exceeded the amount each mer-chant could hope to obtain if he prevailed individually.

Even after the 1980s revolution, the court had still insisted that arbitrating statutory claims is appropriate only "so long as the prospective litigant effectively may vindicate" his statutory rights in the arbitral forum.[32] Scalia now threw that principle to the wind: "The fact that it is not worth the expense involved in *proving* a statutory remedy does not constitute the elimination of the *right* to pursue that remedy."[33] Translation: Although you, the employee or consumer, may never actually get to vindicate your statutory rights in the physical world, you should take comfort that you retain a right to do so in some ideal, Platonic realm of legal forms.

Crying to Heaven

Which brings us back to the ruling in Stephen Morris's case against Ernst & Young (decided jointly with a few other similar cases). Gorsuch and his conservative colleagues recast the entire history of the FAA to suggest that the employers' pro-arbitration arguments were perfectly compatible with the law—that the employees were the ones who had put forth a bizarre and novel interpretation.

Recall that Morris's claim was based on his right to act collectively. Federal law, specifically the FLSA, allowed him to bring a class-action suit to recover overtime that EY owed him and other junior staffers. Otherwise, they would *never* be made whole for the illegal underpayment of their wages. The majority dismissed it. "Until a couple of years ago," Gorsuch wrote, "courts more or less agreed that arbitration agreements like those before us must be enforced according to their terms."[34] This was a shameless assertion: Gorsuch skipped over the decades leading up to the hidden revolution and then blamed Morris for insisting on Congress's clear, original intent.[35]

In the end, Gorsuch showed himself a true believer in liberty of contract in the nineteenth-century mold. He suggested that Morris had "contracted"[36] to forswear his right to seek justice in court (by choosing to show up to work after EY emailed him a new arbitration agreement). The chasmic differential in bargaining power and the take-it-or-leave-it coercion involved in obtaining his "consent" were of no consequence.³⁷ The ahistorical, pulled-from-thin-air "liberal federal policy favoring arbitration" overrode all else.

In a blistering dissent, the late justice Ruth Bader Ginsburg pointed out that the majority had effectively resurrected the *Lochner* era—an era that was supposed to have been swept aside by the New Deal. She quoted one of the legislative architects of the New Deal, Nebraska's Senator George Norris, whose name is memorialized in the Norris–La Guardia Act banning yellow-dog contracts that required workers to forgo union membership as a condition of employment. Such agreements, Norris had declared, render the worker "absolutely helpless," by forcing him to give up "his right . . . to free association" and to "singly present any grievance he has."³⁸

Individual arbitration of the kind the court had come to fetishize did exactly that: It allowed employers to get away with wage underpayment by forcing workers to "singly present" their complaints in a forum where they lacked any realistic means of obtaining justice— where justice meant spending $200,000 to recover less than 2 percent of that amount.

In denouncing this outcome, Ginsburg gave her colleagues an astute lesson in the legislative history of the FAA: that in passing the act, Congress intended merely to "enable merchants of roughly equal bargaining power to enter into binding agreements to arbitrate *commercial* disputes"; that it "did not intend the statute to apply to arbitration provisions in employment contracts"; that it "never endorsed a policy favoring arbitration where one party sets the terms of an agreement while the other is left to take it or leave it."³⁹

Likewise, Ginsburg reminded the conservative majority of the revolutionary nature of its own FAA jurisprudence: how, "in recent decades, this Court has veered away from Congress' intent simply to afford merchants a speedy and economical means of resolving commercial disputes," and how "employers have availed themselves of the opportunity opened by court decisions expansively interpreting the Arbitration Act."⁴⁰

The final result, Ginsburg fumed, was nothing less than "destructive." She cited a 2009 study that found that in Chicago, New York City, and Los Angeles alone "workers lose nearly $3 billion in legally owed wages each year."[41] That last, Los Angeles, was where Stephen Morris had been employed by EY. It was where the mega-firm had ground him down with workdays stretching from dawn to midnight, without coughing up statutory overtime.

It is worth noting that many of the conservative justices behind the hidden revolution, not least Scalia, publicly touted their fidelity to the Catholic faith.[42] In the catechism of the Roman Catholic Church, withholding just wages from workers is one of the grave sins that "cry to heaven."[43] Under the rule of Tyranny, Inc., the highest court in the land has all but given the sanction of law to wage theft.

At the next stop on our tour, we will witness what happens to underpaid workers once the firms they work for are targeted by Wall Street—the command center of private tyranny.

5

The Corporate Eroder

H E W A S N E V E R the book-smart one. That role belonged to his oldest brother, who half a century ago got a job out of college making $32,000 a year, a fat sum then. No, Bruce Miller wasn't clever in that way, but he toiled to make ends meet, to not be a burden. The one-story ranch-style house he bought in Manchester, New Jersey, was a symbol of his determination, the wood and the cement radiating the modest dignity of their owner. The earnings that underwrote Miller's house came courtesy of his employer, one of capitalism's most storied brands: Sears.

"I was pretty proud of that," he told me. "First home that I worked [for], owned it totally. Well, me and the bank did."

As the years wore on, however, his once-secure, well-paying job at Sears slipped away—and with it, his ability to keep up with his mortgage payments. More than two decades after Miller moved in, the sheriff gave him a foreclosure notice and fourteen days to vacate the premises. In a matter of weeks, he would lose his home, his health insurance, and his wages, and all he could think about were the repeated assurances from his bosses that the painful changes afoot at work were to "make the company stronger."

Sears had defined U.S. dynamism and common prosperity for a century. Its onetime Chicago headquarters literally towered over the heartland. Its high-school-educated salesmen doubled the salaries of college-educated men; its warehouse workers could retire with seven-figure assets.[1] It mastered a new way to shop, the mail-order catalog, and built the logistics hub to swiftly deliver any product anywhere in the nation—a system dubbed the "seventh wonder of the business world."[2]

Then it all crumbled. By the time Sears filed for bankruptcy on October 15, 2018, the retailer held $7 billion in assets, against $11 billion in liabilities. Some of its most beloved brands had already been sold off, and the number of stores had dwindled to seven hundred, down from a peak of thirty-five hundred when Sears and Kmart had merged thirteen years earlier.[3] Sears was now best at delivering pink slips, having shed at least 200,000 jobs over the previous decade.[4]

Miller was one of those laid-off Sears workers. Set against the downfall of his employer, his personal tragedy appears minuscule. Yet his travails open a revealing, bottom-up window onto the generational decline of the real economy, where America once made it its business to produce *useful* goods and services.

The demise of Sears was far from a "natural" result of business cycles, rising competition, or sheer bad luck, as the story is often told. Rather, it was the consequence of a relatively recent turn in the historical development of American capitalism. Under this new dispensation, Wall Street financiers acquire going concerns not to sustain, let alone grow, the businesses, but to siphon away productive capital from the real economy into the financial economy—which is to say, into their own asset ledgers, workers and communities be damned.

They call this "investment." But it is far more akin to looting.

BORN IN A small town in southern New Hampshire, Bruce Miller came to live in Jersey after a road trip gone wrong. The year was 1982. Fresh out of high school, he and a few friends were on a cross-country journey when the truck hauling their trailer broke down. With help from Travelers Aid, they towed it to the Garden State, where Miller's friends had family. He was hired by the local Sears, attached to a mall in Toms River, New Jersey, and stayed for good.

His first job was in maintenance, buffing floors for $3.45 an hour. There was no health insurance or other benefits. But Miller was young and single, and the thirty-hour workweek more than sufficed to cover lodging and food, about his only expenses. After a few months, a third-party contractor was hired to do maintenance work, leaving Miller with the choice to either seek a position with the incoming cleaning firm or transfer to another department inside Sears.

Miller resolved to stay. Sears found him a job in the stockrooms at the auto center, unloading and shelving tire inventory. The retailer was relatively new to the auto business in those days, but its service centers had quickly proved a hit with customers, who could pick up, say, camping gear at the main store and have their tires realigned on a single trip. Plus, the Sears name and the premium auto brands associated with it (DieHard, Michelin, Metzeler) telegraphed reliability to the area's large elderly population. Miller's center moved up to fifteen hundred tires a week in addition to offering the full range of services: from batteries and shocks to oil changes and front-end repairs.

Miller's bosses took notice of his work ethic. "The fire inspector one day came in," he recalled, "and he went to my boss, and he says, 'I've never seen the stockroom that clean.'" Eventually, Miller found his way from the stockrooms to the auto bays, "and that was the start of my automotive, fixing-cars career."

He began by changing tires and soon learned more technical tasks, through both formal training and on-the-job experience. Alignments became his specialty. His wage rose steadily, thanks to periodic cost-of-living and merit raises. Because Sears paid hourly, rather than by the job or on commission, it created a "family atmosphere," as Miller put it. Even during busy hours, mechanics didn't hesitate to help each other, which redounded to the advantage of customers.

One summer day, for example, Miller had already finished his shift when the boss approached him in the parking lot with a favor to ask. The evening-shift alignment guy had called out sick, and there were two more alignments to be done. Though he had already changed into his T-shirt and shorts, Miller didn't hesitate to do the extra work, which took about an hour. As he was finally about to leave, the boss signed papers rewarding him with four hours' overtime. "He didn't have to do that," Miller said. "He could've just paid me at my base pay. He realized, hey, I helped him out. Obviously, the next time he needed something, yeah, I'll do that. Not expecting that he'd do that again, but one hand washes the other, y'know?" That was the attitude at Sears back then: "Take care of the people that make you money."

Years passed. Miller went full-time and was able to access health insurance and a pension. In 1996, he tapped into his pension for the down payment on his house, with enough funds left over to cover the addition of a back deck; a new truck came a few years later. By this time, Miller was making $17 an hour, and while he wasn't a social butterfly or the marrying type, he had the joy of tangibly serving his neighbors, paying his bills, and going to bed dog-tired and fulfilled.

Business appeared strong as ever. But while that might have been true locally, things weren't going so well for the company as a whole, which was facing stiff competition from a new class of salesman-free, customer-savvy big-box stores, such as Walmart, Circuit City, Best Buy, and the Home Depot. Amazon, moreover, was well on its way from a gleam in Jeff Bezos's eye to becoming an economy-transforming online-shopping behemoth. Sears struggled to keep up.

Most Americans assume the rise of these rivals alone accounts for the bankruptcy of a legendary retailer. But that isn't even half the story. Yes, Sears faced stiff competition in the 1990s and first decade of the twenty-first century. But its troubles traced to an earlier, and all-too-typical, failure to properly invest in its core retail business. Then came an especially predatory new owner who not only didn't invest but drank the firm's remaining capital to the dregs, disgorging only misery for others.

In all this, Sears tracked, almost to a T, the broader degeneration of the large American corporation: from a source of middle-class

jobs and prosperity and genuine innovation into a capital quarry for
a narrow financial class wielding vast and unchecked coercive powers.

Tower of Wishes

In the 1880s, Richard Sears was a young Minnesota railway agent
with a side hustle selling coal and lumber. One day in 1886, he bought
a shipment of watches that had been rejected by another dealer and
hawked them himself, pocketing a tidy profit. The next year, he went
into business with the Indiana watch repairman Alvah Roebuck to
market watches and jewelry via mail order. A clothier soon joined
the partnership, now based in Chicago. Sears, Roebuck and Company was born.[5]

An ever-swelling catalog formed the foundation of the firm, and
a forty-acre logistics hub in Chicago was its beating heart. The ultra-
efficient hub allowed Sears to not only undersell local general stores
but bring a world of lifestyle possibility to the doorsteps of the rural
middle class. Black Americans especially appreciated the ability to
bypass racist merchants via the catalog. So ubiquitous was the catalog in American homes that, as one legendary story has it, a school-
child told his teacher that the Ten Commandments had been handed
down by Sears.[6]

In 1906, Sears offered shares to the general investor, "the first initial public offering (IPO) for an American retail firm" and "the first
to be handled by Goldman Sachs," as one business reporter notes.
Henry Ford's Model T in the 1920s "would throw a wrench in Sears'
business model, as cars made . . . mail-order catalogs less crucial to
rural customers."[7] In response, Sears built up a network of department stores that in the following decade did better business than the
catalog.

So effective was the firm at logistics and distribution that when
President Franklin Delano Roosevelt needed to mobilize U.S. industry to reinforce the Allies in World War II, he turned to Donald

Nelson, a vice president for merchandising at Sears, to head up procurement at Treasury. After Pearl Harbor, FDR asked Nelson to oversee the conversion of peacetime industrial firms into manufacturers of tanks, aircraft, rifles, and the like.[8]

The postwar era brought still-greater success as Sears became the go-to shop for the appliance- and convenience-hungry U.S. middle class. The retailer created hot new consumer markets for the likes of Whirlpool and General Electric. You couldn't get more "real economy" than this: In a virtuous cycle, Sears spurred demand for products that made life more convenient; the demand, in turn, generated robust, often-unionized working-class jobs that allowed more Americans to access those conveniences. Sears, and the American wage laborer, scored on both ends.[9]

In 1973, Sears touched the sky, literally. That was the year construction was completed on its new Chicago headquarters, the Sears Tower, which at 1,450 feet was the tallest building in the world, a record it held for nearly a quarter century. Former executives who took meetings in the tower still remember feeling as if they were floating above the clouds. From those heights, they continued to fulfill customers' wishes nationwide. Yet customers now had more options, and small cracks were beginning to appear in the firm's retail supremacy. As one manager recalled, it was at that point that a company long accustomed to reinvention was "in need of changing again."[10]

In the 1980s, leadership settled on heavily diversifying Sears's activities. In addition to selling washing machines, televisions, sturdy all-American apparel, and the like, the retailer would now branch out to consumer credit (the Discover card), insurance (Allstate), real estate (Coldwell Banker), financial brokerage (Dean Witter Reynolds), even a proto-internet service (Prodigy), in what became known as Sears's famous "socks and stocks" strategy.

As the former chief financial officer and chief executive Alan Lacy reflected in a *Wall Street Journal* interview after the fall, these new businesses "did create a lot of shareholder value," but they left management "distracted away from the retail business."[11] Just when Walmart, Kmart, the Home Depot, and the like were beginning to make their mark on retail, Sears was hemorrhaging capital from its retail operations to support a bewildering array of unrelated businesses.

"Walmart can't touch us," one manager recalled her fellow executives sneering.[12] They assumed—wrongly, it turned out—that the pick-it-yourself shopping model was too unattractive to compete with Sears's salesmen-led department stores. By the time management got around to unburdening the firm of its various "stocks" businesses and revamping retail, including by retiring the loss-making catalog in 1993 at a cost of fifty thousand jobs, it was too late: Sears was trailing Walmart and Kmart, the No. 1 and No. 2 firms in retail, respectively.[13]

Thus stood Sears at the dawn of the new millennium: down as a result of neglecting its core business—but far from out. Sadly for Miller and his fellow employees, Sears's leadership next turned for "rescue" to a Wall Street boss who epitomized the new general tendency of the U.S. economy: the drainage of capital from the real economy into the financial markets—specifically, into the pockets of hedge fund and private equity managers.

The Eroder

"Hi, I'm Eddie Lampert. I like the story and I'm gonna look at buying stocks."[14] With these innocuous words, the man who would drive Sears to its final ruin introduced himself to Lacy, then the firm's CEO. The year was 2000. Lacy had just held his first investor conference. The "story" he had told was that Sears was an iconic American retailer that could survive and thrive in the new century, provided a farseeing investor or group of investors would back its revival.

Edward Scott Lampert presented himself as that farseeing investor. A Yale roommate of the future Treasury secretary Steven Mnuchin's, Lampert had gotten his start at Goldman Sachs before leaving at age twenty-five to launch his own hedge fund. In its first decade and a half, his fund had averaged an eye-watering annual return on investment of 29 percent, and so when he began to take an interest in distressed large retailers, the financial press was enrapt.[15]

In 2003, Lampert through his hedge fund, ESL Investments, took a majority stake in Kmart—Sears's 1990s nemesis that by the turn of the millennium had gone bankrupt. In the months that followed, Sears, which needed Kmart-style stores, purchased fifty locations from the ESL-controlled Kmart. Then, in 2005, Lampert's Kmart merged with Sears, forming a giant new entity, with thirty-five hundred combined stores and more than 400 million square feet of shopping space. One idea was to transform several low-performing Kmarts into Sears stores, to compete with the rising big-box chains.[16]

Sales revenue jumped during the first year of the Lampert regime, then declined every year thereafter until 2018's Chapter 11 bankruptcy. What happened? To answer the question, we have to explore the evolving structure of the typical American corporation—firms' increasing tendency to use their capital base to service financial markets, at the expense of investment—and the role hedge funds and private equity firms play in hyper-accelerating the waste.

LET'S SAY YOU wish to start a firm to manufacture and market a mosquito lamp you've designed. To raise the capital needed to get going (to pay for machines, labor, advertising, and the like), you turn to financial markets—typically, a bank. If your firm is already established, you might also turn to financial markets to fund, for example, the development of an innovative new mosquito repellent that uses low-frequency sound or what have you.

For its trouble, the bank or other investor receives a return, in the form of dividends on shares of the company you traded away in exchange for the infusion of finance capital. In this way, the financial economy (the bank) helps the real economy (your firm and its customers, suppliers, and workers). Yes, the financier is rewarded for its role. But you, as the manager of your firm, strive to hold on to enough of your earnings to continue investing in and growing the business.

This is the picture most ordinary Americans have of what corporations do, and for a very long time it was an accurate picture. But as the political economist Oren Cass notes, "That's not how the economy works today." The American firm has changed, and not for the better. "Whereas corporations used to retain and reinvest roughly half of their earnings . . . that share has fallen below 10%, with the rest paid out to shareholders. From 2008 to 2017, corporations paid out 100% of their earnings."[17]

Analyzing publicly available information on cash flow for U.S.-based firms traded on Wall Street, Cass divides companies into three categories in terms of what they do with their capital. Let's tackle each in turn.

The first group of firms turn to financial markets to raise funds for investment greater than their earnings before set costs like interest, taxes, depreciation, and amortization (EBITDA, in finance jargon). These are the most ambitious firms, and Cass calls them, appropriately enough, "Growers"; your mosquito-lamp maker above probably acts like a Grower when it turns to financial markets to fund R&D and marketing for the new sound-based repellent. Your ordinary profits wouldn't suffice to develop the innovation while covering your existing costs, so you hope some investor will see the promise of your vision.[18]

Next are what Cass calls "Sustainers." These are firms whose EBITDA allows them to invest in maintaining or growing their business while also paying their shareholders. Every year that a business operates, it wears away some of its capital—its buildings age, its machines wear down, and so on—and so it must continue to invest every year just to maintain the capital base that supports its operations. Growing the business typically requires further investment on top. Assuming your mosquito lamp is a hit with customers, your company will probably end up acting like a regular old Sustainer.

Your profit will be sufficient to replenish your capital base, perhaps invest in growth, and also provide shareholders a return. As Cass notes, "Most companies in a well-functioning capitalist economy should be Sustainers and, historically, most were."[19]

Finally, there are the "Eroders." These firms are profitable enough "to grow their capital bases like Sustainers and still return cash to shareholders, but they choose not to. Instead, they actively disinvest from themselves, allowing their capital bases to erode even while paying to shareholders the resources they would have needed if they wanted to maintain their health."[20] Being an Eroder, as you might guess, isn't a good thing. It may be inevitable if the business becomes unviable for any number of reasons, but it certainly isn't something managers should strive for, since it ultimately puts the firm on the path to failure.

None of this is all that complicated: Just as plants need sunlight and water to grow, so healthy businesses need investment. Starve them of that, and they will soon wither and fade.

These three types of firms collectively accounted for 90 percent of U.S. market capitalization over the past half century. What has changed is the relative composition of that 90 percent. From 1971 to 1985, the vast majority of American firms (82 percent, weighted by market capitalization) were Sustainers. By 2017, however, Sustainers accounted for only 40 percent of market capitalization, while half had degenerated into Eroders, sacrificing their brands, factories, retail spaces, and the like on the altar of short-term shareholder returns. The share of Growers, meanwhile, sank to 3 percent, down from 9 percent in the 1971–1985 period.[21]

This shift has little to do with deindustrialization or the rise of a "softer," information-based economy. On the contrary, the information sector—comprising firms in media, communications, and high tech—has also suffered from erosion. Over the period under analysis, the share of Eroders among information firms ballooned to 52 percent of U.S. market capitalization, up from 2 percent.[22] The digital-communication conglomerate Cisco, for example, has acted like an Eroder since 2003.[23]

Erosion has grave consequences for the nation. Investors are entitled to a return on their investment, to compensate them for providing their capital. But as a share of gross domestic product, the net cash flow out of the real economy and into the financial one has more than doubled in recent decades. This translates to $3 trillion that might previously have supported operating businesses but instead has returned to investor pockets.[24]

The result is firms and industries that are less competitive and less productive. (Innovating and boosting productivity require capital, after all.) It also means a society where the wealthy catch all the upside. When, for example, firms buy back their shares to goose the stock price—the quintessential Eroder maneuver—those who hold corporate equity can watch with satisfaction as their stock portfolios climb in value. Meanwhile, firms stumble, the U.S. economy loses edge, and workers and the political community are thrown into distress.[25]

IF FIRM-LEVEL EROSION and economy-wide resource drainage are the general tendencies of U.S. capitalism today, hedge funds and private equity act as the vanguard of this transformation. They are Eroders par excellence. As the industry critic (and Cass's colleague) Wells King explains, the business model of both hedge funds and private equity is to raise

> large pools of capital from "qualified investors"—high-net-worth individuals, pension funds, university and foundation endowments, and so on—and then pursue complex investment strategies that deliver returns superior to traditional, public equity and bond markets. For their trouble, they charge their investors a flat, annual management fee regardless of performance—traditionally 2% of the amount invested—and also keep a share of any profits—traditionally 20%.[26]

Oxford University's Ludovic Phalippou estimates that private equity managers collected $230 billion in fees over a recent ten-year period while leaving investors with a return no better than a public index fund, a wealth transfer he calls "one of the largest in the history of modern finance."[27]

What do such firms do with that capital? It depends. Private equity firms generally combine some of the funds they have raised and loads more borrowed money to take over a firm. Then they (supposedly) improve the allocation of capital to generate greater value before selling it off. By "levering up"—piling the firm with debt and using profits to pay it down—the partners make nice returns for themselves and their investors, but they also dramatically increase the likelihood of bankruptcy.[28] That's fine for the partners, whose gains on some businesses make up for driving others to ruin. But the employees at the affected company can't afford this risk profile: A worker, after all, can't take ten jobs simultaneously and hope that he comes out well on average.

Hedge funds, meanwhile, deploy any number of byzantine schemes to extract value without producing anything ordinary people might ever consider useful. "Some attempt to generate positive returns regardless of how the market and broader economy perform," writes King, "often taking long and short positions in a variety of publicly traded assets"[29]—hence, the *hedging* in "hedge fund." Others gamble on things no ordinary person would think of as an "investment," including lawsuits, insurance claims, and distressed government assets in the developing world. Still others acquire controlling stakes and either try to force management to do certain things or, as in the case of Lampert's ESL, take the management reins themselves.

The share of the U.S. economy dominated by hedge funds and private equity has ballooned over the past generation. Total assets under their management rose to $2.4 trillion in 2019, up from $2 billion in 1976. More than twice as many Americans now work for private-equity-controlled firms (nine million) as for the federal government and U.S. military combined (about four million). These firms also attract a huge slice of business talent, recruiting a third of 2020 Harvard and Stanford MBA graduates, more than any other industry.[30]

Defenders point to such figures as proof that Big Finance is "investing" in the economy. Yet as King notes, "The buying and selling of companies, the mergers and divestments, the hedging and leveraging, are not themselves valuable activity. They invent, create, build, and provide nothing."[31] On the contrary, financial wizardry of this kind very often destroys businesses, jobs, and communities. The fate of Sears is sadly illustrative.

NOT LONG AFTER the takeover, things started to go downhill for Bruce Miller. For starters, his paychecks now came on a biweekly, rather than weekly, basis, a change presumably intended to reduce payroll costs. That may not sound like a big deal to salaried employees, but for many working-class wage earners, less frequent pay means a harder time managing personal budgets. "I never did get used to that," Miller recalled. "I dealt with it, 'cause I had no choice."

Next came a 6:00 A.M., all-hands-on-deck meeting at which management announced a new, incentive-based wage structure for the mechanics. The upshot for Miller was a reduction in his base wage to $9.50 an hour, down from the $17 an hour that had allowed him to purchase his house and truck. Bosses reassured him that he could make up the difference by doing more jobs. Incentive payments varied depending on the complexity of each task: An oil change might garner him 75 cents in incentive pay, whereas an alignment brought $5. But some days, there just weren't as many complex, high-incentive tasks to be done.

It became harder for Miller to make his mortgage payments, though he still largely managed. Two years later, however, Sears changed the mechanics' pay structure yet again, replacing the incentive payments with commissions. His base pay would remain at $9.50 an hour. But he could earn a commission at rates ranging from 5 percent to 20 percent of the listed price of the service, depending on the technicality of the job. Each mechanic was also required to meet a minimum hourly dollar quota.

Bosses now exerted great pressure on mechanics to "upsell" customers. "We'd get these little old ladies that came in," Miller told me, "seventy, eighty years old, probably drives once a week. They tell me, 'Tell her she needs a coolant exchange and all this extra work.' Obviously, I'd make more money, but my conscience wouldn't let me do it. I wouldn't want somebody to do that to my mother."

He became the shop's black sheep. Bosses each had their favorite mechanics, and they would see to it that the favorites got the higher-commission customers. "They had their ways of tipping [their favorites] off that a good job was coming in, and then I would get sucked into doing a $3 oil change. . . . Because I usually got stuck doing oil changes, I wouldn't make [the quota], and I used to get called into the boss's office all the time for that."

They would scold him, "Why don't you do three oil changes at the same time?"

Toward the end, Miller's answer to the charge was, "Because there aren't enough auto bays."

The growing auto-bay shortage wasn't so much due to a dramatic uptick in the customer load as it was to an understaffing crisis. When mechanics quit, they simply wouldn't be replaced. With less labor power available, bays would fill up and jobs got resolved at a much slower clip. The remaining mechanics felt squeezed, even if there were now more choice jobs to go around. Defenders of private equity and hedge funds claim such management tactics help make the firm more efficient. To Lampert's employees, however, it appeared that he was debilitating a productive and profitable unit.

"If I make a mistake," Miller told me, "that can kill somebody."

One day toward the end of his tenure, the staffing crisis had escalated to such a degree that Miller found himself alone working the entire auto center. Harried and overworked, with the customers growing irate, he jumped frantically from auto bay to auto bay, servicing multiple vehicles. Amid the chaos, he has come to believe, he might have left the lug nuts on a wheel loose, causing the wheel to come off as the customer exited the Garden State Parkway. Luckily, no one was injured, but the incident rankled Miller. "To this day, it bothers me that I did that. I relate it to the amount of pressure they were putting on us to produce."

"Slap in the Face"

Lampert was eroding Sears. Lacy, the firm's last pre-Lampert CEO, recalled, "It became clear early on that Eddie's focus was maximizing cash flow in order to buy back stock."[32] So determined was Lampert to boost the price of shares that he even created a plan for employees to use their pensions to buy stock. Sure enough, the stock surged briefly, peaking at $134.51 a share in April 2007.[33] The high alpha masked, for a brief while, the rot spreading from top to bottom.

To regain its footing, Sears needed, foremost, to develop more attractive, conveniently located stores like those of its rising competitors. That was impossible without investment. But Lampert made it clear that "unless we believe we will receive an adequate return on investment, we will not spend money on capital expenditures to build new stores or upgrade our existing base simply because our competitors do."[34]

He proved true to his word, pushing his managers to refurbish the Kmarts-turned-Sears stores for fractions of what they had expected to spend. "We were taking Kmart stores that were in deplorable condition and trying to put Sears products in them and it was a disaster," one regional manager recalled. Fixtures were broken, lights didn't turn on, and holes pockmarked the parking lots. "The Kmart customers left, and the Sears customers didn't come because the buildings were not in the best places and not in the best shape."[35]

Lynn Walsh, who in 2017 left the company as vice president of profit improvement, recalled Lampert's executive team rebuffing any requests for improvements: "New fixtures? Why can't you use the ones you have? You want to redo that part of the floor? Why do we need to do that?" The result was stores that looked like "war zones," as Walsh put it. She recalled thinking to herself, "What customer would go through this when they can go to so many other stores?"[36]

Advertising dollars dried up, too, thanks to Lampert's notion that underperforming units and product lines didn't deserve that sort of support. This, even though "Sears advertising worked," as one salesman told *The Wall Street Journal*. "When advertising was slimming down, it had an impact on our customer traffic. In the past couple of years [leading up to the bankruptcy], even around Christmas, I don't remember seeing any Sears TV ads."[37]

The Lampert regime did invest in online shopping, the one area that received a measure of help following the takeover. Yet the firm's customer base wasn't exactly tech savvy, and the Sears site was finally too clunky to prove a hit with early adopters.[38]

Instead of investment, Lampert offered a bizarre management model apparently inspired by his juvenile literary tastes—specifically, the novels of the arch-libertarian writer Ayn Rand.[39] He carved up the firm into as many as forty separate divisions that had to compete with one another, even signing contracts for various services. Yes: Lampert would have different divisions of the *same company* bill each other. Each had its own board and senior management, thus multiplying executive-compensation costs and pitting the whole firm against itself.[40]

As the writers Michal Rozworski and Leigh Phillips explain, this vicious dynamic hastened the depletion of Sears's already-malnourished capital stock: "With no company-wide interest in maintaining store infrastructure, something instead viewed as an externally imposed cost by each division, Sears's capital expenditure dwindled to less than 1 percent of revenue, a proportion much lower than that of most other retailers."[41]

Eventually, the underinvestment reached catastrophic levels. One employee wrote to *Business Insider* to complain that "we have a

17-year-old running the office and cash office. He has no experience in either but he is a warm body to fill the job."[42] Other stores weren't able to process cash at all. A Bethesda, Maryland, mattress salesman recalled the shambolic state of the store where he had worked for a decade:

> The lack of staff really disrupted the entire operation. . . . They were seriously cutting the payroll. That was a distraction for the commissioned salespeople because we had no cashiers on our particular level. We were on the top floor of a two-floor Sears, and the few cashiers that were left were all working downstairs. At the end, they weren't even maintaining the registers. A lot of the registers were broken. I didn't even see a cleaning crew at all.[43]

Finally, there was the outright asset stripping. Lampert sold marquee Sears brands like Lands' End and Craftsman tools. His hedge fund, ESL, also created a real estate investment trust, Seritage, that purchased the real estate associated with 266 Sears stores, then leased it back to Sears, in essence forcing the retailer to "pay rent on the stores it previously owned," as critics note. ESL also made $400 million in interest and fees for funds lent to Sears.[44]

Cash-flow data tell the story more simply. To wit, Sears had consistently behaved like a Sustainer going back to the 1970s. But with Lampert in charge, the firm began to act like an Eroder, a strategy it continued to pursue until 2011. Thereafter, Sears "stopped returning cash to shareholders and started recording losses in net income," Cass told me. By then, it was neither a Sustainer nor even an Eroder— "just a dying company."

IN JANUARY 2018, a Sears district manager drove several hours through a terrible Northeast blizzard to inform Bruce Miller and his fellow Toms River employees that their store was being shuttered for good. If the mechanics wished to receive any severance pay, they had to agree to work until April, cleaning out the auto center and the main store and preparing the remaining inventory for liquidation.

"Mathematically," said Miller, "I spent more than half my life in this company. I credit them with being able to buy my house, my truck. When I got the call, it really was surreal. I didn't believe it." An especially sad day came when the lift Miller personally used was sold off, along with numerous other pieces of equipment, all for about $26,000. "That's the cost of one single lift. The liquidation guy might as well have come in with a shotgun under his arm."

As for the severance, Sears capped it at eight weeks' pay at the base hourly wage. "Eight weeks for thirty-five years of service. That was a slap in the face."

It was also far too little to carry him to safer financial harbors. Even before the closure, Miller had been struggling with his mortgage. "Everything was going up," he recalled, "except for my wage," which had been cut. "Classic example is my medical insurance. The last year, the medical insurance—for me alone, nobody else—was going to cost me over $6,600 just in premiums, never mind co-pays and all that. My paycheck wasn't carrying me anymore."

Two weeks after the closure became public, the mortgage company foreclosed on Miller. He begged to have the deadline for vacating the house extended to six weeks. Sears, meanwhile, offered no assistance with filing unemployment. He now had no pay, no insurance, and no housing. He narrowly avoided homelessness thanks only to a modest inheritance left by his parents, which allowed him to buy a mobile home about a mile from his old house. He still drives by his former residence once a week and tries hard not to think about it.

Lampert is as of this writing worth about $2 billion.[45] His $40 million mansion on Miami's Indian Creek Island ranks among the top-forty most expensive homes in Florida.[46] He also owns a nearly three-hundred-foot custom-made super-yacht named *Fountainhead,*

after Rand's literary monument to selfishness. His nonprofit, the
Lampert Foundation, funds the libertarian *Reason* magazine, whose
mission is to advance "free minds and free markets."[47]

Yet for Miller and millions of other workers subjected to the pre-
dations of hedge funds and private equity, the U.S. economy is anything but "free." Coercion, recall, isn't just what the state does to
criminals and taxpayers; it's also what private actors can do to workers and consumers whom they misgovern through economic power.

None of what Lampert and his Wall Street colleagues do is "natural." None of it follows straightforwardly from the ideals enshrined
in the Constitution. Rather, by promoting certain financial policies,
or simply not promoting any policy—itself a form of state action—
our laws have empowered Big Finance to loot the real economy. It's
an especially naked form of private coercion of the many by a very
few.

At the next stop, we will see how Wall Street's private tyrants are
increasingly turning their malevolent attention to the basic public
goods we depend upon to quite literally survive.

6

Privatizing Emergency

IN 1938, THE real estate developer Flora Mae Statler subdivided and sold off a plot of land she owned in Maricopa County, Arizona, about twenty miles northwest of Phoenix. Statler called the new settlement Surprise, because she "would be surprised if the town ever amounted to much," as she once told her daughter.[1] But Surprise, Arizona, succeeded, after all, attracting cotton workers in the early decades and swelling to 150,000 residents today, many of them retirees seeking warmer climes and the senior-living dream. But for Justin Purcell and his wife, Kasia, the town's name took a darker resonance when their mobile home burned down in August 2013.

The Purcells were staying with relatives forty-five minutes away to prepare for the birth of a child when a blaze engulfed their trailer. A neighbor alerted them to the fire, whose cause remains unknown, and the family raced back home. By the time they got there, firefighters were putting out the last of the flames. The Purcells' trailer was almost completely destroyed. And as if that weren't gut-wrenching enough, two weeks later they received a surprise bill for $19,825 from a private firefighting firm that they hadn't called, that had shown up long after the local fire department, and that had barely done anything to help.[2]

Speaking to *The Huffington Post* at the time, Justin Purcell said, "I couldn't believe it. We lost our home, we just had a baby and now we're going through this. It's crazy. We don't know how we are going to come up with the money."[3] The invoice came courtesy of Rural/Metro, a Scottsdale-headquartered firefighting and emergency-services company. Days earlier, the firm had filed for Chapter 11 bankruptcy, following a period of ownership by Warburg Pincus, a Manhattan private equity fund with more than $85 billion in assets under management today.[4]

The family thus joined the growing ranks of Americans who thought of firefighting, ambulances, and other emergency services as common goods, funded by the community and supplied by the government, only to get a rude awakening when Big Finance came collecting.

In the Purcells' case, the local fire department made it to the scene in thirteen minutes, while Rural/Metro, stationed twenty miles away, didn't get there until nearly an hour after the flames started. The Rural/Metro crew included two trucks of three firefighters each. But with most of the work already done by the local department, only two of the Rural/Metro firefighters did much of anything at all. "The other ones were standing around bullshitting," Justin recalled.[5]

Even so, Rural/Metro billed the family at a rate of $1,500 per truck per hour and $150 per firefighter per hour. A spokesman told reporters that those exorbitant rates were based on Rural/Metro's "65 years on [sic] tradition," and claimed the company had a contract with the local department to "provide overhaul and do essentially the mop up" after a fire is put out. Pressed to show this contract, the spokesman said, "We do have what I call a gentleman's agreement."[6]

The Purcells had punctually paid their fire-district assistance tax, but that levy didn't cover Rural/Metro's services. Rural/Metro blamed the family for failing to pay for the company's fire subscription plan, which cost $474 annually. Said a spokesman, "They, along with others across Arizona, in areas we serve, elected to . . . roll the dice that they would not have a fire—they lost. We provided service to them and now they are mad. This is not new. We bill for unsubscribed fires all of the time."[7]

Yet the Purcells insisted they had never previously received a bill or any marketing from the company, and would have happily taken out a subscription had they known it was necessary to stave off a $20,000 invoice. Other families reported they had never gotten a subscription offer, either. Only after the Purcell tragedy did some neighbors receive notices from Rural/Metro warning them that they lacked coverage. The firm conceded it hadn't previously marketed its subscription plans in that area.[8] Still, it wouldn't budge, forcing the Purcells to turn to crowdfunding to deal with their expenses.

The family's story is about more than one emergency-services firm's notoriously underhanded billing tactics. It's about more than even the evils associated with a society where public goods like firefighting and ambulances are increasingly reserved for those who can afford private providers. As we will also see, the story is symptomatic of an even more sinister development: the tendency of public pension systems to invest their contributors' retirement money in Wall Street funds engaged in privatizing those very contributors' jobs.

These investments are no secret. They can be known to anyone willing to pore over the soporific annual reports of state and local pensions. Yet very few public servants are aware that each time they contribute to their retirement plans, they are marginally helping to eliminate their own jobs—or at least to strengthen predatory competitors like Rural/Metro.

Towns and cities contract with privateers like Rural/Metro to cut costs, and working-class people pay the price in the form of lost jobs, wages, and benefits. The winners are Wall Street fee skimmers, who profit handsomely by extracting value out of the public fisc. This has especially dire consequences in the case of first responders. Big Finance, after all, has no compunctions about doing to fire and ambulance companies what it does to any of the other corporations it controls: namely, eroding them, often to the point of paralysis and insolvency.

Heroes No More

Professional, public emergency services—firefighting and ambulances—are among modernity's greatest social achievements.

In colonial America, fires posed a dire social problem. Terrible blazes struck Boston and the Massachusetts Bay Colony throughout the seventeenth and eighteenth centuries, prompting preventative regulations and the formation of "fire societies" armed with engines that could pump water. Many of the most illustrious figures of the founding era served as volunteer firefighters, including Samuel Adams, Benjamin Franklin, Alexander Hamilton, and Paul Revere.

But by the mid-nineteenth century, many volunteer departments had devolved into gangs of privateers that brutally fought each other on the streets for the privilege of being first to stop a fire and collect payouts from insurers. In Cincinnati in 1853, these tendencies prompted the authorities to hire the country's first professional fire department, with an efficient new steam-powered engine as part of its arsenal. After the Civil War, that model was replicated in other cities, with the departments frequently staffed by veterans of the conflict. Volunteers continued to play a major role in firefighting, but they were now funded, and sometimes trained, by public authorities. This didn't mean fires went away; on the contrary, the industrial era only increased the likelihood of terrible accidents. But the real marvel was the evolution of the social response to emergency, from competitive volunteerism toward a coordinated, professionalized, *public* service that ever more people could rely upon.[9]

A similar story could be told about ambulance services, which came about in the gruesome wake of the Civil War and Europe's Napoleonic Wars. The earliest ambulances brought surgeons to the battlefield while sorting and evacuating wounded warriors based on the severity of their wounds. In the civilian realm, America had only a gauzy patchwork of lackluster private and volunteer providers for a century after the Civil War. But like local fire departments, ambulance services were dramatically improved and regularized thanks to federal legislation in the 1960s and 1970s and came increasingly under the ambit of state and local governments.[10]

The upshot is that throughout the twentieth century firefighting was a quintessentially common good, as were ambulances for the latter half of that century. Private providers continued to operate, of course. Rural/Metro, for example, was founded in 1948 and soon won contracts with insurance companies, large private landowners, and some government agencies. A private firefighter made sense for Hollywood studios in need of dedicated, on-site fire services, for example, or far-flung landholdings in the Mountain West not covered by public departments.

But the aggressive push to privatize the firefighting and emergency services relied upon by ordinary Americans—to transform these from "community service to luxury goods," as one critic puts it[11]—began in earnest in the aftermath of the Great Recession. The recession pinched state and local budgets and led some Americans to direct their "anti-elite" ire against government employees and their pensions (rather than, say, Wall Street), lending privateers a golden political opportunity.

Private equity seized that opening. In April 2011, for example, Warburg Pincus acquired Rural/Metro, with its then eight thousand employees, for $438 million excluding debt. The firm offered existing shareholders $17.25 per share, a substantial premium over market value.[12] When the deal was wrapped up a few months later, a Warburg managing director enthused about the industry's "tremendous growth potential," adding, "We believe [Rural/Metro] and its experienced leadership team have what it takes to execute on its organic and strategic growth plans."[13] Warburg wasn't alone. Around the same time, another private equity fund, Clayton Dubilier & Rice, purchased Emergency Medical Services Corporation, a Rural/Metro rival, for $3 billion.[14]

Other funds saw the opportunity even before the recession. The emergency-services firm TransCare EMS, for example, had a decade earlier come under the control of Patriarch Partners, the fund headed by the celebrity financier Lynn Tilton. The star of the short-lived Sundance Channel reality-TV show *Diva of Distressed,* Tilton was known for her raunchy persona—she once sent a client a holiday card featuring a photo of herself dressed in black lingerie and brandishing a whip—and for her supposed forswearing of asset stripping ("It's only men I strip and flip").[15]

All told, at least a dozen ambulance companies were acquired by private equity over the past two decades, with many of the deals taking place after the financial crisis. A quarter of those, including Rural/Metro and TransCare, went on to file for Chapter 11 bankruptcy. Meanwhile, of some eleven hundred traditionally owned firms in the industry, none went into bankruptcy[16]—a disparity that starkly underscores a point we made in the previous chapter: Ownership by private equity dramatically increases the likelihood of a firm's becoming insolvent.

Even if one assumes that profit-motivated firefighting and ambulance services are a net positive to society, the fact remains that Wall Street wasn't interested in properly investing in these firms, or helping them grow in the old-fashioned capitalist way. Instead, as a 2016 *New York Times* exposé concluded, Big Finance turned to its signature "moneymaking playbook: a mix of cost cuts, price increases, lobbying and litigation."[17]

Warburg's ownership was illustrative. For starters, the fund levered up Rural/Metro in typical private equity style, leaning heavily on debt to finance its acquisition and adding $500 million to the company's liabilities at the outset. At first, Warburg did plow some money into the firm and its assets, but it also pushed Rural/Metro to buy out a pair of smaller rivals, compounding debt upon debt and soon necessitating cutbacks. Raises and pensions were slashed. Finances became a "mess," the *Times* noted. Rural/Metro told "investors it would book higher revenue than it ultimately did."[18] As we will soon see, delayed responses became more common, and drug thefts and other staff misdeeds multiplied.

Faced with these difficulties, Warburg spurned investing in its service and other traditional methods for turning around a struggling firm. Instead, it doubled down on savage billing and collection tactics of the kind meted out to the Purcell family in Surprise.

Under the Warburg regime, for example, Rural/Metro mailed a $761 bill to a baby born in one of its ambulances, warning the newborn in a letter that the "matter may be reported to a national credit reporting agency."[19] In many cases, Rural/Metro "didn't bother with regular billing—the first attempt at contact was from a collection agency," as the privatization critics Donald Cohen and Allen Mikaelian note; surprise bills ranged from a few hundred dollars, as in the infant debtor's case, to five-digit sums, as in the Purcells'.[20]

Following the takeover, Rural/Metro trained its EMTs to unfailingly obtain signatures "that approved massive charges and limited the patient's right to appeal" as she was being treated.[21] Posters plastered at Rural/Metro ambulance stations, where staff gathered in between calls, showed a cartoon first responder encouraging his colleagues to get a signature to ensure subsequent billing: "Almost always, if the patient is alert, they will be able to sign." And if not the patient, then family members will sign, "because I don't give up." The campaign was called "Do the *Write* Thing."[22]

EMTs complained that this obsession with billing got in the way of their saving lives just when time was of the essence. But for Rural/Metro, billing and then collecting, including by suing the family members of deceased patients, remained a top priority. Public ambulances, by contrast, generally don't sue patients. Yet with roughly a quarter of ambulance services now in for-profit hands, and medical emergencies being by nature unpredictable, Americans don't necessarily get a choice between public and private when their lives are on the line. Many low-income people dread having to call 911 at all.[23]

Private firefighters cover a comparatively smaller share of Americans, roughly 4 percent of the population, mostly in rural and unincorporated areas. Many have surprise-billing horror stories like the

Purcells'. A Knoxville, Tennessee, family who suffered a chimney fire in 2013, for example, had Rural/Metro place a $15,000 lien against their title—this, even though the privateers arrived an hour after the 911 call. The same year, Rural/Metro took another Arizona family to court for a $7,000 bill related to a mobile-home fire. Like the Purcells, the family had mistakenly assumed that their local taxes would cover them if disaster struck. To pay off the Rural/Metro debt, they switched to eating two, rather than three, meals a day.[24]

IN THE CASE of a corporation like Sears, as we saw in chapter 5, Wall Street–led erosion resulted in empty shelves, unmanned cash registers, broken fixtures, and the like. As bad as these problems were for the mega-retailer's workers, suppliers, and customers, corporate erosion in the first-responder industry is orders of magnitude more serious, because the quality of firefighting and ambulances is a matter of life and death and because taxpayers end up on the hook for these firms' billing misdeeds through Medicare and Medicaid.

For starters, underinvestment inevitably causes delays when time is of the essence. By the time the Patriarch-owned TransCare filed for bankruptcy, for example, a third of its vehicles weren't in working order and had been that way for "hundreds of days," according to a *Times* review of internal documents. A former employee told the paper that it took four hours to get one ambulance started: "You really had to become a MacGyver in the field."[25]

Rural/Metro customers suffered from similar problems. Analyzing publicly available information regarding five of Rural/Metro's major ambulance markets, the *Times* found that "services in four areas suffered under private equity ownership." Response times throughout Arizona were also often slow, leading fire chiefs in Mesa and Apache Junction to raise the alarm about Rural/Metro's aggressive cost cutting. Knox County, Tennessee, officials fined Rural/Metro $110,000 for two instances in which the firm warned them "that it had no ambulances available for emergencies."[26]

Wall Street tightfistedness also results in chronic drug shortages, fostering an atmosphere of desperation among emergency workers. According to the *Times,* for example, TransCare EMTs in the lead-up to the bankruptcy faced pressure to "raid supply carts" at hospitals, "sometimes without the hospital's blessing." EMT teams went so far as to post "lookouts" outside hospital drug repositories, while other members plundered the cabinets.[27] The Drug Enforcement Administration, meanwhile, launched a probe in 2012 into Rural/Metro's Kentucky operation after twenty vials of morphine were replaced with saline solution in company ambulances, "which posed a huge problem," as a DEA supervisor told local reporters (saline doesn't ease pain when a patient has, say, lost a limb).[28]

Third, when Wall Street–dominated firms in their death throes fail to pay their workers, performance crises follow. As it approached bankruptcy, for example, the Patriarch-owned TransCare EMS sent a memo to supervisors coaching them on how to respond to chronically unpaid emergency workers ("Q. When will we be paid? A. We do not know").[29]

Even the most conscientious worker will begin to underperform after putting in inhumane hours as a result of understaffing, with missing paychecks adding insult to injury. It's a dire enough situation for any business but downright catastrophic when it comes to emergency health care. For example, when an eighty-one-year-old resident of Loudon County, Tennessee, couldn't breathe, the 911 call was routed to Rural/Metro, which took so long to put together an ambulance crew that one worker had enough time to smoke a cigarette, according to surveillance footage.[30]

Rural/Metro eventually did manage to bring the woman to the hospital, but she died two weeks later. The company later fired the smoking employee, but she sued for wrongful termination, charging that Rural/Metro was trying to draw a veil over its own "improper scheduling, staffing and response criteria."[31] The employee claimed that by the time the call arrived, she was off the clock, having already put in two successive twenty-four-hour shifts.

Firms that regularly violate labor and safety regulations also tend to underperform on government contracts.[32] Which brings us to the fourth major detrimental effect associated with Wall Street domination of first-responder firms: Medicare overbilling. Rural/Metro, for example, has been the target of numerous Department of Justice probes for allegedly charging the feds for services deemed unnecessary under Medicare and Medicaid rubrics.

In Arizona, the firm agreed to cough up $2.8 million to settle claims that it "violated the federal False Claims Act by submitting false bills to Medicare" before and during Warburg's ownership, according to a DOJ news release.[33] In Florida, Rural/Metro paid $650,000 to settle similar allegations dating from 2010 to 2016.[34] In eastern Kentucky, the firm paid more than $275,000 for allegedly breaching the False Claims Act during Warburg's ownership and afterward, when it fell into other private equity hands.[35] And on and on.

Finally, there are the disruptions to services caused by the bankruptcy process itself as fire and emergency firms collapse from Wall Street erosion. When TransCare went bankrupt in 2016, "cities and towns up and down the East Coast" suddenly lost ambulance services, as the *Times* reported. "Private equity has, in this case, threatened public safety," the mayor of Mount Vernon, New York, told the paper. "It's not the way to treat the public."[36]

The New York City Fire Department was forced to pay overtime to its own ambulances to cover the gaps created by the TransCare bankruptcy. But those public firefighters and EMTs forced to work overtime were probably unaware of a lesser-noticed trend: In many cases, their own retirement contributions were being used to capitalize these shoddy rivals.

Trust Betrayed

In 2006, the *Financial Times* highlighted that public pensions were becoming "a crucial driver of the current boom in the private-equity industry." Hoping to cash in on the supposedly wild returns generated by private equity, pension trustees were pouring their contributors' retirement funds into these investment vehicles. In this way, pensions came to underwrite Wall Street's conquest of the real economy, "feeding the cycle of takeovers, restructurings and sell-offs that define private equity."[37]

The trend has only accelerated since. In recent years, up to half of all private equity assets have come from public pensions.[38] But there remains a more hidden, and especially troubling, fact inside these pensions' embrace of private equity: In many cases, the Wall Street funds in question have a direct, material interest in privatizing the jobs of the very public servants whose retirement contributions are being invested in private equity. "Such investments," as the Boston University law professor David Webber has warned, "lead to reduced working hours and job losses for current employees," yet the negative effect on workers "is almost never taken into account."[39]

A vicious cycle is thus set into motion: Governments increasingly contract with private-equity-owned firms to provide what used to be considered eminently *common* goods, from emergency services to water to street parking, and the retirement contributions of the remaining public employees end up bolstering firms that are trying to privatize still more of their jobs. The public pensions, moreover, end up enabling the Wall Street erosion of the wider real economy.

Quantifying the full scope of this mode of stealth privatization—"investing" away public jobs and services with workers' own pensions—is near impossible. The private equity funds involved, and the privateering firms they control, are legion. The public retirement system is likewise fragmented along numerous jurisdictional lines: federal, state, county, and municipal. But examining just one sector—firefighting and emergency services—is eye-opening enough.

Consider Rural/Metro. As we noted, the firm was controlled by the private equity fund Warburg Pincus from 2011 to 2013. Today, Rural/Metro is owned by a portfolio company of a different New York private equity fund, Kohlberg Kravis Roberts & Co., or KKR. We may therefore safely say that any public pension that held investments in Warburg funds during the Warburg period (2011–2013) or that is currently invested in KKR is at least marginally complicit in privatizing its contributors' jobs.[40]

In Surprise, Arizona, where the Purcells lived, the local fire department's pensions are managed by the state's Public Safety Personnel Retirement System. Sure enough, the Arizona PSPRS has repeatedly shoveled contributor money into KKR funds in recent years—including $40 million directly and $20 million for co-investment in KKR's Asian Fund III, $25 million in KKR's Asian Fund II, and $125 million in KKR's Revolving Credit Partners II.[41]

Notwithstanding the Purcell family fiasco, Rural/Metro continues to operate in Surprise's outlying (Maricopa) "county areas," where its privateering sometimes intersects with the work of the public department. This means that Surprise firefighters, through their pension contributions, have helped capitalize a Wall Street fund that has a material interest in ensuring the growth of private firefighting and ambulances. The amounts involved in this case might be puny, relative to the leviathan assets sloshing around KKR's portfolio. Even so, $25 million soaked up here is $25 million KKR can devote to expanding its privateering efforts over there, and given capital's supremely fungible nature, "here" and "there" are really the same.

Moreover, if we examine similar investments made by public retirement systems across the nation, the numbers begin to add up fast. The picture that emerges is one of pension trustees conspiring, if unwittingly, to replace solid working-class jobs with ones characterized by lower wages, greater insecurity, and flimsy to nonexistent benefits.

Turn to the appendix of this book: A search of annual pension reports and private equity industry publications reveals that at least nine agencies that invest the retirement contributions of public emergency workers in eight states—Florida, Kansas, Minnesota, New Jersey, Ohio, South Carolina, Washington, and Wisconsin—and one city, New York, collectively poured $1.74 billion into Warburg Pincus during its ownership of Rural/Metro. KKR, Rural/Metro's current owner, has benefited from even larger investments. As documented in the appendix, at least eight state agencies have collectively shoveled nearly $8 billion into various KKR funds.

That list is almost certainly far from exhaustive. Rather, it offers a snapshot of public pensions in a few states and big cities and counties, out of some six thousand such retirement systems nationwide.[42] Even so, the privatization-complicit investments of just these few retirement systems over the past decade or so amount to nearly $10 billion. And even assuming that firefighters and EMTs contributed only 10 percent of the total invested amount, it follows that over the past decade just a few pension funds contributed $1 billion to the privatization of their own members' jobs.

The same sort of investment has also resulted, for example, in school cafeteria workers and janitors losing their jobs or having their wages and benefits slashed after the food- and facilities-services company Aramark, then controlled by Warburg, entered into contracts with their (public) employers. These workers' own pension plans had invested their contributions in Warburg funds.[43]

In making these destructive investments, pension trustees are motivated by the often-mistaken belief that private equity firms (and hedge funds) invariably generate hefty returns, and by a wrongheaded notion of what it means to be "loyal" to their contributors.

Start with the dreams of big returns. Surveys show that the overwhelming majority of America's institutional investors expect private equity to generate returns at least 2 percent to 4 percent higher than the public stock market. Yet the hype is very often just that. As the author Daniel Rasmussen, himself a private equity alumnus, noted in a 2018 essay, "since 2010, private equity has, on average, underperformed the public equity market," with one key performance index showing that "PE" has "lagged . . . the S&P 500 by 1.5 percent per year over the past five years."[44] Then, too, scholars and even some private equity insiders increasingly call into question the industry's preferred performance metric—the so-called internal rate of return—owing to its opacity and susceptibility to manipulation by managers trying to stand out in a crowded market.[45]

While private equity did yield high returns from the 1980s to the early years of the twenty-first century, that hasn't been the case since the financial crisis. The reason? It's in large part, Rasmussen argues, because pension funds and other institutional investors have been throwing so much money at these funds, driving up valuations and thus "eliminating the formerly large gap between private and public market valuations."[46]

Put another way: There is so much capital deluging private equity that funds end up paying too much for buyout deals (so much for Wall Street bargain hunting). This naturally results in diminishing returns, but it also goads yet more institutional investors to join the rush, lemminglike.

Even assuming private equity were a golden class of low-risk, high-returns assets—which is almost certainly *not* the case, not anymore, at any rate—it still wouldn't morally justify the self-privatizing investments forced on public servants by pension administrators who are supposed to manage labor's capital in trust.

Defenders of this strategy argue that trustees' duty involves maximizing returns for the retirement plan, nothing more, nothing less. This, as you might be saying to yourself, is crazy. How can the interests of pension-plan contributors—that is, workers—be partitioned off from whether or not they get to keep their jobs? They can't. And as Webber rightly insists, when such investments result in job losses for workers, never mind the corrosion of public services, that can only be described as harm to plan "participants and beneficiaries."[47]

Workers' interests aside, this pallid account of the duty of loyalty can undermine the long-term interests of the *fund* itself. Job-destroying, returns-only "loyalty" can leave pension funds hanging out to dry when older cohorts of workers suddenly hit retirement age and there are no new positions for younger and newer workers who could contribute.[48]

The overwhelming majority of public pension contributors are unaware that any of this is going on, and the very few who wise up to it are often reluctant or powerless to speak up. For the rest of us, meanwhile, the debate over public pensions is obscured by billowing clouds of artificial smoke generated by privatizers and their political and media apologists.

We are told that privatizing public goods, including by "investing" workers' retirement funds in private-sector rivals, is necessitated by public pensions' underfunding crisis. And we are told that privatization is inevitable—"There is no alternative," the forever mantra of free-market fanatics—and so pensions might as well try to maximize returns with help from Wall Street, which retains its aura of mastery even after having triggered the 2008 crisis.

Nonsense.

For starters, the public pension underfunding crisis is overstated. To calculate the health of a retirement plan, public or private, experts divide the value of all of its assets on a given date by the plan's payout obligations on the same date, called the funding ratio. The federal government recommends a funding ratio of at least 80 percent. And while it's true that the 2001 downturn and the Great Recession devalued assets and left many retirement systems short of that recommended target, the nationwide funding ratio has stabilized since. There were even signs of small improvements by 2021.[49]

Plus, privatizers underestimate the paradoxical *negative* effects of public job losses on the health of pensions—paradoxical, because the normal expectation might be that fewer workers mean smaller payout liabilities down the road. Yet according to recent research on the wave of job losses associated with the pandemic, that is not the case: COVID layoffs—that is, staffing cuts—not only failed to improve but might have worsened pension health.[50]

As for the supposed "inevitability" of privatization, that is nothing but the insidious voice of Tyranny, Inc., speaking. In truth, there is *nothing inevitable* about a family having to pay $20,000 for lousy private firefighting services they never asked for, just weeks after having lost their home. There is *nothing inevitable* about patients being deprived of urgent care because a thirtysomething Harvard MBA sitting in an office on Lexington Avenue loaded up the local ambulance service with unsustainable debt, causing vehicles to fall into disrepair and staff to be laid off. And there is *nothing inevitable* about public firefighters and EMTs being forced to capitalize their own dispossession. All of these are the consequences of public-policy choices and the failure of our laws and policy makers to properly regulate the market as a zone of coercion.

If you are wondering why you have never heard about *any* of this, you aren't alone. Turn the page. On the next stop of our tour, we will see how Wall Street, with an assist from Big Tech, has helped to extinguish the one democratic candle that was supposed to illuminate the doings of the mighty: your local newspaper.

7

Parched for Truth

THE STORY READ like a harrowing report from a drought on the Horn of Africa: scenes of a mother and father and their five children praying desperately for rain and then, once it finally came, rushing to gather as much of the miraculous precipitation as they could, in buckets and pots and pans and a small plastic pool, rejoicing and wondering when the weather might be so generous to them again.

Except these scenes took place not in Africa but in modern-day Appalachia, where decrepit, underfunded infrastructure has deprived many families of reliable access to potable water at high enough pressures to allow them to bathe or drink. The subjects of the story were Tim and Jessica Taylor, pig farmers residing in Martin County, Kentucky, one of the poorest in the nation, with an average family income of $30,000 a year.[1]

Before the rain came in October 2018, the Taylors had gone without water for a week, reported the *Lexington Herald-Leader* newspaper, based some 150 miles west of Martin County. The state water department hadn't kept good track of the number and duration of these outages. But over the preceding twenty-two months, the local water district issued thirty-two advisories urging residents to boil their water. That suggests residents could expect line leaks, which cause shortages and risk contamination, every three weeks on average.[2]

Losing water was a constant source of communal misery. For one thing, families had to use Styrofoam dishes, because they never knew if they would have water for dishwashing. For drinking, they expended large chunks of their meager incomes on bottled water. As for bathing amid "long outages like this one, the Taylors shower as often as they can at the homes of friends and family." Jessica would skip doctor's appointments when she couldn't shower beforehand, while the kids would often be barred from playing outside, lest they got dirty before school and were unable to wash it off. "In a nation awash with technological advancement," observed the *Herald-Leader*, "many families . . . are dominated by the absence of one basic thing: reliable water service."[3]

The causes were neither unique nor all that complex: Mismanagement and underinvestment had left many pipes leaky, wasting as much as 75 percent of plant-treated water before it flowed into homes, a problem compounded by the area's hilly topography that made it hard to restore pressure whenever there was an outage. It was an all-too-typical failure of the low-tax, low-investment model championed by influential libertarian brain trusts.[4]

More remarkable was the fact that the story of the water crisis saw the light of day at all. Will Wright—the cub reporter who published a series on it in the *Herald-Leader*, eventually marshaling national attention to the story—had ended up at the paper thanks to a nonprofit called Report for America. Inspired by the older Teach for America program, RFA recruits promising recent graduates to serve as reporters at understaffed local newspapers for two-year stints, partially funded by RFA and partially by the papers where its corps members are hired.

The mission: to curb the spread of news deserts, vast swaths of the nation where residents don't have access to trustworthy local news.

RFA was the brainchild of Steven Waldman, a journalist and media entrepreneur who served as the lead author on a landmark 2011 Federal Communications Commission report on the challenges facing local journalism in the United States. His research opened his eyes to the sheer scale of the problem. The report warned, "The independent watchdog function that the Founding Fathers envisioned for journalism—going so far as to call it crucial to a healthy democracy—is in some cases at risk at the local level."[5]

Among the many other developments examined in his 2011 FCC report, Waldman highlighted Wall Street's conquest of America's dailies, noting that by the end of the first decade of the twenty-first century "14.9 percent of daily newspapers were owned by lenders or private equity firms, and those papers accounted for 20.4 percent of daily newspaper revenue." At the time, Waldman concluded that hedge fund and private equity ownership needn't spell doom for newspapers.[6]

A decade later, he would render a much darker judgment. In the intervening years, Big Finance dramatically expanded its footprint in the newspaper industry, with twelve hundred papers now owned in whole or in part by Wall Street firms and half of all U.S. daily circulation controlled by hedge funds.[7] Far from injecting new life into the business, Wall Street was starving it of resources, turning many outlets into shells of their former selves.

In 2021, Waldman, now writing as head of RFA, published an op-ed in the *Los Angeles Times* sounding the alarm about Wall Street "wrecking local news." The occasion was the acquisition of Tribune Publishing, a national newspaper chain, by the Manhattan-based hedge fund Alden Global Capital. With the takeover, Alden seized several iconic papers, including *The Baltimore Sun,* the *Chicago Tribune,* the New York *Daily News,* and the *Hartford Courant.*

The problem, wrote Waldman, isn't that funds like Alden are "run by evil people. It's that when it comes to newspapers, their aim has been to maximize cash flow by slashing costs" without making investments to sustain, let alone grow, the businesses.[8] Managing for cash flow should by now be familiar to readers of this book: It's Wall Street's marquee strategy, and it frequently results in firm-level erosion, as we saw in chapters 5 and 6.

Waldman's critique didn't go unnoticed on Wall Street. Soon after his op-ed appeared, the McClatchy newspaper chain signaled that its dailies wouldn't recruit RFA journalists for future stints. A few months earlier, a hedge fund called Chatham Asset Management had acquired McClatchy, and the decision to shun RFA going forward was widely viewed as retaliation for Waldman's impudence in questioning Big Finance's role in the industry.[9]

As it happens, McClatchy's portfolio includes the *Lexington Herald-Leader*, where the RFA journalist Will Wright had exposed eastern Kentucky's water woes. This turn of events raised disturbing questions: What other urgent stories about public or private malfeasance were going unreported because much of the nation is parched for truth? And what did it mean for self-government that even modest reform efforts like Waldman's could be iced out by Tyranny, Inc.?

Who Killed the Local Paper?

Newspapers were once a lively and profitable medium. Then came the internet, which dried up print advertising and made it much easier for consumers to directly access information at the click of a mouse, without the need for journalists acting as gatekeepers and mediators.

To many Americans, this narrative sums up the rise and fall of the American daily. And much like the story we tell ourselves about the decline of brick-and-mortar retailers like Sears (see chapter 5), this one is overly simple. The truth is that the American newspaper, especially the local paper, didn't have to go the way of the phone book. News deserts didn't have to proliferate across the American landscape, especially in rural areas, desiccating the sort of enterprise- and accountability-oriented journalism of which only experienced journalists with meaningful ties to the local community are capable. Yes, an older generation of newspaper owners were caught blindsided by technological change. But to overlook Wall Street's (and Big

Tech's) share of the blame not only obscures the truth but also makes it difficult to reverse this profoundly un-American trend.

AMERICA'S FOUNDERS CONSIDERED newspapers so essential to a democratic republic that they explicitly protected a "free press" in the Bill of Rights. And they didn't consider it enough merely to restrain the state from censoring journalists. To further the circulation of "such easy vehicles of knowledge," as George Washington called them, Congress enacted laws in the early republic facilitating discount postage for periodicals. The postal service went so far as charging more for other types of mail to subsidize the shipping and handling of magazines and newspapers.[10]

In his 2011 FCC report, Waldman noted that it wasn't uncommon for local papers in the nineteenth century to have more subscribers outside their circulation areas than inside.[11] All this fostered a sense of *national* consciousness among the far-flung citizens of a new country, where local and regional loyalties could run thick.

Early papers were financed by partisan factions. For this reason, it's common among historians to unfavorably compare that era's journalism with the kind of supposedly "objective" journalism that emerged in the twentieth century. My own experience as an ink-stained wretch inclines me toward Christopher Lasch's skepticism of the later model, which tends to depoliticize fundamentally political questions, smuggling in various agendas under an authoritative tone.[12]

But professionalized, "objective" journalism got the upper hand thanks to a major shift in the industry, away from newspapers as an artisanal, independent trade and toward a business dominated by large and highly lucrative monopolies. In 1920, at least two papers competed for dominance in nearly half of American cities. Eighty years later, only 1.4 percent of cities had two or more competing papers, with the number of competitive markets dropping to just 20 cities, down from 552 in 1920.[13]

During the same period, corporate chains consolidated many local outlets, cutting the share of independently owned papers from 93 percent in 1920 to 23 percent in 2000. The chains did introduce greater efficiency—multiple dailies could rely on a single HR department, for example—but they also displaced the civic-minded family owners of old, who had been "rooted in the communities they served," as Waldman observed in his 2011 report. The new bosses "often lacked a connection to their readers and to the journalists who reported the news, and they focused more on overall corporate financial performance."[14]

Daily circulation exploded during this period of corporate consolidation, peaking at sixty-three million in the mid-1980s. But while readership was expanding absolutely, in relative terms it lagged American demography: Total subscriptions grew by two million between 1940 and 2010; the number of U.S. households swelled by eighty-three million in the same period.[15]

Despite this failure to capitalize on population growth, the corporate-monopoly papers proved tremendously profitable. From the late 1980s until the turn of the millennium, the chains achieved double-digit cash-flow margins. In 2000, for example, Gannett managed an eye-popping margin of 34 percent; Knight Ridder, 30 percent; Lee Enterprises, 31 percent; McClatchy, 30 percent; E. W. Scripps, 28 percent; and so on.[16]

Corporate owners came to think of these margins as the norm, though they would have been considered extraordinary in any number of other industries. A few owners, chasing after even-higher profits, began sacrificing quality. Foreshadowing the bloodbath to come in the following decade, they slashed jobs and the physical size and thickness of the papers, among other steps. One editor recalled talk of a "harvest strategy" in the 1990s—"milking a declining business for all the cash it can produce until it dies."[17] Still, the old corporate titans did for the most part continue to invest in journalism. To reporters and editors, it seemed the age of the three-martini lunch and the bottomless expense account could go on forever.

★   ★   ★

THEN THE INTERNET struck its blow, with print-ad spending dipping to $23 billion by 2005, down from nearly $50 billion in 2000. Newspapers' websites were often popular, but they failed to translate the eyeballs they attracted into revenue even close to sufficient to offset print losses. As Waldman's FCC report lamented, "Each print dollar was being replaced by four digital pennies."[18]

Some large national papers, such as *The Wall Street Journal* (where I began my career in journalism), foresaw a more heavily subscription-based model, including digital subscriptions, and moved quickly to make it work. More recently, the Minneapolis *Star Tribune* and *The Boston Globe* have also expanded their online subscriber rolls, proving the model can bear fruit not just for national and international papers like the *Journal* and *The New York Times* but also for more regional outlets.[19] But monetizing digital content required investments that many other papers weren't prepared to make; they turned, instead, to still more cost cutting just when quality content mattered most.

This, by the way, was just the damage done by Web 1.0, by the likes of Craigslist, Monster, and Zillow wreaking havoc on traditional classifieds pages. Web 2.0, led by ruthlessly monopolistic search and social giants like Google and Facebook, posed an even more serious problem. Readers were exposed to a great deal of local-news content on these platforms, but the entire reading experience could take place on Big Tech's turf. Many people never clicked through to the underlying source, depriving the original news gatherers of eyeballs, subscriptions, and ad revenue. Local outlets were thus forced to compete with Big Tech not just for ad dollars but as suppliers of content. This, even as they remained utterly dependent on these platforms for spreading their content and growing their audience online.[20]

Disaster ensued. As a 2020 Federal Trade Commission study on Big Tech's anticompetitive behavior reported, "The United States has lost nearly 1,800 newspapers since 2004 either to closure or merger, 70% of which were in metropolitan areas. As a result, the majority of counties in America no longer have more than one publisher of local news, and 200 [are] without any paper."[21] More bad news: Today, newspapers are bleeding jobs faster than even supposedly obsolete industries like coal mining, with total employment down at least 60 percent since the year 2000 and nearly a thousand jobs disappearing every month.[22]

The destruction of local outlets and the spread of news deserts is only speeding up. For her latest study, Penny Abernathy, the nation's foremost scholarly expert on this phenomenon, found that an average of two newspapers shutter every week. It's a statistic so startling and depressing that it's almost hard to believe, but it's all too true. "Since 2005," Abernathy concludes, "the country has lost more than a fourth of its newspapers (2,500) and is on track to lose a third by 2025."[23]

Do you remember the *Albuquerque Tribune, The Ann Arbor News, AsianWeek, The Baltimore Examiner,* the *Boulder City News,* the *Carson Times,* the *Chicago Free Press, The Christian Science Monitor,* the *Corpus Christi Business Journal,* the *Detroit Daily Press,* the *Franklin Chronicle,* the *Greenville Press,* the *Hershey Chronicle,* the *Hyde Park Townsman, The Kansas City Kansan, The Lakota Journal,* the *Los Angeles City Beat,* the *Maricopa Tribune,* the *New York Blade,* the *Peoria Times-Observer,* the *Rocky Mountain News, The San Juan Star,* the *Seattle Post-Intelligencer,* the *South Idaho Press,* the *Tucson Citizen,* or *The Washington Blade?*

In most cases, unless you lived in one of the communities served by these papers, your answer is likely no. But these were a few of the two hundred or so papers that closed or went online-only in just the years 2007 to 2010.[24] They were beloved in the communities they served; some were legendary journalistic enterprises with multiple Pulitzers under their belts for investigations that shined beams of light where powerful interests preferred murk and mud.

Now add hedge funds and private equity to the mix. As the story so far shows, the failure began with previous owners' pursuit of huge short-term margins, even in the teeth of looming technological change and the aggressions of Big Tech. But while hedge funds and private equity didn't cause the crisis, "once they got in, they accelerated it and made it harder to fix," as one high-ranking industry insider told me (he declined to be named for fear of Wall Street punishment).

Consider Alden Global Capital. The hedge fund launched its newspaper-takeover spree toward the end of the 2008–2009 financial crisis. Today, its portfolio of two hundred papers makes it the second-largest newspaper owner in the nation. But this is anything but a civic-minded rescue operation. Indeed, editors and reporters familiar with its business model have dubbed Alden "the vulture."[25]

After seizing *The Denver Post*, for example, Alden slashed jobs by a devastating 70 percent.[26] That prompted the paper's own opinion editor to publish a job-risking editorial condemning Alden. He railed against the hedge fund's "cynical strategy of constantly reducing the amount and quality of its offerings" and raising its subscription prices all while hiding "behind a narrative that adequately staffed newsrooms and newspapers can no longer survive in the digital marketplace."[27]

Moral opprobrium has given Alden no pause, however. As we saw, it went on to acquire Tribune Publishing—the event that impelled Waldman to pen his own denunciation. In just six weeks after its conquest of Tribune, Alden eliminated 22 percent of jobs at the *Chicago Tribune;* 17 percent at *The Virginian-Pilot* (of Norfolk, Virginia) and the *Daily Press* (of Newport News, Virginia); 22 percent at *The Morning Call* (of Allentown, Pennsylvania); and 12 percent at the New York *Daily News.*[28]

After the job cuts comes the mining of real assets. Alden has set up a number of real estate firms whose sole purpose is "efficiently buying, selling, leasing and redeveloping newspapers' offices and printing plants," as *The Washington Post* reported in 2019.[29] Dozens of newspaper facilities have been bought and sold by these Alden affiliates, suggesting the hedge fund views the core functions of the newspapers it acquires—exposing inconvenient truths, holding power to account, connecting communities—as secondary, at best.

From the point of view of ensuring these papers continue to serve their civic function, the triple-strategy pursued by the likes of Alden—job cuts, real estate sales, subscription-rate hikes—makes little sense. But the point isn't to buy an asset in distress, improve it, and then sell it off, the supposed purpose of private equity and hedge funds. Indeed, Alden has *never* sold a paper it acquired, because the fund merely makes "cash-flow bets," as the industry insider told me. "You cut costs right away, and that almost immediately goes to the bottom line. You cut 70 percent of staff, sell buildings, and fill the paper with wire copy. Eventually, the quality goes down. But there is cash flow."

Alden's corrosive management of the nation's media assets is far from isolated. If Big Tech monopolists killed off (and continue to extinguish) scores of local papers by drying up their ad revenue, Wall Street tends to keep them alive—albeit frequently in a degraded, comatose state. As recent research by scholars at Caltech and New York University has shown, following a private equity buyout, "the composition of news shifts away from local governance, the number of reporters and editors falls, and participation in local elections declines."[30]

Of the 1,610 newspapers they examined, the 262 controlled by private equity published fewer articles overall, devoted significantly less attention to local issues, and shed editorial staff far more aggressively than did papers under other forms of ownership. "Instead of local news, private equity firms may produce more national news content, which can be syndicated across many different papers" and involves lower labor costs.[31]

Gutting newspapers, turning them into shells of their former selves, and then charging more for the lackluster product may keep some papers going longer while allowing Wall Street to extract rents and profit margins not available to more traditional owners. But it doesn't serve local communities or civic engagement. As the authors of the Caltech-NYU study found, total votes and turnout levels both decline in counties when a given county's local paper ends up in private equity hands—an "unambiguously negative" effect.[32]

And the aggressive strip-mining means that even an ambitious editor determined to revamp local coverage won't have the resources to do so. But as the industry insider told me, "From the logic of private equity and hedge funds, this all makes sense."

Uninformed, Disempowered, and Atomized

So far in this book, we have examined the workings of private tyranny as they manifest themselves in different realms of American life. In each case, we were able to anchor our discussion to a human narrative, the stories of men and women whose lives were injured, and in some cases ruined, by the system.

That is harder to do with Tyranny, Inc.'s capture of the local newsroom. Here, the story is about what happens when the story isn't reported. We are trying to prove a negative, to distill an absence. The good news—or bad news, really—is that in recent years scholars have done an enormous amount of research measuring the effect of local journalism's demise, paying special attention to which types of communities suffer the greatest harm when the story isn't told.

About two hundred counties in the United States, as we noted earlier, go entirely without a local newspaper. These are the most parched regions of America's fast-spreading news deserts. What are the chief characteristics of these counties?

It's difficult to draw conclusions about such a vast number of places, spread across a continental nation. Still, some commonalities stand out. A 2019 study conducted jointly by the *Columbia Journalism Review* and the Expanding News Desert project at the University of North Carolina selected ten counties with no news publication and compared living conditions there with national averages. The researchers found that the median household income in these counties is 13 percent lower than the national average, while the poverty rate is 5 percent higher. These news-parched counties also have a 10 percent lower college-graduation rate than the national average, and residents are more likely to lack broadband access.[33] These are communities that eminently need information and robust exchanges of opinion—that is, if we accept the Founding Fathers' premise about the free press's role in social uplift.

Even many communities that still have newspapers can't access meaningful local news. The conduct of "the vulture" and similar financial firms means that many remaining local newspapers have become "ghost papers." They continue to operate, but the offices are largely vacant, most staffers have been laid off, and the remaining editors and reporters struggle to make do with scant resources. Much of the copy they print tends to be national, rather than local or regional, in scope, whether original or borrowed from wires.[34]

To quantify this dimension of the news-deserts crisis, Philip Napoli of Duke University and his fellow researchers analyzed more than sixteen thousand news stories published in one week across a hundred random communities with populations ranging from 20,000 to 300,000. Of the hundred communities, roughly 10 percent had no stories addressing critical information needs (those touching upon emergencies, health, education, transport, the environment, civic matters, and politics). Another 10 percent received zero original news, while 20 percent went without local news altogether. The researchers also found that just "17 percent of the news stories provided to a community are truly *local*—that is, actually about or having taken place within—the municipality."[35]

The Americans who reside in news deserts are poorer, less educated, and culturally and physically distant from centers of power and commerce, which renders them all the more needful of accountability-oriented journalism. Yet it is they who are most likely to go without such journalism.

SOME CONSERVATIVES RELISH the demise of traditional journalism. The media, especially national media, are unquestionably the

dominion of cultural progressives, and some outlets and personali-
ties have more than earned the opprobrium that attaches to their
names among half or more of the population, what with their hyper-
partisan journalism that always cuts one way, their punditry passed
off as neutral "fact-checking," and the like. Yet the experience of the
past two decades amply demonstrates that there is no substitute for
the vigilance of traditional journalistic institutions—especially local
and regional papers targeted by the same tech and financial elites the
right these days claims to oppose.

For one thing, a dearth of local news coverage leads to festering
government corruption and waste. To belabor the obvious, when
public officials don't face media scrutiny, they tend to misbehave more
and to get away with it. Consider the appalling graft that afflicted Bell,
California, a working-class, and heavily immigrant-settled, suburb of
Los Angeles. Bell's city council hired one Robert Rizzo in 1993 to serve
as interim municipal CEO, for a salary of $72,000 a year. Seventeen
years later, he was earning nearly $800,000 annually, money he used to
buy a beachside mansion and a horse ranch in Washington State. Bell's
police chief, meanwhile, was getting paid $457,000 a year. The median
annual household income in Bell: $30,000.[36]

Unfortunately, the local newspaper, the *Bell, Maywood, Cudahy
Community News,* shuttered a few years after Rizzo took control of
the public fisc and began using it to grossly enrich himself. It was the
Los Angeles Times that eventually exposed Rizzo, leading to criminal
charges against him and other town officials. But as one local activist
told Waldman for his FCC report, "Residents tried to get the media's
attention [earlier], but it was impossible."[37]

It should come as no surprise, then, that borrowing costs for local
governments jump by five to eleven points, or roughly $650,000 per
bond issue, following the closure of the local newspaper, according
to a 2018 study: Local media's watchdog function—asking questions
like, *Why did the city council choose such and such contractor for such
and such service? Isn't the CEO related to Councilmember So-and-So?*—
fosters efficiency and transparency. Removing that function results

in greater municipal-wage bloat, higher deficits, overpayments, and the like, all of which boost borrowing costs and lower bond ratings.[38]

Similar patterns hold at the state level. Researchers, for example, have established a correlation between the geographic isolation of a capital city—think of Annapolis, Maryland; Jefferson City, Missouri; Springfield, Illinois; Trenton, New Jersey; and other obscure state capitals you struggled to memorize in elementary school—and the likelihood of state-government corruption. That's because capital cities that are close to a metropolitan newspaper's readership area receive more robust coverage, while far-flung capitals tend to be subject to weaker scrutiny from smaller, weaker papers.[39] Now consider the fact that these days many state capitols are covered by far fewer reporters than they were ten or fifteen years ago.

Relatedly, the growth of news deserts disempowers ordinary people relative to larger, more sophisticated actors, be they government bureaucracies or private corporations.

In theory, ordinary Americans today enjoy instant access to an infinite trove of data through the internet. Paradoxically, however, bureaucrats and corporate managers these days are often more likely to get away with withholding information from the public: *Everything is on the internet—you figure it out.*

Raw data alone aren't useful in terms of countering bureaucratic or managerial power. Most public firefighters, for example, wouldn't have the time or energy to go through their pension plan's annual reports to connect the dots between a particular private equity investment and a Wall Street predator seeking to privatize their jobs. And even if a firefighter went to the trouble, he would still struggle to be heard without traditional media's enduring power to amplify citizen voices and to put pressure on public and private authorities.

An individual might be aware of some instance of corporate misconduct in his town—say, illegal toxic-waste dumping. He might take to social media to complain about it (though, depending on the power dynamics, he may hesitate to do so, for fear of running afoul of the local powers that be). Yet recent research points to the limits of such so-called citizen journalism. In 2021, Jonas Heese of Harvard Business School and his colleagues found that after a local paper shuttered operations, companies in the area violated regulations more brazenly, suggesting that "the closures reduce firm monitoring by the press."[40]

For example, not long after the *Haverhill Gazette,* the paper serving Haverhill, Massachusetts, switched to weekly publication from a daily format, the municipal hospital lost $15 million to a private operator's incorrect filings. As the (ironically downsized) *Christian Science Monitor* reported, that amount, piled atop preexisting debt, "led to the hospital's sale in 2001. Citizens are still on the hook, repaying $7 million annually until 2023." A Haverhill antipoverty activist lamented that a local paper might have caught the issue earlier.[41]

There is something about the newspaper format, as a stern community conscience with a physical presence in the councils of power, that prevents it from being rolled over by self-interested bureaucrats and managers inclined to hide information in plain sight.

Plus, when local journalism is diminished or lost altogether, public goods like utilities, health, education, and the environment go down in quality. It's true that a smaller tax base usually translates into a lower quality of public goods and services. Still, it's also clear that media coverage can galvanize public opinion around demands for reform, while in its absence crises in the poorest communities fester. We already saw this in the case of the Appalachian water crisis. But for a dogged RFA journalist, there to supplement a McClatchy paper's thin staff, the story might have gone underreported if not altogether unreported. There is much more where that came from.

In 2018, a Swedish-based scholar examined the top-twenty polluters in each U.S. state and found that "only 4 percent . . . received any coverage at all, perhaps owing to a lack of environmental specialists at local papers." Meanwhile, "among those that were subjected to negative press," polluting emissions dramatically *decreased.* For example, the *Pacific Standard* reported that in the year 2000

a coal- and oil-fired power plant in Massachusetts, was responsible for almost a million pounds of toxic emissions, the bulk
of which came from hydrochloric acid. . . . In 2002, the *Herald
News* reported that the Somerset plant was the third-biggest
emitter in the state. The data submitted by the plant later that
year showed that emissions had suddenly dropped to
400,000 pounds—a reduction of around 60 percent.[42]

In other words, local newspaper coverage can swiftly improve air
quality. As the news deserts grow, our natural environment, among
the most fundamental common goods, is bound to suffer.

Then, too, news desertification degrades the competitiveness of
our elections and the civic and political competence of citizens. To
wit, Americans who follow local news are also more likely to regularly vote in local elections. A 2016 Pew Research Center study found
that the quarter of adults who profess to always vote in local elections have "strikingly stronger local news habits" than those who
don't regularly visit the polling booth.[43]

Local news coverage also correlates, not surprisingly, with greater
voter sophistication. The University of Chicago's Daniel J. Moskowitz, for example, has found that voters who reside in counties with
out-of-state media markets—meaning they typically receive their
news from nonlocal sources—are less likely to assess down-ballot
candidates on their own merits; instead, they vote along strict party
lines, according to whichever national candidate they prefer at the
top. By contrast, voters in counties with in-state media markets tend
to uphold an older and more venerable American tradition: split-
ticket voting, a great antidote to polarization.[44]

The loss of local news, in other words, intensifies the gravita-
tional pull of national politics on local elections. This is deplorable,
because it means that national partisanship is obscuring local problems, even as it elevates down-ballot politicians to national power
who might not have garnered ballots but for insufficient local oversight. Incumbents tend to do better under such conditions, including

on Capitol Hill, where nearly half of states don't have a local news-paper reporter to cover their own congressional delegations.

Finally, when the local story isn't told, we become less engaged with our local communities. Americans who don't follow local news are also less likely to know their neighbors and more likely to report feeling alienated from their community.[45] To authentically take part in a local political community means to jointly confront economic and other problems that don't lend themselves to Libs of TikTok videos or angry Occupy Democrats messages.

This isn't to suggest that national debates over hot-button cultural issues aren't important, or that the ideological barriers dividing us would melt away if only we would put our heads together to solve local issues. But it is to say that to solve critical local issues, we need the kind of context-rich, accountability-oriented reporting that neither your favorite Twitter personality nor the citizen journalist of social media lore can supply.

The local newspaper failed owing not just to "natural" market developments but to decisions made by those occupying the commanding heights of our system—not least Silicon Valley monopolists and Wall Street looters. These actors also happen to be the ones to benefit the most when the story isn't told. On the next, and final, stop on our tour, we will see how Tyranny, Inc., has mastered legal coercion in the bankruptcy process so that when companies fail, it is aggrieved consumers and other weak parties who end up holding the bag.

8

"Broke" Billionaires

I N T H E B O O K of Job, Satan hatches a plan to test the faith of a good man by subjecting him to misery. God approves, and soon a flurry of misfortune falls upon Job and his family. In the modern world, some lives more than others seem to trace the same pattern. Yet unlike the biblical figure, few latter-day Jobs are redeemed and restored to happiness following their ordeals. Not in this world anyway. Such is the story of the Sandy, Utah, resident Kimberly Naranjo.

Born to a drug-addicted single mother, she was abused as a child and thrown into foster care before striking out on her own at age fifteen. As she later testified before the U.S. Senate, all this childhood turbulence left Naranjo dreaming of nothing but "stability"—having it for herself and being able to offer it to her children. Between the ages of nineteen and twenty-six, she had five kids out of wedlock; two more came later. Having inherited "the unhealthy behavior patterns that I had been exposed to in my early years," Naranjo explained, she possessed neither the means nor the ability to care for them.[1]

Naranjo had one person in her life willing to help carry her burdens. That was her aunt Cathy, who adopted the young mother and took over full-time care of her children, allowing Naranjo to enter a long-term inpatient treatment program to overcome her addiction. Naranjo got sober. She attained an associate's degree in drug counseling and began serving wounded men and women like herself as a counselor with the local sheriff's office.

"I have worked really hard to break the cycle for my children who I am blessed to have a wonderful relationship with today," Naranjo told the senators. Ever since getting clean, she acted as a "supporting participant in all their lives." And not just that, but thanks to the counseling job she was finally able to afford her "forever home" after years of bouncing between various residences.[2]

Then, one day, she woke up to a mysterious stabbing pain in her side. Before long, Naranjo was diagnosed with mesothelioma, an especially deadly form of cancer associated with exposure to asbestos, a toxic substance once used in many consumer and industrial products. Doctors gave her twelve to sixteen months, "which puts my expiration date at March of 2023," just short of her fiftieth birthday. Two of her kids would still be underage then, including one diagnosed with autism.[3]

How, she wondered, had she contracted mesothelioma? Reviewing her life and occupational history, doctors determined that the source of her asbestos exposure was the Johnson & Johnson talc baby powder she had used to care for her children, a link the megafirm strenuously denies. As a consumer, Naranjo said, she had "no idea I was exposing them and myself to the deadly asbestos inside that white plastic bottle I associated with motherly love."[4]

The financial blows soon compounded the medical ones: Naranjo lost her job, and unable to pay down her mortgage, she was forced to sell her "forever home." Still, there was hope. She figured she could "use my constitutional right and be heard in a court of law"—to bring her case before a jury that would award damages for the harm caused by J&J's talc powder, funds her family could use to care for her underage kids.[5]

That's when fate—or the legal system, more precisely—twisted the knife in true Jobean fashion. J&J had brainstormed a neat way to escape courtroom liability for Naranjo and thirty-four thousand other asbestos claimants like her. All it took was to file for bankruptcy. Yes, J&J—a profitable firm with a market capitalization of nearly half a *trillion* dollars—claimed to be broke.

Specifically, J&J used Texas corporation law to divide itself into two parts, off-loading its asbestos liabilities onto a new unit called LTL, which then filed for bankruptcy, putting a stop to all asbestos litigation and shielding the rest of the firm from the normal legal process for resolving such claims. This is the awesome—and highly coercive—power of corporate bankruptcy: The process is designed to bring legal claims to a halt, giving a struggling firm a respite to reorganize, seek fresh financing, and do right (as best it can) by creditors. Yet in this case, the "struggling" firm happened to be one of the largest, most successful corporations on earth. J&J had figured out a clever way to effectively plead, "I'm broke," when it was anything but. Lawyers call this the "Texas two-step" (first a division, then a bankruptcy). J&J's two-step is the biggest, most prominent example of this new maneuver.

Naranjo and other alleged victims would have to wait for a bankruptcy court to approve LTL's debt-discharge plan. Upon approval, they would all receive the same payout, likely to be pennies on the dollar compared with the huge jury awards handed down in the few cases that did go to trial before J&J pulled its two-step (a single group of twenty-one women with ovarian cancer had won a $2.12 billion verdict).[6]

The elements of justice and due process we associate with normal trials—the giving of testimony, the discovery of facts, ordinary citizens serving as jurors, and the sense of fairness that comes with all that—would go out the window. The pharma giant, as the "debtor," would be fully in control of the process at every stage. Even so, Michael Kaplan, chief bankruptcy judge for the U.S. District of New Jersey, allowed the move to go forward, holding that the unusual scheme was acceptable notwithstanding "allegations of bad faith."[7]

That's what compelled Naranjo, using "every ounce of strength" she had left, to testify before the Senate. As she asked the assembled lawmakers in Washington, "Johnson and Johnson is a really big and thriving company. How could they be bankrupt?"[8] How, indeed.

What Naranjo and other J&J plaintiffs faced was a symptom of what scholars have widely criticized as the "breakdown" and "lawlessness" that now characterize U.S. bankruptcy law when large corporations are concerned.[9] In addition to the Texas two-step, the legalized abuses include a process that lets shareholders, officers, and others who themselves aren't going through bankruptcy to shield their assets and reduce their liability for wrongdoing, or avoid it altogether. And it's all made possible by aggressive and barely disguised court and judge shopping by large debtors.

Today's corporate-bankruptcy regime is an especially insidious component of our system of private tyranny. For it co-opts a process meant to help genuinely distressed debtors to keep their businesses going—and uses it to defer, diminish, or outright deny justice to weaker creditors and claimants.

Dirty Dancing

On the surface, corporate bankruptcy appears to be one of the less pugilistic aspects of our legal system. At its best, it brings peace to what could be a scene of war. A company facing unsustainable liabilities is menaced at every side by lenders, shareholders, employees and retirees, landlords, suppliers, and others. These creditors are prepared to tear apart the debtor's assets, and claw out each other's eyes, to recover as much of what is owed them as they can. And that's exactly what would happen in many cases but for the filing of a reorganization petition under Chapter 11 of the U.S. Bankruptcy Code.[10]

At that point, the court imposes an immediate and automatic pause, known as a stay, against all lawsuits, foreclosures, and collection actions, while a judge considers the reorganization plan. In some instances, the court may ultimately hold that reorganization isn't feasible, in which case the debtor's assets end up being liquidated and divvied up among the creditors. But in many others, a re-organization goes forward, with the debtor allowed to remain in possession of its assets in the meantime, to operate the business as before, and even to seek fresh financing.[11]

There are good reasons to let companies do this. For one thing, the automatic stay prevents an ugly "race to the courthouse" among creditors, facilitating a calmer, more rational process for satisfying their competing claims against the debtor. Plus, reorganization safe-guards the value of assets that might otherwise be condemned to the auctioneer's hammer. Crucially, Chapter 11 lets a viable business that has run into a patch of trouble to remain a going concern, sav-ing jobs, supplier contracts, and consumer value that would be lost if it were allowed to go under.

But don't let the cooperative appearance of the process fool you. As the Georgetown University law professor Adam J. Levitin has commented, Chapter 11 bankruptcy "is by its nature coercive."[12] Bankruptcy *forces* rival groups to act collectively for the good of all, limiting property rights that creditors would be entitled to outside this unique process. A debtor might owe you $2 million plus interest. But under Chapter 11, you might end up recovering only $250,000—a big haircut—after negotiations with other creditors and after the court weighs all of your claims against the debtor's need for a clean start and the viability of the restructuring plan. If you don't like the outcome, other creditors whose claims enjoy higher priority may be able, with perfect legality, to cram it down your throat, all the same.

This is all nakedly coercive. As we argued in chapter 1, supposedly noncoercive market societies are, in fact, full of coercion, and bank-ruptcies of all kinds are a great example of that. Not every instance of coercion is necessarily bad, however, nor would a society orga-nized along more socialist lines be able to eschew all coercion. Rather, the point is to notice that market power *is* coercive power, often relying on the state's backing and benefiting those blessed with legal sophistication at the expense of those who lack it.

When a system denies this reality, ignoring the power inequalities to which market societies are especially prone, we end up with the sorts of *unjust coercion* explored in this book. It's how we get private tyrannies enforced by state action (or, crucially, inaction).

J&J's dirty two-step is just one symptom of this tendency in the bankruptcy domain. The current U.S. Bankruptcy Code was enacted in 1978, and as the Harvard legal scholar Michael Francus notes, lawmakers didn't anticipate it turning into "a forum for resolving mass torts" (that is, civil actions by numerous plaintiffs against a single company, often involving defective products). Yet large entities soon began using bankruptcy to deal with such claims. Still, as Francus observes, "bankruptcy is unpleasant." While plaintiffs forced to press their claims in bankruptcy may recover only pennies on the dollar, from the firm's perspective it would be better still to "eliminate the tort payments altogether" or bargain for even cheaper terms.[13]

Hence, the allure of the Texas two-step. The central operation is a so-called divisive merger, which creates two companies out of one. "Bad Company" (in lawyers' parlance) gets laden with all the liabilities, while "Good Company" remains asset rich. While Bad Company gets put into bankruptcy and has its liabilities discharged, Good Company "goes on its merry way," as Francus summarizes.[14]

Normally, such a move *should* meet with courts' cold disapproval. If a company shifts assets to another entity with an intent to prevent creditors from being able to get at them, that company would be guilty of making a fraudulent transfer and compelled to restore the assets to the debtor entity that transferred them. Yet J&J and a few other corporate debtors have learned to use divisive-merger laws to repackage what looks plainly like a fraudulent transfer.

Even if courts eventually see the maneuver for what it is, the Texas two-step will have achieved its purpose: namely, wasting time. "Fraudulent-transfer claims," explains Francus, "must be litigated in an adversary proceeding, with the full trappings of a trial. That means service, pleading, counterclaims, discovery, summary judgment, and trial, all of which take time"—precisely what Naranjo and women like her lack. J&J can grind them down to "extract settlement value, reducing the claimants' ultimate recovery."[15]

Defenders of the maneuver insist the two-step isn't tantamount to fraudulent transfer. In theory, Good Company agrees to cover Bad Company's liabilities. Yet, Francus warns, that coverage can be much narrower in practice than the "on-paper" promise.[16]

In the baby powder case, J&J has offered to pay "amounts the Bankruptcy Court determines are owed" by the spin-off division onto which J&J off-loaded its liabilities. J&J has set aside a $2 billion trust for this purpose, as well as "certain royalty revenue streams with a present value of over $350 million to further contribute to potential costs," according to a corporate website.[17] That amount—$2.35 billion in total—suggests that J&J anticipates coughing up *far less* than it would, but for the two-step. After all, the group of twenty-one women whose case went to trial won a $2.12 billion jury award— almost as much as the entire amount the firm has set aside for tens of thousands of similar cases now barred from the courtroom.

The corporate optimism is warranted: In return for relatively trifling contributions to the spun-off entity's bankruptcy, J&J can win a so-called third-party release. Such releases allow people or firms who aren't going through bankruptcy themselves—in this case, J&J—to avoid getting sued in the future as part of the Chapter 11 settlement. Although the legality of third-party releases is a matter of dispute among courts, in asbestos cases they are explicitly permitted under the Bankruptcy Code. Writes Francus, "The result is that a two-stepper, and especially one with asbestos liability, can extinguish claims against the asset-rich business through the bankruptcy of the liability-laden one, cutting off tort claimants from any further recovery."[18]

Even without the explicit blessing of the code, corporate wrongdoers in non-asbestos cases have managed to use third-party releases in bankruptcy to shield their shareholders. Indeed, that's precisely what happened in one of the most consequential American bankruptcy cases of all time: that of Purdue Pharma, the disgraced firm that played an outsized role in the ongoing opioid crisis.

The Sacklers' Last Trick

The story of the opioid crisis is by now all too familiar. It is both a symptom and a leading cause of misery in working-class America, predating the coronavirus pandemic by at least two decades and likely to long outlast it. Opioid overdoses claimed more than half a million American lives from 1999 to 2020, according to the Centers for Disease Control and Prevention, and exceeded 100,000 in 2021 alone. Opioid addiction and overdoses have also exacted a heavy economic toll on the nation, totaling $142 billion in health-care, criminal justice, and lost-productivity costs each year, according to one estimate.[19]

Equally notorious is how the opioid manufacturer Purdue Pharma enriched itself off this suffering. Purdue "produced some of the most powerful opioids, most notably an extended-release version of oxycodone called OxyContin," as Levitin, the bankruptcy scholar, summarizes. More than twenty-six hundred lawsuits lodged by governments and private actors allege that the firm "downplayed the dangers of addiction and pushed doctors to overprescribe the medications."[20]

Less well known, however, is how the Sacklers—the billionaire family who owned Purdue Pharma and closely oversaw its business— used the Chapter 11 process to dramatically limit their personal liability for the crisis. The legal operation was as audacious as it was enraging in its effectiveness. To understand what Purdue and the Sackler family did, it is helpful to view the operation from *their* point of view, as Levitin does in a 2022 article.

The Sacklers' chief goal was to squirrel away, and render untouchable, as much as possible of the reported $13 billion the family had amassed from Purdue's toxic business. To achieve it, they turned to Chapter 11.

As a firm, Purdue had no major liabilities—save for the various lawsuits filed against it (or threatened to be filed) by state and federal authorities and by individual plaintiffs whose lives were damaged by opioids. Those lawsuits were the basis of its petition for reorganization under Chapter 11. Before filing for bankruptcy, however, Purdue reached a tentative settlement with some plaintiff groups, including two dozen state attorneys general, that would release the family from "all claims and causes of action of any nature" in return for the Sacklers' pitching in $3 billion toward the firm's liabilities.[21] The idea was that in return for helping pay for a share of the ruin wrought by their company, the Sacklers would get to keep the rest of their assets.

It would take many more highly complex legal maneuvers, involving a vast range of public and private actors, for the Sacklers to finally get what they wanted all along. But that early agreement lent the Purdue bankruptcy its fundamental mold: If opioid victims and the public were to receive any restitution for the harm caused by Purdue, the Sacklers' personal liability had to be limited—crucially, without the family (as opposed to the firm) going through bankruptcy.

The Sacklers, in other words, got to take advantage of one of Chapter 11's most potent features—the blocking of courtroom claims—without themselves being the bankrupt debtor or submitting their assets for reorganization. Other actors, including many well-meaning public officials, would fail to break the mold. This, owing to the remarkable extent to which Purdue and its lawyers mastered the coercive dimensions of U.S. bankruptcy law.

As Levitin notes, once the reorganization petition was filed, Purdue faced three problems. The first was how to divvy up payouts between thousands of creditors, including the state attorneys general, hospitals, insurers, and individuals and families harmed by opioid addiction. The second quandary was Purdue's "liability to the federal government related to Medicare and Medicaid payments and violations of the Food and Drug Act"—liabilities that triggered the feds' robust power to take over the assets of a wrongdoer. And finally, there was the family's liability, given that the Sacklers were personally and closely involved with Purdue's business operations.[22]

Faced with these challenges, Purdue placed various pieces on the bankruptcy chessboard in such a way as to checkmate the public interest. A third-party release for the Sacklers, obtained on the cheap, became the essence of the reorganization. Rather than being treated as a mere reorganization *proposal,* that early settlement—the one that permitted the Sacklers to escape personal liability—came to be pre-ratified as the "map for Purdue's restructuring," with other claims forced to bend to its demands.[23]

How? Purdue used the feds' power to seize assets in its criminal and civil cases against the firm to solve the most critical of its problems: the Sacklers' personal liability. To grasp this, we need to briefly review what the firm owed the feds before explaining how Purdue leveraged those federal claims to get what it wanted.

Purdue Pharma owed the U.S. Department of Justice $2 billion as part of a criminal asset-forfeiture claim related to its Medicare, Medicaid, and drug-safety violations. But the DOJ agreed to let Purdue count a $1.775 billion payout to state and local governments against this amount, slashing its criminal liability to the feds to $225 million. Purdue also owed the DOJ $2.8 billion in civil liabilities, which was treated as a separate claim in the reorganization. In this way, Purdue won the "alliance" of at least one group of creditors, the federal government, whom it could rely upon to help force through its reorganization plan, even if state governments or individual plaintiffs objected (bankruptcy is inherently coercive, remember?).[24]

Then the pill maker concocted its ultimate "poison pill." A poison pill is a clause in a contract that triggers some sort of negative outcome if a certain condition is (or isn't) met. In this case, the $1.775 billion distribution to states would "snap back" to the feds unless Purdue was allowed to avoid liquidation and transform itself, instead, into a "public benefit" company, whose profits going forward would be used to address the opioid crisis.

If Purdue's deal with the feds, including the release for the Sacklers, didn't go through, the DOJ would gobble up the $2 billion, and the other creditors would be left with very little. *This* was the Sacklers' poison pill. But why would the DOJ or the states care if Purdue was turned into a "public benefit" company? The states were indifferent to what became of Purdue, whether it dissolved or became a charity or something else. That suggests to Levitin that "the poison pill was included in the settlement at Purdue's behest, meaning that Purdue created the very exigency"—the prospect of states and others ending up with mere scraps—"that it argued necessitated the settlement."[25]

Or think of it this way: The Sacklers built a Rube Goldberg machine that would only work if everything happened *just so*—that is, to their personal benefit.

Presto! By leveraging the rival interests of various creditors against each other, Purdue paved the way for a third-party release for the Sacklers. In the end, after some haggling, the family's personal contribution ended up being $6 billion, pending appeals court approval. It's a hefty amount for an ordinary person, to be sure, yet one that meant the Sacklers would keep their place in the billionaires' club, without even an admission of wrongdoing.[26]

Draining Justice

So far, we have spoken as if Purdue's successful and surprisingly painless glide through the Chapter 11 gauntlet were foreordained as a legal matter. But that was hardly the case. As we noted, outside the asbestos context, third-party releases are the subject of intense controversy, dividing the bankruptcy bench between judges who approve of them as a normal part of their bankruptcy powers and others who treat them as illegal.[27]

Knowing this, Purdue handpicked not just the right district in which to file its Chapter 11 petition but the right jurist: Robert D. Drain, a bankruptcy judge for the Southern District of New York who until his retirement in 2022 sat for many years in the city of White Plains, transforming the once-torpid courthouse into a bustling Chapter 11 mecca. Drain was the judge of choice for many corporate debtors, because he rarely disappointed them.

Courthouse shopping has long been a moral stain on the U.S. bankruptcy system, with debtors filing their petitions in specific circuits and districts in search of legal advantage. J&J, for example, located its LTL subsidiary in North Carolina, of all places, in the apparent hope of exploiting the Fourth Circuit's high bar for good-faith challenges to maneuvers like the Texas two-step. Under Fourth Circuit precedent, which governs in North Carolina, talc plaintiffs like Naranjo would have a harder time proving that "Bad Company" LTL was formed just for the purpose of bankruptcy (later, the bankruptcy was removed to New Jersey, in the Third Circuit).[28]

The law allows a debtor seeking bankruptcy protection to file a petition

(1) in the district in which it has been headquartered for the previous 180 days; (2) in the district in which its principal assets have been located for the previous 180 days; (3) in any district in the state in which it or its general partner has been incorporated for the previous 180 days; or (4) in any district in which one of its affiliates or its general partner or its partnership has filed.[29]

This wide range of options means that debtors can file almost anywhere. As Levitin comments, if the choice of venue is appropriate for a single firm in a corporate family, then it's also appropriate for the rest of the entities, "even if those entities have neither assets nor operations nor incorporation and perhaps not even creditors in the district."[30]

This has led to most so-called mega-cases—80 percent of them in 2020—being forum shopped. That is, "they were filed in a district other than that of the debtor's headquarters."[31] The Southern District of New York in particular has proved a hit with large debtors, owing to its judges' mastery of the admittedly labyrinthine, facts- and numbers-heavy analysis required in complex Chapter 11 cases. More recently, Delaware has also won corporate favor.

The advantage—or the problem, from a fairness perspective—is that these districts tend to rubber-stamp large debtors' requests and plans. Meanwhile, workers and other weak creditors are compelled to trek to inconvenient locations if they wish to be heard.[32]

Purdue went to astonishing lengths to hand its bankruptcy to a judge who would go on to rule for it and the Sacklers. How did Pur- due manage this? The key was to strategically use the local rules each district applies when deciding which case should go to which courthouse and which judge.

As Levitin notes, "Some bankruptcy courts have separate geo- graphical divisions, and local rules assign cases among those divi- sions on the basis of the address on the debtor's petition. Some divisions have but a single judge, so any case assigned to the division is guaranteed to have that judge."[33] Given the permissive choice-of- venue rules (see previous page) and the address-based assignments, corporate debtors can get their preferred judge by doing little more than renting temporary or virtual office addresses with the right zip code. No wonder that in 2020 just 3 of the country's 375 bankruptcy judges handled nearly two-thirds of the 155 restructurings involving companies with more than $100 million in assets.[34]

From a powerful debtor's perspective, what matters isn't just a judge's philosophy on contentious issues such as third-party releases or the Texas two-step but also his desire to have so-called mega-cases assigned to him. Some judges more than others seem to enjoy han- dling big, news-making, prestigious cases. To consistently do so, they must prove that they will "sign off on major transactions" and otherwise use their discretion to ease things for corporate debtors.[35]

Such a judge was the Honorable Robert D. Drain.

Yale and Columbia Law School educated, Drain was "among the most prominent bankruptcy judges in the nation," according to

Levitin. Following his appointment to the Southern District of New York bankruptcy bench, he sat initially at the district's Manhattan courthouse; there, he oversaw 18 percent of all big cases in the district, double what he should have received if such cases were assigned evenly among the district's eight judges. In 2009, Drain was moved to the district's White Plains courthouse, where for nearly a decade he attracted about 10 percent of mega-cases, an unremarkable share. "Then, something changed around 2018, and megacases started flocking to Judge Drain's White Plains courtroom." Indeed, from 2018 to 2020, he oversaw nearly two-thirds of all mega-cases in the whole district.[36]

The reason for this lies in a combination of Drain's own pro-big-debtor opinions on certain issues, other district judges' unfavorable views on third-party releases, and the fact that debtors couldn't be sure about the worldviews of newer judges appointed to the district in 2015.[37] In any event, debtors began maneuvering to have their bankruptcies filed in White Plains—which is to say, to have them heard by Drain.

They claimed, for example, to hold property in Westchester County, though it wasn't clear if these properties amounted to these debtors' main assets, as required by law. In other cases, debtors simply created new affiliates and then waited a hair more than the requisite 180 days to file for bankruptcy in White Plains. Still many others used short-term or virtual addresses to parachute into Drain's courtroom. And some simply did so without any good reason for being there.[38]

Even against this backdrop, Purdue's case assignment to Drain was especially dubious. As Levitin explains, "Purdue is headquartered in Connecticut and has a major manufacturing facility in Rhode Island." Meanwhile, "Purdue's holding company, Purdue Pharma L.P., is a Delaware limited partnership with a set of subsidiaries, all of which are Delaware or British Virgin Island entities." None of these locations would suggest the Southern District of New York as the obvious or appropriate venue for Purdue's bankruptcy. Yet the firm used its New York–incorporated general partner—an entity called Purdue Pharma Inc., which "has no equity interest in Purdue Pharma L.P. or any of its subsidiaries" and acts more like a fee-collecting contractor—as the basis for filing for Chapter 11 in the Southern District of New York. And the rules, of course, permitted the entire corporate family to file there once this strange contractor–cum–general partner got its foot in the door.[39]

So far, so good. Next, Purdue needed to make sure its Southern District of New York filing would be assigned not just to any courtroom but to Drain's. Using the district's electronic case-management system, Purdue must have picked White Plains as the appropriate courthouse.

But hang on, Purdue Pharma Inc.—the New York–based contractor entity used as a camel's nose to get the whole corporate family into the Southern District of New York—had been based in New York City since 1990. So by what right did Purdue pick Westchester County, as opposed to the district's Manhattan division, when it filed its petition? As it happens, on March 1, 2019, "Purdue Pharma changed its official corporate address from New York City . . . to White Plains." This, even though the company had "*never* conducted business at the White Plains address."[40]

Count forward from the change of corporate address for Purdue Pharma Inc. to the date of Purdue's Chapter 11 filing, on September 15, 2019, and you end up with 198 days, or just a couple of weeks longer than the 180-day minimum required under the venue rules.

Sure enough, the Purdue bankruptcy landed on Drain's desk. Indeed, as sleuthing by Levitin shows, so confident were Purdue's lawyers that they would end up with the judge they wanted, the initials "RDD"—for Robert D. Drain—were prefilled out on their earliest motions before the electronic system "had indicated a judicial assignment."[41]

And Drain delivered for Purdue. As Levitin concludes, the judge "gave Purdue all the major rulings it sought," including by approving the poison pill and stopping lawsuits against the Sacklers and releasing them from future liability. In addition, Drain barred the appointment of an independent examiner to scrutinize the deal's finances until negative publicity forced his hand, at which point he granted the examiner $200,000, an "unprecedentedly" pitiful budget relative to the complexity of the task.[42]

IN 2021, IN the aftermath of the Purdue-Drain debacle, the Southern District of New York inaugurated a new system for assigning $100-million-plus cases. Going forward, the district would route such cases to random judges, rather than letting debtors pick. Yet as Levitin told Bloomberg at the time, "It comes too late. The cow's already out the barn door": The judge-shopped Drain approved everything important that Purdue and the Sacklers wanted out of the Chapter 11 process.[43] The case remains on appeal before the Second Circuit as of this writing.

Meanwhile, as her life was crushed and her wounded cells multiplied, Kimberly Naranjo arranged a "living memorial" so her loved ones could wish her farewell before death. As a parting gift, she gave each a picture of herself standing next to a sign that read, "Do Not Quit."[44]

Her own determination paid off in February 2023, when the Third Circuit dismissed the bankruptcy of LTL—the spun-off entity where Johnson & Johnson had tried to house all of its talc liabilities—on the ground that the mega-firm had failed to show "good faith." The Texas two-step has yet to be tested in the Supreme Court, however, and even the Third Circuit ruling leaves open the door to the maneuver, as long as corporate debtors can muster greater subtlety than J&J's lawyers managed.[45]

Part II

ANOTHER WAY

9

An Unspeakable Problem

I N   A   B O O K of this kind, it would be customary at this stage to present a litany of public-policy "fixes" to the crises we just witnessed: Close the carried-interest loophole, legislate greater transparency about private equity fees, and so on. But to do so would defer a reckoning with the more fundamental forces behind private tyranny, from Alicia Fleming's scheduling hell to the Sacklers' evil triumph in bankruptcy, not to mention more headline-grabbing instances like Big Tech censorship or money in electoral politics. While these might appear as a miscellaneous grab bag of social ills, they all trace back to class-based inequalities in power and income that are inherent to the workings of unrestrained capitalism.

Before we go on to explore how those inequalities might be addressed, it's worth asking: Should Americans even worry about social class and the lopsided spread of the economy's blessings, so long as the economy is growing? Is it un-American or "socialist" to care?

These days, concerns about class-based inequality are usually associated with the progressive wing of the Democratic Party. On the mainstream right (and even much of the center left), the only kind of equality that matters is *equality of opportunity.* "Social mobility" is the North Star of such politics, and a good society is one that affords all people a fair shot at rising up.

Paul Ryan, then a GOP congressman on his way to becoming House Speaker, gave voice to these sentiments in a 2011 address to

the conservative Heritage Foundation. Those who believe in equality of opportunity, Ryan declared, "follow the American Idea that
justice is done when we level the playing field at the starting line and
rewards are proportionate to merit and effort." By contrast, those
who promote equality of outcome blame "most differences in
wealth and rewards" on "luck or exploitation" and believe "that few
really deserve what they have"—"a false morality that confuses fairness with redistribution and promotes class envy instead of social
mobility."[1]

Yet there is very little that is "conservative" or traditional about
Ryan's way of thinking. Indeed, it is more properly characterized
as laissez-faire or libertarian. Conservatives who worry about the
sorts of injustices documented in this book—not to mention the
rule of "woke capital" and Big Tech—must reject it. Fortunately,
they would find sound reasons for doing so in the American tradition.

In the eighteenth and nineteenth centuries, in the wake of the
democratic revolutions that swept the West, a tension arose between
the promise of equal citizenship in the *political* sphere and the yawn-
ing material inequalities that characterized the *economic* sphere. That
was certainly true of the world's leading democratic republic, the
United States.

The likes of Paul Ryan insist that "equality of opportunity" was
how the American tradition resolved this tension between politics
and economics. But the historical record is more complicated, and it
cuts against attempts to reduce the "American Idea" to mere social
mobility. Rather, the constant anxiety was that Americans couldn't
encounter each other as political equals if many millions of them
lacked enough property and material security to be invested in the
system.

The earliest American statesmen thought a virtuous, self-
governing republic required a modestly propertied and competent
citizenry. They fretted about an industrial, urban economy that

would breed "men without property and principle," as the Founding Father John Dickinson put it. James Madison fearfully prophesied "future times" when "a great majority of the people will not only be without landed but any other means of property," an oppressed rabble that would either destroy liberty or "become the tools of opulence and ambition." Thomas Jefferson considered it an urgent task of government to ensure "that as few as possible shall be without a little portion of land."[2]

It is true that "equality of opportunity" ran through the early tradition. Yet as the historian Christopher Lasch showed, this wasn't a rags-to-riches ideal. The mere possibility that a few of the poorest could attain grand wealth, Horatio Alger–style, wasn't what bound Americans to their newborn nation. Rather, equality of opportunity, Lasch argued, meant that most Americans "owned a little property and worked for a living."[3]

It wasn't until after the Industrial Revolution that something resembling the Paul Ryan ideal of social mobility began to edge out the older account of equality. By the late nineteenth century, a little ownership and equality increasingly eluded the masses. Describing the political-economic conditions of the era, one contemporary observer lamented,

> We discover that the fortunes realized by our manufacturers are no longer solely the reward of sturdy industry and enlightened foresight, but that they result from the discriminating favor of the government, and are largely built upon undue extractions from the masses of our people. The gulf between employers and the employed is constantly widening, and classes are rapidly forming, one comprising the very rich, while in another are found the toiling poor. . . . We discover the existence of trusts, combinations, and monopolies, while the citizen is struggling far in the rear, or is trampled to death beneath an iron heel. Corporations, which ought to be care-

fully constrained creatures of the law and the servants of the people, are fast becoming the people's masters.[4]

That observer was Grover Cleveland, no radical leftist, in an address to Congress in 1888, a remarkable admission of social failure by a sitting president. This was the America that witnessed furious railroad and mining strikes, the America of proletarian squalor set against plutocratic opulence, of farmers who still considered themselves frontier yeomen but who were, in truth, the near slaves of creditors and the "money power."

The more entrenched these great concentrations of corporate power and wealth became, the more the idea of "social mobility" gained steam. Indeed, Lasch noted, the phrase itself entered common parlance just "when the hierarchical structure of American society could no longer be ignored."[5] As far as some intellectuals were concerned, though, it no longer mattered whether workers as a class could enjoy the older equality—that is, as long as the gifted among them could be recruited to the top, reinvigorating the elite class with fresh blood and lending legitimacy to the whole order.[6]

In this line of thinking, if the education system molded *some* children of the poor into future entrepreneurs and professionals, the invisible hand would take care of the rest. Markets would carve pathways from the bottom to the top, and those who failed to crawl through them could be written off for having lacked "merit." Ignoring the complex lessons of the American tradition they championed, modern conservatives like Ryan, and not a few liberals, came to embrace the private economy as *the* solution to—rather than a major cause of—the challenge of inequality.

In doing so, they succumbed to one of the most seductive and enduring utopian visions: the dream of a market system in which coercion is the rare exception, rather than the norm. After all, a great deal of inequality could be morally tolerated, provided the economic order that brought it about was characterized by consent, choice, and merit—rather than power and coercion.

The Market: Trouble in Utopia

Americans pride themselves on being allergic to utopian thinking and barmy visionaries of all stripes. There is a reason the celibate and pacifist Shaker religion, which peaked in the nineteenth century, is down to three single practitioners today. Or why most 1960s hippie communes soon withered away. That this anti-utopian attitude is shared by many individual Americans makes it all the more ironic that as a society we are captives of market utopianism.

Market utopianism has given rise to a twenty-first-century U.S. society that is fast taking on the aspects of an economic *dystopia*. Like every would-be utopia, this one remains as elusive as it was when it first took shape in the writings of its visionaries more than two hundred years ago. But its enduring hold on the public mind, especially on the political right, makes it nigh impossible to discuss, much less address, the problem of economic power.

To begin to reverse these trends, we must return to market utopianism at its origins, to examine how it rendered economic coercion invisible and unspeakable, even as such coercion pervaded America and the West in the nineteenth and early twentieth centuries. The crisis finally came to a head in the Depression. Afterward, the United States joined the great, transatlantic experiment of socially managed capitalism, in which lawmakers aimed to strengthen the hands of the many against the economic power of a few.

In the bargain, the nation enjoyed three decades of widely shared prosperity, uplifting millions of formerly impoverished Americans, before the forces of private tyranny launched an even more radical counteroffensive in the 1970s that persists to this day. The Paul Ryan speech quoted on page 132 was but one expression of this ongoing counteroffensive.

This political-economic story holds the keys to understanding and, perhaps, improving our condition today. The next three chapters of this book are devoted to recounting it. The history is ultimately about the virtue of limits, a value on which conservatives, especially, pride themselves. For traditional Jews, Christians, and Muslims, for example, adherence to a divinely ordained day of rest regulates acquisitiveness and hyperactivity, thus liberating the believer from his own baser appetites. Timeworn moral maxims about fidelity in marriage can keep us out of all sorts of trouble. In both cases, what at first appears as a restriction is, in truth, a source of freedom. Likewise in complex market economies, regulation and control can be the friends, rather than the enemies, of freedom.

As we will see, it is pure idealistic folly to believe that freedom and regulation can be neatly sifted apart, with the market being a zone of pure freedom and the evil of regulation belonging solely to government. The realist accepts that coercion is to be found everywhere, very much including the market—the only meaningful questions being who gets to exert it, to what ends, and against what limits. Recovering this wisdom is essential if our political system, left and right, is to meaningfully challenge today's system of private tyranny.

The Competitive Model, Myth and Reality

Economic liberalism—the laissez-faire ideology of the eighteenth and nineteenth centuries—has a fetish for spontaneity. The more its advocates can attribute market trends and social phenomena to the interplay of impersonal forces, the more they view such phenomena as legitimate—as compared with state action, which "classical" liberals deem illegitimate in all but a few narrow areas. Adam Smith's "invisible hand" remains *the* emblem of this preference.[7]

Smith attributed the development of market society to human beings' irrepressible yearning to "truck, barter, and exchange one thing for another."[8] Yet market societies weren't, in fact, an organic outgrowth of human nature. As the Austrian economic historian Karl Polanyi pointed out in his 1944 classic, *The Great Transformation*, "Laissez-faire was the product of deliberate State action." It came about as a result of "a conscious and often violent intervention on the part of government which imposed the market organization on society."[9]

For Polanyi, no event evoked market society's coercive origins quite so clearly as England's early-modern enclosure controversy, when enterprising noblemen divided up (or "enclosed") fields that had been freely accessible to peasants for grazing. They then employed the newly subdivided land for commercial farming. Enclosure was achieved, Polanyi noted, "sometimes by means of violence, often by pressure and intimidation."[10] Despite some initial resistance, this brute privatization took place with state approval, with Parliament eventually codifying into law what had taken place in fact.

This was all very far from the picture many Anglo-American free marketeers have of early capitalism. The resulting suffering was undeniable. As Polanyi explained, the enclosers

> were literally robbing the poor of their share in the common, tearing down the houses which, by the hitherto unbreakable force of custom, the poor had long regarded as theirs and their heirs'. The fabric of society was being disrupted; desolate villages and the ruins of human dwellings testified to the fierceness with which the revolution raged, endangering the defences of the country, wasting its towns, decimating its population, turning its overburdened soil into dust, harassing its people and turning them from decent husbandmen into a mob of beggars and thieves.[11]

The erstwhile "decent husbandmen" and their descendants would soon find themselves ground down in prison-style workhouses and factories, their bones and tears forming the working-class sediments that underlay the glories of Victorian capitalism. Far from a "natural" process, proletarianization—the birth of a class with no other means to sustain and multiply itself but to sell its labor power—was the result of coercion, the traumatic unsettling of a way of life.

Enclosure wasn't the only form of state-directed or state-backed coercion used to bring about market societies. There was much else of the kind, on both sides of the Atlantic (though the British question is especially germane in these discussions, since it was Englishmen and Scots who pioneered market-utopian ideology). To develop export-based industrial economies, for example, Britain and the United States both erected protective tariffs, while the British went so far as to criminally prosecute foreign agents who poached skilled textile workers.[12]

Then there were imperialism and colonialism. Britain and other European powers "enclosed" much of the rest of the planet for the benefit of their market systems, transforming indigenous societies into resource pools for domestic industry, as well as captive markets for the products of their manufactures. In India, the British not only seized a colonized people's natural resources for the benefit of their empire's burgeoning industrial economy. They also used tariffs and duties to keep Indian fabrics out of Britain's domestic market, turning an Indian economy capable of manufacture and export into one heavily reliant on imports.[13]

In the colonies, one important aim was to will into being the types of labor markets that had been theorized by the market utopians, and that had already been violently imposed upon poor whites in the imperial core. This was no small feat. Indigenous societies might have been impoverished, but within their means they generally saw to it that no individual starved. That had to change. "Ironically, the white man's initial contribution to the black man's world mainly consisted in introducing him to the uses of the scourge of hunger," wrote Polanyi. "Thus the colonists may decide to cut the breadfruit trees down in order to create an artificial food scarcity or may impose a hut tax on the native to force him to barter away his labor."[14]

We needn't romanticize indigenous life or feudal patterns of social organization. Those societies had their own ruling classes and power hierarchies; coercion, especially the use of physical punishments, was openly practiced. But that's just the thing: Before capitalism, the economy was but one component of the social order.

Pre-market societies didn't recognize the impulse to "truck, barter, and exchange" as human beings' most important trait, and they took steps to circumscribe this propensity.[15] Then came a movement that sought to partition off the autonomous market from the political imperative to maintain a just and stable order. The advocates of this new movement preached noncoercion. And yet all this was itself brought about by coercion, frequently directed by the state.

SO MUCH FOR market society's origin story. But even if one ignores the means by which the market system was established, its everyday functioning has posed a still-greater challenge to the laissez-faire utopia.

Market utopianism described an economy in which coercion simply couldn't take place, "because no one had power to misuse," as the Canadian American economist John Kenneth Galbraith summarized the laissez-faire view.[16] Everyone was supposed to be subject to impersonal market forces crystallized in prices, over which no single actor exercised influence to any appreciable degree, and certainly no undue influence.

What guaranteed this state of affairs was relentless competition. The existence of many producers in any given industry meant that no one of them could wield significant economic power over other market actors, be they consumers, suppliers, or workers. The arch-laissez-faire theorist F. A. Hayek, for example, hailed "competition as superior not only because it is in most circumstances the most efficient method known but even more because it is the only method by which our activities can be adjusted to each other without coercive . . . authority."[17]

Milton Friedman had a similar confidence in competition as a bulwark against coercion. "So long as effective freedom of exchange is maintained," he wrote in *Capitalism and Freedom*,

the central feature of the market organization of economic activity is that it prevents one person from interfering with an-

other in respect of most of his activities. The consumer is protected from coercion by the seller because of the presence of
other sellers with whom he can deal. The seller is protected
from coercion by the consumer because of other consumers
to whom he can sell. The employee is protected from coercion
by the employer because of other employers for whom he can
work, and so on. And the market does this impersonally and
without centralized authority.[18]

There was one big problem: Even as the market utopians extolled
perfect competition, most of America's major industries were falling
into the hands of a few humongous corporations thanks to a merger
frenzy that began in the latter decades of the nineteenth century.
The U.S. consolidation bonanza spanning 1895 to 1904, for example,
saw 157 firms emerge out of the combination of some 1,800. Many
of the resulting giants controlled 40 to 70 percent of their respective
industries. Among these were the likes of Nabisco, Kodak, U.S. Steel,
and Otis Elevator. Still more staggering was the extent of control
exercised by GE (90 percent of its market), International Harvester
(70 percent), and American Tobacco (90 percent).[19] A similar trend
toward concentration was afoot in the major industrial powers of
Europe—Britain, Germany, and France—around the same time,
particularly in banking and heavy industry.[20]

By 1933, just two hundred nonfinancial firms and their subsidiaries controlled 57 percent of all U.S. nonfinancial corporate assets, according to a groundbreaking study by the economist Gardiner
Means.[21] The economists E. H. Chamberlin and Joan Robinson
coined the term "oligopoly" to describe this situation, one in which
only a few producers dominate most industries. Its chief characteris-
tic was the absence of real price competition: that is, the one thing
supposedly needful to prevent some market actors from coercing
others.[22]

Worse, from the standpoint of laissez-faire purists, all this combination made *good sense* for national development. For one thing, it

was the semi-competitive (at best) giants that could fund industrial-scale research and development.[23]

The chaotic early years of America's railroad industry, moreover, exposed the inadequacy of laissez-faire policy to national development. In the railroad context, the ferocious competition between multiple firms had led to track overproduction, throwing a quarter of firms into bankruptcy by 1895. Stability was soon to be found in consolidation and, eventually, a federally sanctioned cartel system for limiting price competition.[24]

In response, some devotees of laissez-faire, and not a few progressives, called on the government to bring down the hammer of antitrust, to shatter the giants into smaller, more competitive pieces. But what was to forestall the return of topsy-turvy competition and the eventual absorption of most of the players by new giants? The threat of a return to oligopoly hadn't really gone away, as the market utopians had hoped. "If there are only a handful of firms in the typical industry," wrote Galbraith, it follows that "privately exercised economic power is less the exception than the rule in the economy."[25]

The modern capitalist wasn't a hapless marionette, yanked this way and that by the mysterious movements of some invisible hand above. To a remarkable extent, it was *he* who decided what to charge for products, how much to pay in dividends to shareholders, and how to treat workers and suppliers. True, the capitalist structure constrained his range of rational choices (the firm would soon fail if he neglected to maximize profits). But his vast coercive powers were plain to see in the actually existing economy—even if they remained invisible to the market utopians peering out on the world from the high towers of their fantasy castles.

The Class Structure

As we emphasized in the early chapters of this book dealing with labor and employment contracts, two classes sharply divided market societies following the Industrial Revolution: the capitalist few who controlled productive assets, on the one hand, and the multitudes who lacked any means of survival but to sell their labor power for wages, on the other. A third class, technocratic managers who service the assets of the first, has received a great deal of attention from thinkers across the political spectrum since at least the 1930s, from New Deal liberals like Adolf Berle to conservatives like James Burnham.[26]

But the distinction, and the alleged tensions, between owners and managers needn't detain us long here. If managerial theories are correct, and technocrats have overtaken the old-school capitalists as the dominant class, it makes little difference for our purposes, since the managers have every rational incentive to deploy coercion against workers on behalf of their firms (as indeed they do) and even if they personally profess progressive attitudes (as many also do). That last tendency was crisply illustrated recently when the chief diversity officer for REI, the outdoor-gear chain, began a company podcast by declaring, "I use she/her pronouns and am speaking to you today from the traditional lands of the Ohlone people."[27] The aim of the podcast: browbeating REI workers into not joining a labor union.

Class-based coercion of this kind kindles tensions in market societies that can turn explosive. At the same time, the power asymmetries between the two camps usually compel workers to submit, all else being equal. (We will explore the structural asymmetries and what it might mean for all else *not* to be equal in the next chapter; suffice it to say for now that it is an uphill battle.)

To be sure, there are individuals who resist the constraints this situation imposes upon them: the unusually generous boss, the worker who strikes out on her own as an entrepreneur and succeeds against long odds, and so on. But as the New York University sociologist Vivek Chibber has shown, these are deviations from an inexorable general tendency. For the rest, market reality compels them to choose certain goals (coercion for bosses; submission for employees).[28]

Here, a certain kind of conservative might insist that a more virtuous culture suffices to rechannel economic behavior into more humane grooves: If only the church did a better job of morally forming managers, for example, the workplace would become a less oppressive place. A certain kind of progressive, meanwhile, might object that this is guilty of "essentialism," of privileging one narrative at the expense of many other incommensurable lived experiences.[29]

These arguments, though typically raised by partisans at opposite ends of the ideological spectrum, are mirror images of each other. Both underestimate the material realities that confront workers regardless of their religious beliefs or the other identities that define who they are. Class, as Chibber notes, implicates their "physical survival."[30] Regardless of the cultural context, workers have to put food on the table.

The employer likewise faces an economic compulsion that forces him to coerce the worker, regardless of his cultural outlook. A private equity partner today might be a conservative Catholic, a devotee of the traditional Latin Mass, a fierce opponent of abortion, and so on. And insofar as running his fund doesn't obtrude upon these things, his cultural and religious convictions will retain their primacy in his mind. What's at risk are only those aspects of his faith that clash with his economic imperatives, such as the church's social teaching, with its pesky insistence on the obligation to furnish a living wage to one's employees.

In the nineteenth century, many expected the class structure to collapse under the weight of its contradictions. The starkly uneven distribution of income between coercive asset owners and the asset-less workers whom they coerced, and the sheer misery that was the near-universal lot of the latter, were supposed to awaken a revolutionary spirit. Mass upheaval would lead to the overthrow of the entire social order and the dawn of a new society—one that would finally fulfill the freedom and equality promised, but never quite delivered, by the democratic revolutions of the previous (eighteenth) century.

Karl Marx, for example, spoke of a "conflict now raging," as a result of the "changed relations between masters and workmen" and the "enormous fortunes of some few individuals, and the utter poverty of the masses." These conditions had brought about "increased self reliance and closer mutual combination" among workers, as well as a "prevailing moral degeneracy."

Actually, those words were penned not by Marx but by Pope Leo XIII in his 1891 encyclical on capital and labor, *Rerum novarum.*[31] Yet half a century earlier, Marx and his friend and frequent co-author Friedrich Engels had similarly prophesied in *The Communist Manifesto* that the "advance of industry" promoted by employers and the intimate "association" of employees in the workplace would combine to assure the downfall of the whole system.[32]

The more the masters of industry developed the economy along the competitive lines promoted by laissez-faire theory, the more people they would proletarianize, swelling the ranks of the many who lived hand to mouth, at the mercy of the labor market and the vagaries of nineteenth-century capitalism, with its frequent bankruptcies, currency crises, and unruly business cycles. Radicalized together in this crucible, Marx and Engels believed, workers would inevitably emerge as the "grave-diggers" of the capitalists.[33] Eventually, private property itself would be abolished—the prospect dreaded by Pope Leo and welcomed by Marx and Engels.

Events took a different course. The crises of capitalism in the nineteenth and early twentieth centuries catalyzed social change. But in the industrial nations of the West, the change brought about was a modification of the status quo, rather than its complete overthrow. Political leaders across the West came to welcome, rather than suppress, the ability of the weak to *act collectively and politically* to counterbalance the power of the strong.

What followed were three decades of socially managed capitalism on both sides of the Atlantic. The new arrangement was neither

the laissez-faire utopia of the free marketeers nor the classless society imagined by orthodox Marxism. What mattered was that it
achieved its purpose, safeguarding the weak and the political community as a whole against private tyranny, however imperfectly. Its
rise was a grand achievement, its loss an epochal setback.

IO

There Was *an Alternative*

THE BRITISH HISTORIAN Tony Judt described social democracy as "a practice in lifelong search of its theory."[1] Rooted in nineteenth-century Europe and flowering in the three decades after World War II, social democracy was defined, above all, by its pragmatic approach to the problem of economic coercion. And it is precisely that pragmatism that commends its lessons to us today, when market utopianism has plunged us into a state of private tyranny, all while the supposedly "realist" prophets of laissez-faire still insist that "there is no alternative."[2]

Against the backdrop of a cynical "capitalist realism"[3] that seeks to foreclose even the possibility of reform, the achievements of social democracy remind us that there once *was* an alternative—and that there could be one again. In those first three decades postwar, this mix of policies and practices brought about hitherto unseen levels of mass comfort and prosperity, earning the era the moniker "the thirty glorious years."

Judt was writing of the European context, and specifically western and northern Europe, where political parties had garnered mass support under the banner of social democracy going back to the nineteenth century. The leaders of these movements were emphatically men and women of the socialist left. What set them apart from *revolutionary* socialists was a commitment to peaceful reform and democratic politics, an approach that stood out especially after the bloody savagery of Russia's 1917 revolution. Instead of going down the Bolshevik route, as Judt wrote, European social democrats resolved to "use the resources of the state to eliminate the social pathologies attendant on capitalist forms of production and the unrestricted workings of a market economy: to build not economic utopias but good societies."[4]

The U.S. variety was never as comprehensive as Europe's, and it would be more apt to talk of socially managed capitalism—or better yet, political-exchange capitalism—in the American context. The early model was laid down by progressives like Woodrow Wilson, whose World War I–era policies showcased the state's indispensable role in directing private activity in a complex economy, as well as conservatives like Herbert Hoover, who as secretary of commerce encouraged business, labor, and governmental leaders to cooperate to improve the wages and conditions of workers and to mitigate ruthless price competition in certain industries.[5]

Yet it was Franklin Delano Roosevelt and his New Deal that gave full expression to these insights. By the time our only four-term president was done, he and his allies had refounded the U.S. political economy to reflect the realities of the market, as opposed to the theories of the market utopians. The New Deal came to form a broad consensus, with even FDR's Republican successors upholding its logic and expanding it through the Nixon era. Having witnessed the crises of pre–New Deal capitalism, conservatives of that generation understood why these policies had been necessary.

We can't offer a full history of the New Deal, the subject of innumerable studies and endless debates among journalists, historians, and economists. Much less can we present a detailed comparison between the New Deal and its more comprehensive analogues across the Atlantic. What matters for our purposes is examining how it managed to defang—or at least, to soften the bite of—coercion in the marketplace.

Much as is the case today, the U.S. economy in the decades leading up to the Great Depression was rife with many varieties of private coercion, some of which we have already discussed: chaotic industrial development; entire sectors dominated by a handful of colossal firms that could more or less set their own prices; the overweening influence of Wall Street financiers who funneled capital toward dangerous speculation, rather than useful production; and outright fraud and hucksterism that not infrequently harmed consumers and small-time investors.

There was *one* coercive relationship, however, that underpinned most of these others and that elicited the greatest moral outrage at the time. That was the relationship between asset-less employees and asset-owning employers—the coercion, in other words, that was embedded in the class structure of market society.

The New Deal's "alphabet soup" of novel federal agencies addressed a wide range of economic problems, some more successfully than others. But the program's most transformative element, the one that touched the lives of the greatest share of wage earners, was bolstering labor's ability to bring collective action to bear against employers' power. In this way, the New Deal helped catalyze what the Belgian political theorist Chantal Mouffe calls a "subject of collective action"—a class of people prepared to make the mutual sacrifices needed to reform "a social order they experienced as unjust."[6]

The benefits, as we have said and will show in greater depth presently, redounded to the whole of society.

The Wages of Asymmetry

It's worthwhile restating what exactly the problem was (and is): why under "normal" market conditions, the power dynamics generated by the economic structure itself prove almost impossible to overcome for employees.

It comes down to the fundamental asymmetry in power we have been discussing, and which we illustrated repeatedly in the contemporary world on our tour of today's system. Even Adam Smith, the godfather of laissez-faire, betrayed glimpses of this asymmetry in

The Wealth of Nations, first published in 1776—that is, before the Industrial Revolution massively widened the power gulf between capital and labor.

Describing conflicts between employers and employees, Smith observed that it isn't hard to "foresee which of the two parties must, upon all ordinary occasions, have the advantage in the dispute, and force the other into compliance with their terms." The reason has to do with the uneven distribution of income inherent to capitalist production. Not to put too fine a point on it, employers get to keep more of the profits, and this means that even if they stop production, they can "generally live a year or two upon the stocks which they have already acquired." By contrast, noted Smith, "many workmen could not subsist a week, few could subsist a month, and scarce any a year without employment. In the long run the workman may be as necessary to his master as his master to him; but the necessity is not so immediate."[7]

A second asymmetry is carved into the employment agreement. Economists have long recognized that the employment contract is necessarily incomplete. What is put to paper and signed is never the operative agreement. This is because, as Vivek Chibber, the NYU sociologist, says, bosses "have to constantly adjust the pace and intensity of work as market conditions change; they have to redirect labor in accordance with changing exigencies and as they discover the actual abilities of individual workers."[8]

While the incomplete contract may be understandable from the employer's perspective, it implies a profound instability for workers—a daily renegotiation of how they spend large chunks of their lifetimes, with the ever-looming possibility that they will be deemed redundant, have their wages slashed, or be subjected to that bullying new manager with an ax to grind.

Laissez-faire theory welcomes this constant renegotiation, as we have seen: If management hands down a new and unpleasant workplace diktat, employees are always "free" to push back and, failing that, to find another job. But as we have also seen throughout this book, that is simply not an option for the vast majority of ordinary working people, given their need to pay for basic necessities, care for kids and elderly parents, seek treatment for health problems, and so on. More than that, most ordinary people aren't radical entrepreneurs of the self, ready at a moment's notice to adapt, move around, and seek new opportunities. They long, rather, for stability and order.

Which brings us to a third, and related, asymmetry that bears down especially hard on workers on the lower rungs of the economic ladder: low wages and the ready availability, in many markets, of people willing to toil for still less. Under "normal" market conditions, workers "seek out employment in order to defend their well-being," writes Chibber, "but once they acquire the job, it delivers on the promise only partially or opens up entirely new fronts that threaten their well-being."[9] They might be able to cover their life expenses (if barely), so long as they work. But they lack a fundamental sense of security: Any mishap—an accident on the job, a misunderstanding with the boss, and so on—can suddenly put a stop to their earning ability, pulling the rug out from under their lives.

Laissez-faire is prepared to allow wages to fall drastically, if necessary. Indeed, this is the theory's "solution" to the problem of unemployment: Allow the price of labor power to decline to low enough levels, and everyone will have a job. But for individual workers, low wages set the terms of a game they can never win, a promise of security they can never quite grasp. As Chibber argues, the competitive wage structure is precisely what gives the boss the power "to direct his labor as market conditions demand." The competitive structure itself tells the worker that he can be replaced at any moment and left unable to feed himself. Thus, for the worker, the insecurity of low wages "endows his employer with an arbitrary power over him" and "destabilizes much of his life outside the workplace in that the rest of his life choices have to be subordinated to ensuring that he prioritizes his attractiveness to a current or future employer.

The loss of power at work is complemented by a general anxiety at home."[10]

All else being equal, the combined force of these asymmetries pushes most workers to eschew union organizing, workplace political activism, and other forms of collective action. Instead, they do their best to get by, and maybe even get ahead, on their own. As Chibber emphasizes, this is an emphatically rational choice from the point of view of the individual worker, much as meting out coercion is rational from the point of view of the individual employer (the rare "nice boss" excepted). And the bottom line is that getting workers to organize around demands for better wages and benefits, greater autonomy, and so on is a *very difficult* business.

These class-based power asymmetries were very much present in the American workplace in the decades before the New Deal. Writing within living memory of pre–New Deal U.S. labor conditions, John Kenneth Galbraith declared, "Not often has the power of one man over another been used more callously than in the American labor market after the rise of the large corporation."[11]

To prevent workers' collective action in those days, employers deployed not just what Galbraith called compensatory power ("If you refuse to work, I will starve you!") and conditioned or ideological power ("Unions are a harbinger of Bolshevism!") but also outright physical violence:[12] The history of the labor movement in the nineteenth and early twentieth centuries is, in some respects, one long sequence of uprisings put down, sometimes murderously, by the soldier, the police officer, and the Pinkerton detective.[13]

All this repression worked its intended effects: to keep wages down and to impose a low ceiling on union density—that is, the share of the workforce belonging to labor organizations, the one vehicle available to wage earners seeking to act collectively against employers. As Michael Lind notes, the "percentage of Americans who belonged to labor unions, only 2.7 percent in 1900, had risen to 12.1 percent in 1920, only to fall to 7.4 percent in 1930."[14]

This turned out to be a very lousy outcome not just for workers but for the economy as a whole.

The same lopsided distribution of income that so strengthened the hands of employers against employees at the firm level also weakened the economy. Chronically underpaid workers couldn't afford to buy the things they helped produce, leading to a purchasing-power deficit that would ultimately hurt the asset-owning class as well. Put another way: The power inequalities that kept workers down at the firm level ended up breeding material inequalities that threatened the system.

The disparities between manufacturing productivity and overall profits instantly tell the story. Thanks to technological developments, U.S. manufacturing productivity jumped by a third in the 1923–1929 period, whereas manufacturing wages in the same period rose by only 8 percent. Indeed, "labor's share of income in manufacturing *declined* from 77.9 percent to 72.9 percent" in that period, "while the share going to capital rose from 19.6 percent to 25.5 percent."

Translation: Industrial workers just before the Depression were producing much more than they had a decade earlier, but earning less for it. Likewise, overall profits (not just in manufacturing) spiked by 62 percent in this period, while the 11 percent increase in wages didn't come close to keeping pace. Indeed, as Lind notes, unskilled wages fell absolutely amid the opulence of the 1920s.[15]

Then came the 1929 stock market crash and the Great Depression. While many theories have been floated to explain the cataclysm, the demand-based account still commands a great deal of mainstream scholarly respect. And for good reason, for it was by bolstering demand that the New Dealers finally pulled the nation out of the Depression.

Many leading American figures at the time recognized that the Depression had something to do with income inequality, which, in turn, came out of power inequalities. Marriner Eccles—the Mormon banker tapped by FDR to head the Federal Reserve for much of the Depression period through World War II—was no socialist. Yet he saw the devastating mismatch between mass production on the supply side and mass impoverishment on the demand side. The U.S. economy, he argued, had to strike some measure of parity between the two.[16]

Faced with a crisis sparked by the power asymmetry between labor and capital, New Dealers pursued two broad types of reforms. The first—massive public-works projects intended to put the unemployed back to work and leave more spending cash in their pockets— was urgent to the demand crisis of the moment. The second was more long-term, and it involved government encouraging, where hitherto it had suppressed, workers' ability to exercise *countervailing power.*

The Triumph of Countervailing Power

"Countervailing power" is a common term on the labor left. But we owe the concept to Galbraith, a figure who eluded easy ideological categorization but was certainly no leftist. He was, above all, a realist: In his 1952 classic, *American Capitalism: The Concept of Countervailing Power,* he wasn't so much advocating for some new economic ideology as he was describing trends that were already unfolding in the U.S. economy in the aftermath of the New Deal.

Recall from chapter 9 that competition was laissez-faire's all-purpose solution to the problem of coercion. Or rather, the existence of competitive markets was taken to mean *there was no such problem at all.* Competition among a multitude of producers would spare the consumer the danger of any one of the producers exerting control over price. The common price, of which every market actor was supposed to be aware, would soon sound the death knell for any one firm that tried to put one over on buyers. Price manipulation was simply impossible. Likewise, competition among employees (as sellers of labor power) would ensure that wages were efficient, that everyone who wanted one could get a job, and that the individual worker was always free to find a new gig, not least by offering to work for less.[17]

Only, real-life market economies weren't the "delicately adjusted Elysium" described by this account, as Galbraith sardonically commented.[18] Rather, typical industries were lorded over by a very few firms that exercised a great deal of control over the prices they charged for their products, the prices at which they purchased supplies, and the prices they paid for the labor power of their employees. The common price was their toy, a situation that cried out for limits on economic power of a kind that competition, classically understood, just couldn't provide.

But there was another way, as the New Deal had shown. The counterpressure would be exerted not on the same side of a given market—not between producers, between employees, and so on—"but on the opposite side, not with competitors but with customers or suppliers." In this way, "private economic power is held in check by the countervailing power of those who are subjected to it. The first begets the second."[19]

In some markets, the formation of countervailing power was an almost automatic process. In retail, for example, big department stores exercised countervailing power against corporate producers and passed on the savings to consumers without any governmental actor helping or any political movement urging them to do so. If there were going to be large appliance manufacturers like GE, for example, then bulk buyers like Sears (in its heyday) were likely to countervail their oligopolistic influence over the price, in pursuit of their own self-interest and to the happy benefit of shoppers.[20]

Yet it was the labor market that presented the best example of how one group of people (sellers of labor power) could push back against the unjust power of those on the other side of the market (buyers of labor power). There, the concentration of power on the employers' side—the fact that in the most developed industries a multitude of workers found themselves competing against one another, with very few buyers on the other side of the market—had compelled labor to join forces, acting collectively to secure higher wages, better working conditions, greater autonomy, and so on.[21]

Unlike in retail, however, the formation of countervailing power in the labor market couldn't be taken for granted. Galbraith observed that "the development of countervailing power requires a certain minimum of opportunity and capacity for organization" that some market actors can't muster on their own.[22] The labor market was one such area. Owing precisely to the asymmetries we discussed earlier, workers couldn't take the risks involved in mounting countervailing power.

"In light of the difficulty in organizing countervailing power, it is not surprising that the assistance of government has repeatedly been sought in this task," wrote Galbraith. "Without the phenomenon itself being fully recognized, the provision of state assistance to the development of countervailing power has become a major function of government—perhaps *the* major domestic function of government."[23] Indeed, the New Deal could only be fully understood in light of the need for government to bolster countervailing power in certain markets, most notably labor.

To foster workers' countervailing power, New Dealers enacted two hugely significant pieces of legislation. One was the Wagner Act (the National Labor Relations Act), which sought to encourage unionization and collective bargaining. The other was the Fair Labor Standards Act, which created federal minimum-wage and overtime protections.

Galbraith saw the Wagner Act as a form of government support for unionized workers, and the FLSA as offering similar support for nonunionized workers.[24] But the two operated mutually, along with the welfare nets the New Dealers wove at the bottom of society, to strengthen labor's countervailing power. Scholars have long recognized, for example, the role of welfare nets in boosting labor's position: If workers don't have to worry about basic health care, dire joblessness, and the like, that can allow them to demand, with less fear, a greater say in the management of their companies. A modicum of security breeds boldness.[25]

Sure enough, these laws enhanced the proportion of workers belonging to labor organizations. Union membership peaked in 1945 at 33 percent, up from its turn-of-the-century nadir (2.7 percent), and remained high throughout the 1950s and 1960s.[26] In concentrated, mass-production industries, especially, labor gained a seat at the table, sometimes joined by government. At its best, this arrangement promoted long-term planning and yielded decisions aimed at the well-being of the firm, its workers, and the economy as a whole.[27]

It was perfectly reasonable for governments to reinforce labor's ability to mount countervailing power against capital. In doing so, Galbraith insisted, "government action supports or supplements a normal economic process. Steps to strengthen countervailing power are not, in principle, different from steps to strengthen competition"[28]—something laissez-faire was committed to. It's just that, here, the pressure came from the other side of the market, from *sellers going up against buyers*, rather than *among sellers*.

Larger consequences flowed from this. State support for countervailing power led asset-less workers and asset owners to strike a political compromise, leading to what might be called political-exchange capitalism. Under pre–New Deal conditions, workers and the asset-less masses either went along (to survive) or found themselves locked in pitched battles against bosses that undermined the stability of society as a whole. Post–New Deal, workers could channel their demands through recognized unions and mass political parties (including Republicans, who competed for the labor vote as recently as the Nixon era). Labor had now "bought in" to the system. In a way, this model made more explicit what ordinary people already knew: that economic life involves coercion. But it also gave them a measure of power to negotiate the coercion to which they had long been subjected.[29]

Whether we think about it in terms of countervailing power, po-

litical exchange, or class compromise, mid-century political economy went a long way toward returning markets to their proper place
as a component of politics, the shared quest for the common good
of the whole. It recognized that the pursuit of profits isn't, and
shouldn't be, autonomous from other human imperatives, not least
that of a living wage. And it accepted that the market, like any other
human institution, involves coercion. In a good society—if not a
utopia—this coercion should be subject to the give-and-take that
characterizes our other public endeavors. This, socially managed
capitalism set out to do, and this it achieved to an admirable extent.

The advocates of the laissez-faire utopia refused to grant any of
this back then. Their editorial pages and PR statements were rife
with fevered warnings that the New Deal had set the United States
on a course to totalitarianism. In their less temperate moments,
laissez-faire advocates went so far as to link the social democratic
elements of the new consensus with the horrors of Fascism and Nazism.[30] To be sure, the tone was more elevated, the lines of argument more nuanced, as befitted the literary culture of that era. But
the core message was often scarcely different from the rantings of a
talk-radio host today: Americans were poised to lose not only their
freedom but also their prosperity.

Except things didn't pan out that way. These years were called
"glorious" for a reason. A statistical snapshot, drawn from the economic historian Judith Stein, explains why:

> However we explain it, in the fifteen years following the war
> rising productivity advanced the GDP 37 percent and the wage
> component of the national income rose. The country attained
> growth and mild redistribution. Between 1947 and 1973 dispos-
> able income increased 15 percent in real terms. For the first
> time in history, large numbers of workers had discretionary
> income, money that they could decide how to spend. Most
> unionized workers, over one-third of the working class, en-
> joyed paid vacations, holidays, pensions, and health insurance,

which became norms of working-class life. The low unemployment seemed miraculous. Throughout the 1930s unemployment never fell below 14 percent, peaking at 25 percent in 1933. In the 1950s the average was 4.6 percent.[31]

Equality and growth, unions and low unemployment, planning and innovation, limits on speculation and material abundance—with prudent political intervention, principles that had formerly been treated as enemies turned out to be friendly. Or as Lind puts it, America's "middle class enjoyed its zenith under a system of highly regulated . . . capitalism" and "suffered under the less regulated capitalism that preceded it and followed it."[32]

What followed it was a new order—neoliberalism—that not only rejected political constraints on the market but called for remaking civic and political institutions in the image of the market. Its practical effect has been to reset class relations back to where they stood before the rise of socially managed capitalism. The comprehensive system of private tyranny described in this book came about as neoliberalism's inner logic unfolded beginning in the 1970s. We will explore that logic in the following chapter, then turn to consider how it might be rolled back.

II

The Neoliberal Counterpunch

A GOOD SCIENCE-FICTION WRITER can be so much more far-seeing, and so much wiser, than the typical pundit or think-tank expert. More than any white paper, the best imagined futures can reveal the deeper currents shaping our age and greatly assist us in understanding why we feel powerless or unsettled in the present.

The British writer J. G. Ballard's novel *Super-Cannes* is one such novel–cum–seeing stone. Published in 2000, it offers an arresting mix of paranoid noir, science fiction, and social commentary. The setting is a fictional business park in the South of France called Eden-Olympia, and our protagonists are Dr. Jane Sinclair, a British pediatrician hired to replace one of the park's physicians, and her husband, Paul, a pilot convalescing from a plane crash.

The management at Eden-Olympia recruits Jane because her predecessor in the job, another Brit named David Greenwood, went postal, shooting up ten colleagues, many of them senior managers at the park, before turning his rifle on himself. As Jane gets absorbed in her work at the park, it falls to the jobless and bored Paul to unravel what really happened with Greenwood, what led a gentle pediatrician to murder innocents in cold blood.

Eden-Olympia is as much a character in its own right as Ballard's human figures. The weather might be Mediterranean, but the cultural atmosphere at the park is all Silicon Valley. Imagine an environment similar to the real-world campuses of today's tech giants: Sleek structures of steel and glass are set against carefully manicured greenery; high-end cars whiz by private roads; stately villas sit mostly empty, because the owners are too busy to actually enjoy their big pools.

These new masters of the universe—managers with expertise in tech, the hard sciences, and even psychology—are bringing forth a borderless world of capillary supply chains spread across the planet, a world of consumer products tailored to buyers' individual DNA, a world where the role of tangible, physical labor is minimized, if not altogether eliminated. It's a cold, alienating environment, to be sure, but then again, given the managers' "corporate puritanism" and obsession with bodily health, they don't view interpersonal distancing as such a bad thing.[1]

In Eden-Olympia, the author distills many of the elements we have come to associate with the lifestyles of the capitalist and managerial ruling classes worldwide. For one thing, the managers are what they do, their identities having almost completely merged with their professional functions. They are a multicultural bunch, to be sure, hailing from Britain, France, Mexico, Japan, and beyond. But there is nothing particularly British, French, Mexican, or Japanese about them. Rather, what unites them, as one critic of the park tells Paul, is that they are all "paid-up members of the new elite. They're the corporate chosen people."[2]

In the all-too-brief hours when the managers don't work, they party—hard. The Eden-Olympia ruling class's idea of relaxation includes synthetic drugs, sadomasochism, and random ultraviolence. Meanwhile, much like real-life counterparts such as Amazon's headquarters in Bellevue, Washington, Eden-Olympia is a place utterly bereft of children. As one manager tells Paul, the "corporate city is superbly talented, adult and virtually childless. . . . You define yourself by the kind of trainers you wear."[3]

Yet the most important feature of Eden-Olympia, for our purposes, is that it is a profoundly *antipolitical* place. Throughout the novel, we hear of Sophia-Antipolis, a real-world, Silicon Valley–style corporate park located in the same region. The name is telling. Antipolis is the ancient Greek name for nearby Antibes. But the ancient name happens to be nicely evocative of what these business parks are like, to Ballard's mind: anti-polises, anti-cities, the opposite of what the ancient city represented, the ideal of the city as a genuinely political community and a space for cultivating civic virtue. "There were no town councils or magistrates' courts, no citizens' advice bureaux," Paul observes. "Representative democracy had been replaced by the surveillance camera and the private police force."[4]

Again and again, Eden-Olympia's architects drive home this point. In a revealing exchange, Paul tells one manager, "There's no drama and no conflict [at Eden-Olympia]. There are no clubs or evening classes. . . ."

"We don't need them [the manager responds]. They serve no role."

"No charities or church fêtes. No fund-raising galas."

"Everyone is rich. Or at least, very well off."

"No police or legal system."

"There's no crime, and no social problems."

"No democratic accountability. No one votes. So who runs things?"

"We do. We run things."[5]

The managers boast that there is no poverty, but that isn't quite true: Outside the park's gates ranges a squalid urban landscape populated by poor North African migrants, petty criminals, and drug-addicted working girls, including not a few child prostitutes. The two classes, however, come into contact only when the executives set out on periodic hunting parties, in which they beat and torture these lumpen characters—their perverse way of letting off steam.

At Eden-Olympia, the private has swallowed the public, eaten it from the inside out. Rival classes don't contest the public square in any meaningful way, let alone strike a class compromise of the kind discussed in chapter 10. There is no public political culture, no insti-

tutions devoted to sustaining it. To the extent a vestigial public political realm exists, it is totally devoted to serving the needs and
preferences of the corporate ruling class.

Just as Eden-Olympia has no progeny, so it has no history. As Jane
tells Paul, "There's no ground already staked out, no title deeds
going back to bloody Magna Carta. You feel anything could happen."[6] Jane exults in this sense of historical amnesia. She somehow
intuits that it is good for the cosmopolitan class of managers and
meritocrats to which she belongs. But it isn't good for others, who
suffer what they must at the hands of the shockingly sadistic managers.

Places with "deeds going back to bloody Magna Carta" impose
inherited obligations on members of the political community. There
are competing claims to social justice and ancient rivalries, there is
historical memory, there are moral authorities and romantic heroes.
But all that stands in the way of the smooth functioning of the market system and the rule of oligarchic capital and managers—and so
must be liquidated.

Super-Cannes offers a portrait—exaggerated, to be sure, as if in a
funhouse mirror—of our situation since social democracy went on
the wane. From the privatization of public services to widespread
cultural alienation, and from unchallenged corporate power to the
decline of solidarity, Ballard's fictional business park depicts many of
the pathologies of our real world. And the novel hints that behind
these disparate phenomena lies a deeper logic, according to which
law and government abjectly serve the market.

In social theory, that logic has a name: neoliberalism.

It's an ideology that arose during the heyday of socially managed
capitalism among a narrow clique of European (mainly, German-
speaking) intellectuals but soon won adherents on both the mainstream right and the mainstream left. Ronald Reagan and Margaret
Thatcher were neoliberals par excellence, but so were the likes of
Bill Clinton, Tony Blair, and Germany's Gerhard Schröder (a nomi-
nal Social Democrat), among many other left-of-center politicians.

Neoliberalism is a true *uniparty* ideology, whose diktats are often treated as the only "responsible" position on both sides of the aisle; to stray from them is to violate a ruling consensus.

Neoliberal theory, the successor to laissez-faire ideology, is arguably *more* utopian than the original. Yet put to practice, neoliberalism has yielded a brute "restoration of class power," as the economic geographer David Harvey puts it.[7] More than that, neoliberalism has transfigured what it means to belong to a political community and what states are for, dramatically narrowing the scope for resisting economic power.

We will tackle neoliberal theory first, practice second.

Neoliberal Theory: "Spontaneity" Versus Coercion

What is neoliberalism? Harvey defines it as "a theory of political economic practices that proposes that human well-being can best be advanced by liberating individual entrepreneurial freedoms and skills within an institutional framework characterized by strong private property rights, free markets, and free trade." Where these elements are lacking, neoliberalism calls on the state to create them, forcibly as the need may be.[8]

Yet while this is a sound working definition, it is necessarily incomplete and in some ways hardly distinguishable from regular old market liberalism. Neoliberalism is this, but it is also much more. As we will see, it is ultimately a theory and practice aimed not just at liberating markets from politics but at turning politics itself into a tool of the marketplace and of neutralizing any political claims that don't fit the logic and needs of capitalism.

Defenders of our current order like to dismiss the very term "neoliberalism" as a catchall piece of rhetoric used to demonize a wide range of controversial practices and institutions. There is something to this. Like any loaded political label, neoliberalism has become an increasingly fuzzy cultural signifier. For some, it evokes anti-homeless architecture, such as the public bench in Calgary, Canada, with metal bars designed to make it impossible for the indigent to find rest but decorated, in a supremely neoliberal touch, in LGBT rainbow colors.[9] For others, it's epitomized by hedge funds' recent conquest of the entry-level housing market. And so on.

Yet for its intellectual architects, neoliberalism had a distinct political-economic meaning (even if many never used the term). In his 1944 book, *The Road to Serfdom,* the neoliberal bible, F. A. Hayek identified himself with plain, old "liberalism," which he defined as the belief "that in ordering our affairs we should make as much use as possible of the spontaneous forces of society, and resort as little as possible to coercion."[10]

For Hayek, writing in the heat of World War II, spontaneity, and the "individualism" it fostered, could be traced all the way back to the West's deepest origins, never mind classical and Christian thought's emphasis on the primacy of the common good. Almost in the same breath, however, he celebrated the moderns for "freeing the individual from the ties which had bound him to the customary or prescribed ways."[11] So was the ancient tradition a fount of market individualism, or a hidebound bastion of tyranny blessedly overcome by modern capitalism? Hayek tried, implausibly, to maintain both positions.

In any event, market-driven spontaneity and individualism were the best Western civilization had to offer, Hayek insisted, and in his time these principles were under threat not just from the Nazis and Soviets but from Europe's boring social democrats and America's would-be central planners. For Hayek, all of these tendencies, from the mildest of New Deal reforms to the horrors of Auschwitz, sprang from the same depraved impulse: "collectivism."[12]

While social democrats might have spoken benevolently of people's need for a measure of economic stability and security to enjoy real freedom, what they really desired was a will to power and the same "old demand for an equal distribution of wealth." This brought them into a tacit alliance with the Nazis and fascists against whom they were ostensibly waging a world war. All these partisans would override the ordinary person's "freedom from coercion, freedom from the arbitrary power of other men."[13]

That the market itself could occasion the arbitrary power of some men over others wasn't a premise Hayek was prepared to seriously entertain. He conceded that some individual market actors might do bad things, and he was happy to see state power used to curb, say, industrial pollution and unsanitary food production. Unlike some of his cruder latter-day disciples, he was also prepared to allow unspecified "social services" to be supplied by government.[14]

What he and other neoliberals couldn't abide was any intervention that got in the way of competition—that is, the "spontaneous" way that human beings under natural conditions supposedly coordinate their activities. Neoliberals could grant that good societies need rational planning. The question was *who* got to plan things: Governments? Or ordinary men and women who were closer to the action, as it were, and who knew their own interests better than any expert?[15] (Hayek unfailingly celebrated the individual person, as opposed to, say, the megacorporation, a move with obvious rhetorical advantages for his cause.)

Hayek forswore a "dogmatic laissez-faire attitude" that rejected any intervention in the preexisting state of economic affairs. On the contrary, he saw a *major* role for government in promoting a competitive society. The primary, even sole, purpose of the state, in this telling, is to create a comprehensive order of predictable rules, preferably spanning the whole earth, so that anyone anywhere would be "free to sell and buy at any price at which they can find a partner to the transaction," and so all people could "be free to produce, sell, and buy anything that may be produced or sold at all."[16]

Public education? Trade unions? Financial regulations? Economic planning? Protection of security-sensitive industries? Borders and trade barriers? Redistributive welfare programs? Restrictions against commercialized vice? In the neoliberal frame, all have to justify themselves in market-competitive terms or face slashing "reforms," if not outright demolition.

In this way, neoliberalism, while appearing somewhat more pragmatic than old-fashioned or classical liberalism, in fact pursues a far
more radical transformation. Neoliberalism is just as insistent as earlier market utopianism that restraints on market actors be minimized. But more than that—and this is the "neo" in neoliberalism—it
turns government itself into a mere appendage of market power.

As the University of California, Berkeley, political theorist Wendy
Brown has argued, old-school laissez-faire was merely content to
have "the state leaving the economy alone" (even if, as we saw with
Polanyi in chapter 9, the bringing about of such an autonomous
market itself required violent state coercion). But neoliberalism calls
for much more. It "activates the state on behalf of the economy, *not*
to undertake economic functions or intervene in economic *effects*,
but rather to facilitate economic competition and growth and to
economize the social." Or in the French philosopher Michel Foucault's pithy formulation, whereas classical liberalism sought to limit
social regulation of the market, neoliberalism seeks to "regulate society by the market."[17]

Where obstacles to "competitive" markets persist, the state under
neoliberalism would take a very strong hand indeed, freely using its
coercive capacities to bring about market-friendly "rule of law";
where the market already prevails, government is to conceive of itself as one more market actor, a preemptively suspect one, which
has to justify its presence and interventions according to market-
based metrics—or do away with itself.

Coercive Depoliticization

Hayek earnestly saw himself defending freedom—"that condition
of men in which coercion of some by others is reduced as much as
is possible in society."[18] And who could begrudge an Austrian thinker
his abhorrence of coercion in the wake of Nazism? The problem
was that he and his neoliberal cohort mistook the private economy
for a general safe harbor from coercion, rather than a site of ubiqui-

tous coercion, mostly meted out by a powerful few to the powerless many. By playing down (at best) the possibility of private coercion, they set the stage for private tyranny—Eden-Olympia on a national and global scale.

In the 1970s and 1980s, politicians like Margaret Thatcher in Britain and Jimmy Carter and Ronald Reagan in the United States were elected to solve the very real crises racking their nations in that era. But rather than pursue targeted, prudential reforms, they followed Hayek and company's blueprint wholesale, ignoring its category errors on the question of economic coercion. In so doing, that generation of leaders ended up repealing the postwar compromise between classes, raising new barriers against workers' exercise of countervailing power, and reinstating the more lopsided income distributions that had characterized industrial economies before the rise of socially managed capitalism.

It was a fortuitous turn of events for the hitherto marginalized neoliberals and a testament to the fact that ideas rarely have consequences unless they align with particular material conditions and historical moments.

Like many other successful ideological movements, neoliberalism began with a small group of disgruntled intellectuals advancing their arguments when the wider world appeared least receptive. Hayek's *Road to Serfdom,* as we noted, was published in the waning days of World War II—just when government, big business, and big labor had joined hands to forge FDR's "arsenal of democracy,"[19] in the process showcasing the productive genius of highly regulated, heavily unionized capitalism in which the government coordinated private economic activity.

Immediately postwar, Hayek and sympathetic thinkers such as Milton Friedman, Ludwig von Mises, and Karl Popper launched an organization, the Mont Pelerin Society, to warn of the danger to freedom posed by moderate reforms to income distribution and attempts to check private power. In their opening manifesto, they lamented how faith in "the competitive market" was sadly declining and how this had made it "difficult to imagine a society in which freedom may be effectively preserved."[20]

The views of the Mont Pelerin neoliberals were echoed by sundry U.S. "free enterprise" lobbies and publicists agitating against the "totalitarian" and "statist" horrors of the New Deal. All the while, however, socially managed market economies were booming, and big business largely accepted the need for some sort of compromise between the classes. This was seen as the rational, consensus way to do business, while the neoliberal ferment was decidedly fringe.[21]

Things began to change in the 1970s, however, when the neoliberals finally won over enough influential officials to begin to make a difference. This wasn't so much because their ideas had grown more persuasive with age as because the 1970s proved to be a period of crisis for the social democratic model.

Entire books have been devoted to explaining the confluence of economic and geopolitical developments that set the stage for the so-called neoliberal turn. We can offer only a brief sketch. Chief among the causes was the shock of free trade. In the immediate postwar era, the U.S. government was happy to see American consumers absorb European (especially German) and Japanese exports—even if it cost U.S. industrial workers dearly, and even if U.S. exporters lacked reciprocal access to consumer markets in Europe and Asia, owing to protectionist trade barriers and mercantilist policies there. Cold War priorities thus overrode New Deal commitments: Damaging trade imbalances were worth it, if growth and prosperity kept these former bloodlands pacified and out of the Soviet column.[22]

To these competitive pressures were added a number of other factors: the wage-price-driven inflation of the 1970s; oil shocks triggered by the 1973 Yom Kippur War and Iran's 1979 Islamic Revolution; the complacency and sclerosis of some U.S. manufacturers and labor unions; and the urban malaise and crime that fueled some wonderful independent cinema in that era but also rendered American cities miserable to inhabit in real life. The overall impression was that political-exchange capitalism "was clearly exhausted and was no longer working," as Harvey notes.[23]

Critics of the mid-century model, including some leftists, argue that these developments merely laid bare a more structural flaw: It worked during a brief window after 1945, while Europe's industrial economies remained devastated by war and the United States enjoyed overwhelming supremacy in every arena and could therefore afford to be generous with its workers. But once the rest "caught up," so to speak, America had to abandon the model to compete.

History belies this line of argument. After all, various forms of socially managed capitalism took hold across the West, in war-devastated Allied winners and former Axis losers, including Germany, France, Britain, Norway, Denmark, and Japan. Neutral-but-war-affected Sweden built one of the world's most generous welfare states. Spain, Portugal, Taiwan, and South Korea pursued similar programs, albeit initially within undemocratic political frameworks.

This suggests that the principles underlying managed capitalism—countervailing power and class compromise—are transhistorical, meaning they can be applied across many different contexts. Should America have preserved in amber every element of its postwar political economy, heedless of changing global conditions? No. But the gap between American workers' productivity and pay since the neoliberal era leaves no doubt that the United States could have afforded to maintain workers' countervailing power and a relatively more equal distribution of the social income. Instead, policy makers and corporate leaders chose to restore inequality.[24]

Having been forged as a pragmatic response to the crises of nineteenth- and early-twentieth-century capitalism, social democracy had ample room to adapt to new conditions; adaptability was of its very essence. Yet neoliberalism wasn't interested in pragmatic reform. Posing as the "realistic" alternative, it was, in truth, a revolutionary program: a revolution of the top against the bottom and middle. Its message: that the poor and working classes had gained too much of a say over the use of productive assets and the relative distribution of the social income, and this threatened "liberty"— which is to say, the economic power of a few to coerce the many.

THE NEOLIBERAL POLICY mix is all too familiar: drastic privatization, deregulation, and the removal of barriers against free trade. As Harvey notes, the disciples of Hayek and Friedman haven't been able to implement that mix to the same extent everywhere; the earth's political-economic geography is too "uneven" for even the most ambitious ideologues, over there presenting tough resistance in the form of angry French farmers, over here smooth ground thanks to anti-union sentiment in the American South.[25]

Still, a pattern is discernible. In the developed world, neoliberalism is associated with the strengthening of the financial economy relative to the real economy; the weakening of manufacturing and the spread of rust belts in formerly vibrant industrial heartlands; a decline in labor unionism, particularly in the private economy; the opening up of borders to the free movement of capital, very much including "human capital"; the forcible injection of markets into zones of life that most people consider either part of the commons (water rights, utilities, and so on) or too sacred to be traded (the leasing of wombs via commercial surrogacy); and the derogation of nation-states in favor of distant transnational bodies dominated by elites.

But all of these are mere symptoms of a more fundamental neoliberal disease: namely, *depoliticization*. By this, I mean a systematic attempt to foreclose the very possibility of ordinary people using political power and workplace pressure to get a fairer shake out of the economy. This is brought about by conditioning us to accept private coercion as a matter of competitive rationality, rather than to see it for what it is: a political choice, made by the asset rich for their benefit, frequently at the expense of the asset-less.

In this way, neoliberalism perpetuates class-based domination but takes away politics as a tool for ameliorating, much less resolving, class conflict. Neoliberal politicians' uncritical embrace of globalization in the final decades of the twentieth century, for example, meant that workers and the public at large lost their democratic say over the future of America's manufacturing sector. Competitive "rationality" told us that the future was in information-based industries, that we couldn't build *stuff* anymore. Meanwhile, high-school-educated Americans were told to seek refuge in the service economy, where, as it happens, it's much harder to organize labor.

Then, too, public goods of all kinds—from education and elder care to toll roads and parking—were placed on the auction block. Often, as we have seen, this redounded only to the advantage of predators and middlemen, raising costs without noticeably improving services, if not causing deterioration.[26] Yet neoliberal logic barreled past such pesky facts. Today, that logic has advanced to such a degree that even the remaining public services have to justify themselves on "competitive" grounds, including in areas where the market-knows-best mentality makes no sense, such as mental health and care for people with intellectual disabilities. Even hospice chaplains, called by faith to accompany the dying, now find themselves being evaluated using "productivity scores."[27] If workers in these areas find so little time for interactions with their patients, one big reason is that they have to spend much of their time completing "data based" paperwork showing "quantifiable gains," as neoliberal management dictates.

There is a reason neoliberalism operates in this way—why, as Brown argues, the ideology extends "economic values, practices, and metrics into every dimension of human life," politics very much included.[28] The more private, competitive rationality expands its domain, the harder it becomes to politically challenge the imperatives of the powerful: You, as a parent, might be struggling to find quality time with your children because your work schedule is an algorithmic hell. But this is no longer an issue to be contested between employers and employees as social classes with rival interests. No, it's up to you, and you alone, to strike the right "work-life balance"—

speaking of which, there is an app that can help you do just that, for a mere $4.99 a month. Under neoliberalism, in short, only political claims that can be articulated in terms of market rationality are heard and granted legitimacy. Those that fail this test fall by the wayside.

Far from restoring the Western tradition, as Hayek claimed to be doing, neoliberalism's depoliticizing tendency represents a radical rupture not just with classical and medieval accounts of politics but even to some extent with post-Enlightenment liberal modernity.

In the Greco-Roman political tradition, which medieval Christianity took up as its own, politics was emphatically about the pursuit of common goods: goods like peace and justice that only the community could secure. The common good thus conceived wasn't a "collectivist" imposition on the individual, because it was also the good of each individual as an individual. Classical politics recognized, moreover, the existence of rivalrous classes, arrayed against each other along lines of wealth and ability. It was the role of the ancient statesman to govern these classes for the good of the whole, taking into account the virtues and vices peculiar to each.[29]

In this framework, it would have been inconceivable to claim, for example, that lending money at inhumane rates of interest is okay because it's the only way to "rationally" induce creditors to take a chance on riskier classes of borrowers. Such a narrowly economistic rationality would have run afoul of a more comprehensive *political* rationality, one concerned not just with autonomy and efficiency but also with justice and social harmony.

Modern politics broke with premodern political rationality. Where the ancient tradition saw human beings as naturally social, and order as "heaven's first law,"[30] the moderns began with a picture of human beings as brutes thrown into a brutish world. Order could no longer be taken for granted, but had to have been the result of some mythical social contract, in which men consented to be governed in exchange for state protection of their rights. Political liberalism and market liberalism both rested on this account of the human person.

And yet, as Brown notes, even the original liberals didn't go nearly as far as their neoliberal heirs in seeking to subject the one (politics) to the other (markets).[31] *Market* liberalism—or market utopianism, as we have called it—sought to insulate economic activity from politics, based on the false assumption that markets are inherently noncoercive. But *political* liberalism—the tradition represented in sometimes-clashing ways by thinkers like Locke and Smith and practitioners like the American founders and Lincoln—still saw a legitimate domain for politics. Politics, in their telling, was no longer about pursuing the common good of the whole, classically understood. But it *was* concerned with securing self-determination and equality, rights that inhered in human beings by their nature.

Socially managed, political-exchange capitalism, the tradition we have been celebrating in these final pages, was an extension of this line of thought. It supplemented the modern quest for self-determination with the recognition that unchecked private coercion makes a mockery of equality and self-determination; that class-based subjugation and democracy are inimical to each other; and, therefore, that democracy and capitalism, politics and economics, must be brought into some measure of coherence, through the prudent regulation of market forces.

Politics, in short, had to tame economics. The result, as we have seen, was a prolonged period of broad-based prosperity and political consensus. Were there crises? Yes—but compared with what? Relative to the cataclysms of the competitive model—the Depression and two world wars—1970s stagflation was but a blip. Was some targeted deregulation called for in specific industries, such as telecommunications, that had been transformed by technological advances? Sure. Did some labor unions' intransigence lead to sclerosis, needlessly constricting workers' flexibility? Even David Harvey, an eminent Marxist, grants that.[32]

But neoliberalism, as I have argued, wasn't about tweaking socially managed capitalism. It was about reintegrating politics and economics on a totally new basis, one in which private profit seeking utterly lords over public politics. Lost was the recognition that society is divided between classes with conflicting interests and power asymmetries, and that there needs to be a public battleground where they can contest their claims.

Hayek, for example, detested all talk of class as a permanent, objective reality. For him, there was no fundamental distinction between progressives who spoke of the working class as a class—an objective, measurable reality—and fascists who demonized various ethnicities on arbitrary, irrational grounds. "Anti-Semitism and anti-capitalism," he wrote, "spring from the same root." Though speaking of the German context, he was making a general point: For Hayek, there were only competing individuals, and any politics that dared to take cognizance of power asymmetries within a class structure was tantamount to a false and immoral "collectivism."[33] All class talk led to the gulag and the concentration camp.

It is hard to overstate how dramatic a departure this represents from Western political theory stretching from Plato's *Republic* to even Adam Smith's *Wealth of Nations* (see chapter 10). It is equally hard to overstate how useful a picture of society neoliberalism presented to the more zealous advocates of private power, such as Thatcher, who in 1987 declared, "Who is society? There is no such thing!"[34]

If there are no permanent classes, and no possibility of private coercion generating class conflict, all that remain are competing individuals and firms, and our picture of who people are, and what politics is for, must shift accordingly. As Brown notes, under neoliberalism, each of us is an individual "human capital" seeking to increase its value and to attract investment. Each becomes a "member of a firm" and, indeed, "a firm itself."[35]

If we fail as human capital, if we struggle to maintain and grow our "value" through the ups and downs of the competitive market, then we plunge: through a thinned-out welfare net and down into personal and financial ruin.

TO SUMMARIZE ALL this more bluntly: The classically liberal state was mostly indifferent to private tyranny (chapter 9). The social democratic state sought to curb it by empowering workers and other weak market actors, winning their consent to the system in the bargain and thus stabilizing market and society (chapter 10). The neoliberal state, however, *actively abets private tyranny.*

It does this by turning state and law into instruments for promoting market values everywhere, and by rendering the power asymmetries generated by the market immune to political or legal challenge. Not even bothering with the pretense of a "neutral" terrain that can be contested by different classes, neoliberalism terraforms and flattens the very landscape of our politics, bulldozing through once-familiar landmarks like "Class," "Solidarity," and "Common Good."

At their most extreme, the neoliberal state's operations look something like the economic rules imposed by the Bush administration on Iraq in the immediate aftermath of the 2003 invasion. The so-called Bremer Orders, named after the Coalition Provisional Authority administrator Paul Bremer, opened every Iraqi asset except oil to foreign investors, permitting them to repatriate every cent of profit. Tariffs were steeply cut, to zero in the case of "humanitarian" goods like food, pharmaceuticals, and books. Personal and corporate taxes were capped at 15 percent. *The Economist* gushed at the time, "If it all works out, Iraq will be a capitalist's dream."[36]

At the same time, Bremer's imperial diktats sought to chill trade unionism with severe restrictions against workplace organizing and strikes—not just for Western contractors, mind you, but throughout the Iraqi economy. This last move was the neoliberal coup de grâce: The Bush administration used U.S. military power not only to enact *The Economist's* tax-and-trade fetishes in a newly conquered land but to actively make it harder for workers to organize countervailing power in response. And Bremer sought to insinuate his orders into Iraqi legal structures in such a way as to make them nearly impossible to reverse. As Harvey comments, "Bremer invited the Iraqis . . . to ride their horse of freedom straight into the neoliberal corral."[37]

Another glaring example of the neoliberal state in action is the U.S. Supreme Court's 2010 opinion in *Citizens United v. Federal Election Commission*, in which a narrow majority held that fictitious legal persons—corporations—have a free-speech right to spend unlimited money on political campaigns. Corporate America had to be allowed to spend to its heart's content on elections, Justice Anthony Kennedy argued, lest government impede the circulation of capital in markets for ideas and politics.[38]

For Brown, the political theorist, the distinctly neoliberal aspect of *Citizens United* is how it "remakes the political sphere as a market." The decision refashions *"homo politicus"* (political man) into *"homo economicus"* (economic man). Under the court's logic, once-familiar political terms—"rights, equality, liberty, access, autonomy, fairness, the state, and the public"—take on a strange new, market-oriented meaning. "Access," for example, refers not to the ability of the poor or excluded to be heard in political debates but to something like the uniform access to developing markets demanded by transnational corporations; only here, the "market" in question is democracy itself. "Whether the speaker is a homeless woman or Exxon, speech is speech, just as capital is capital."[39]

Yet we needn't look as far afield as U.S.-occupied Mesopotamia or relitigate *Citizens United* to see the neoliberal state in action. We saw its everyday workings up close earlier in this book. How else to explain, for example, the distortion of a commercial arbitration law, meant to ease trade between merchants of relatively equal bargaining power, to prevent workers from vindicating their rights under a New Deal statute? Or the abuse of bankruptcy to allow billionaires to avoid courtroom justice and hold on to ill-gotten gains?

How else to account for a heavily deregulated financial industry using public servants' capital to fund the privatization of their own jobs? Or the use of that same financial power to ravage and hollow out real industries—not least newspapers, the quintessentially democratic medium, without which political contestation is impossible, since we can't contest what we don't even know is going on? How else, finally, to describe the genuinely dystopian Fortune 500 employment agreement requiring the worker toiling for a paycheck to permanently give up the right to her own image and singing voice for commercial exploitation?

Scanning our political economy, we can't be blamed for wondering if we inhabit a sort of Eden-Olympia writ large. Indeed, we do. But there is one difference. In Ballard's fiction, no trace remains of messy class rivalries, historical memories, and political limits on capital accumulation. Nature itself, as Paul says in the concluding pages of the novel, has given way "for the last time to the tax shelter and the corporate car park."[40]

Our reality, by contrast, is strewn with the detritus of an older world: hulking shells of mass political parties now captured to varying degrees by corporate interests and neoliberal maximalism; gleaming shards left over from the shattered edifice of middle-class dignity; space-age memorials to the industrial achievements of the socially managed market; above all, the remnants of the labor union, the indispensable catalyst of worker empowerment and class compromise.

This haunted landscape renders our condition more tragic, by reminding us of what has been lost, but also more hopeful, by pointing us to what still might be. It tells us that to bring about a better economy, we needn't rally to the banner of utopia but merely take up *politics,* in the full sense of the term, as our forebears did within living memory.

12

In Defense of Politics

A T BOTTOM, THE message of this book is a simple one: Coercion is inevitable in human affairs, not least the significant portions of our lives we spend as workers and consumers. A political-economic order that would wish away this truth only allows coercion to proliferate unchallenged: pressure unmet by counterpressure, a system that grants every advantage to those who control most of society's productive and financial assets.

That, I have argued, is the system under which we labor today in the United States. We are subject to pervasive coercion in the economy—coercion we too often can't challenge politically (or legally), because our system fails to treat what happens to us in the workplace and the marketplace as political. More recently, neoliberal elites have made it still harder to bring the market under political control, by remodeling politics and law to resemble the market.[1]

That much of this has been done to us in the name of "noncoercion" renders the real state of affairs not less painful but only more so: Market tyrants playacting as benefactors are fast swallowing up American liberty, and they won't restore our birthright unless we insist that politics and economics go together.

That is, we must restore a political give-and-take in relations between the asset rich and the asset-less. Whether we call this arrangement by its twentieth-century names—social democracy or socially managed capitalism or political-exchange capitalism, or something else—what matters are the underlying principles: the recognition that a decent society should strive to ameliorate the effects of coercion, not least by empowering the coerced to mount countervailing power in response.

This is a more ambitious agenda than even many progressives are prepared to contemplate. Owing in part to the recent domination of the left by professionals and NGO types, the constant temptation is to pursue legal or technocratic fixes to the crises documented in this book. In this frame, for example, the "solution" to the commercial-arbitration crisis (chapter 4) is to lodge just the right lawsuit or tweak the Federal Arbitration Act. And the "solution" to Wall Street's stealth privatization of first responder jobs (chapter 6) is to use the law to change how pension administrators think about their fiduciary duty, or to impose stricter disclosure requirements on private equity firms. And so on.

Far be it from me to forswear such strategies, as far as they go, when the financial lives and basic well-being of millions of ordinary Americans are at stake. In some cases, especially the abuse of bankruptcy (see chapter 8), legal tweaks might indeed go a long way: With a little push from Congress and committed legal scholars and activists, courts themselves might put a stop to the worst of these abuses. Likewise, the Federal Trade Commission's proposal, under Chairwoman Lina Khan, to ban noncompete agreements must be counted an important triumph for American workers.[2]

But I fear that without something more, legal tweaks aren't up to the full scope of the problem of coercion in today's economy. That something more is *politics:* more precisely, a politics that empowers workers and the asset-less to the point where they can give genuine consent to the economic order as a whole, rather than despondently resigning themselves to its coercive operations, as they do today.[3]

Instead of waving competition and the price mechanism as a mystical talisman against coercion, the state must actually counter coercion, by encouraging (rather than hindering) labor organizations. The goal should be a labor market in which most sectors are

unionized, while workers in those few industries that resist unionization enjoy higher minimum wages, giving them the security
needed to mount countervailing power in the absence of labor organizations.

The state must also take a far more active role in coordinating
economic activity for the good of the whole community. Not every
speculative asset or novel takeover strategy cooked up by Wall Street
deserves preemptive government approval until things go wrong.
America is a great country, and firms that wish to take advantage of
its bounty, its diligent workers and stable legal order, must work
with the state to develop U.S. productive capacity—rather than
blackmail Americans into a race to the bottom against the developing world over taxes and labor rights.

The closest we have gotten to such a point was during the "glorious" three decades immediately postwar. It was a time of heavy
regulation and close coordination between different classes and the
government. It was also when government made it its business,
however imperfectly, to encourage workers to exert countervailing
power against their employers. And as your grandparents will tell
you, it was a generally happy time of broad prosperity.

RAISING UP WORKERS' countervailing power is the most important element in all this.

Countervailing power, as we saw in chapter 10, is strictly analo-
gous to competition. Only, in this case, the competitive pressure
comes from the "other side" of a market—that is, from workers
going up as a team against a smaller number of employers. And just
as dealing with abusive monopolies calls for state antitrust action,
something even laissez-faire types admit, promoting countervailing
power in the labor market requires government backing, to alleviate
the power asymmetries otherwise inherent to the class structure.

When workers exert countervailing power, they can secure
higher wages, greater autonomy in the workplace, better benefits
and working conditions, less lopsided contracts, and a tangible sense

of stability in their lives that isn't easy to measure except by its absence today, when "working class" is often a byword for opioid addiction, out-of-wedlock birth, declining life expectancy, and deaths
of despair.

Most important, political-exchange capitalism alters the distribution of the social income for the better. It promotes *equality*, in a
word. A more equal distribution of income has salutary benefits beyond the material welfare of workers and the asset-less as a class,
though that in itself is a most worthy goal. It can also check the
compensatory power of an asset-rich few to coerce the many in
realms outside the workplace.

Several of the crises documented in the first part of this book
would be alleviated under the conditions of political-exchange capitalism, while others wouldn't arise in the first place:

- Workplace tyranny would be much easier to resist when the
  union is there to block managerial caprice, and when employees
  aren't forced to tread fearfully on the thin ice of our neo-*Lochner*-
  ist labor regime.
- The employment agreement would be negotiated at the level of
  the firm—or better yet, across a given region or industry—rather
  than being imposed on the lone employee who has no option but
  to assent to the terms.
- Commercial arbitration would return to its true purpose: facilitating transactions between parties of relatively equal bargaining
  power. As it is, management and labor organizations in unionized
  sectors arbitrate disputes all the time, both formally and infor-
  mally ("on the job"). The process is infinitely fairer than the dia-
  bolical brand of "justice" meted out by corporate America to
  workers in today's privatized courts.
- There would be far less scope for destructive financial engineer-
  ing as banking returns to its proper and limited role: supporting
  the activities of managers and laborers in the real economy. Bank-
  ers and financiers would no doubt continue to profit reasonably

for their trouble, but they wouldn't act as the (often drunk) drivers of the economy.

- In a political-exchange financial market, private equity and hedge funds would be severely disciplined, as Senator Elizabeth Warren proposes to do with her Stop Wall Street Looting Act. When the future of productive firms in the real economy is at stake, the financial industry's speculative wizardry would be subject to the oversight—and veto—of not just the government but workers, local communities, and other stakeholders.

- Acting together, unions and policy makers would protect public pension plans, stanching the mindless deluge of workers' capital into private equity and hedge funds, which use it, in turn, to further erode the real economy and extend the privatization of public goods.

- Americans who devote decades of their lives to toil should be able to retire in dignity and safety, period. A stronger labor movement, with government backing, could demand that large firms restore the older model of retirement based on defined *benefits*, rather than defined *contributions*. This would help reverse the distortion of private-economy retirement from a secure bastion into something precarious and terrifying from workers' standpoint, an issue not explored in this book.[4]

- There would still be pockets of individual wealth among investors and managers. We aren't talking about "full socialism." But owing to the more equitable distribution of the social income, there would simply be a little less money to go around for dangerous speculation, and workers' organizations would have a little more money to counterbalance the compensatory power of the rich in politics and civic life. That "little less" and "little more" can go a long way toward taming today's private tyrannies.

- Finally, what a "more equitable distribution of the social income" means would be up for negotiation, reflecting changing economic conditions. What can be stated with confidence is that today's shockingly lopsided distribution—with CEOs making hundreds of times more than the average worker, for example—is not it.

What I'm suggesting, in other words, is that while smaller legal or technical fixes might address some of these problems, the shape of the economy as a whole cries out for a structural overhaul in the direction of greater political control and class compromise. With the overhaul complete, what operate today as blunt and unjust instruments of coercion can emerge as the rational components of a more humane economy tomorrow, with less need for piecemeal reforms.

All this and much more can be done if we would but retrace our steps to the wisdom of the past. I speak not of a distant and misty past, mind you, but of economic achievements that took place when our parents and grandparents were in prime working age—achievements whose neglected and cobwebbed remnants still to a degree benefit working people: monuments to economic and political realism awaiting repair, renewal, and service to the common good in a new century.

Neither Nostalgia nor Utopia

A call for renewing political-exchange capitalism is bound to rankle two groups. The first are market utopians of various stripes: libertarians, neoliberals, and laissez-faire advocates clustered in business schools, at libertarian think tanks, and on the mastheads of publications that still advance the idea that neoliberalism has "no alternative." Their faith in competition as a panacea against private coercion is exactly that: a religious faith. It is to shaking that faith that this book is largely devoted, though I'm not holding my breath.

The second group likely to be disappointed are harder-left socialists. One strand of socialist thought has always treated political-exchange capitalism as, at best, a temporary stop on the path to a classless society and the abolition of private property. At worst, political-exchange capitalism is viewed as bosses' concession to workers when the system was internally in crisis and externally rivaled by the Soviet alternative—a concession withdrawn as soon as economic and geopolitical conditions permitted a return to prewar patterns of accumulation and class domination. In this telling, social democracy or political-exchange capitalism was fundamentally a *conservative* project, aimed at forestalling more radical change.

There is something to this line of thought. While militant labor unions helped bring about the New Deal, not all of its leaders and intellectuals were progressives. They were men and women largely drawn from elite ranks who had come to believe that in order for everything to stay the same, *some things* had to change. But at the risk of sounding blasé, my answer to this long-standing leftist objection is: So what? And (again) compared with what?

We needn't be detained by abstract arguments for the inherent morality of private property (within limits of the common good, of course). Fact is, American workers did best under the combination of large private enterprise, high union density, and a vigilant administrative state that mediated between classes and coordinated economic activity (western and northern Europe added thicker welfare nets and nationalized certain industries). By contrast, in nations like Russia where the left ventured to build "full socialism," the result was the continued subjugation of workers by bosses, who now called themselves commissars and *nomenklatura,* and who had recourse not just to the pink slip but to the gulag.

Others might object that my preference for political-exchange or socially managed capitalism bespeaks a hankering for a bygone era of cultural comity. In this telling, I'm guilty of looking back wistfully at a recent age, the 1950s, with its stolid conformity upheld by all elements of national power, from television and newspapers to unions and churches. But this book hasn't touched on cultural concerns, not directly at any rate. I'm not advocating for the particular cultural forms that prevailed in those years. I would only insist that the broad social consensus of the era rested, at least in part, on rising living standards for working- and lower-middle-class Americans that purchased their "buy-in" to the system.

The hard left laments this fact, since workers' buy-in is seen as an obstacle to revolutionary change, while the right would prefer to altogether ignore economic equality's role in stabilizing culture. But in any event, it should be clear that the program laid out here steers clear of "culturalism": the notion that all we need are healthier cultural norms, as either liberals or conservatives would have it, rather than material reforms aimed at making the market fairer. Any cultural improvement that may come about as a result would be a welcome knock-on effect of political-exchange capitalism, not the primary goal.

The more serious counterargument has to do with whether the conditions that gave rise to political-exchange capitalism could be replicated in our time. Perhaps the biggest obstacle involves activating the type of labor militancy that characterized the late nineteenth and early twentieth centuries. Political-exchange capitalism might have been an elite response to the crises of market societies governed along competitive lines. Still, it helped to have fierce mass movements demanding workers' empowerment. These movements came to form the core of the New Deal coalition in America and the electoral base of social democratic (and Communist) parties in Europe.

Such militancy appeared not out of the blue but in response to certain industrial conditions. Unions benefited almost as much from sheer scale as did the large manufacturers they set out to organize. Militancy glowed hottest in factories jammed with workers, toiling side by side and sharing in close intimacy the misery of subjugation. These conditions prepared the ground for a clash of giants: a mass labor movement capable of taking on enormous concentrations of corporate power. While union density ebbed and flowed before the New Deal, it surged decisively when political leaders came to see the wisdom of giving worker power an extra push.[5]

That's a tall order today, and even a reader sympathetic to my call for restoring political-exchange capitalism in theory might despair of how far we are from its necessary preconditions in practice. The disappearance of manufacturing jobs as a consequence of globalization, the rise of a low-wage and heavily services-based economy, and the corollary collapse in private-economy union membership—all of these developments have the aura of world-historical inevitability about them. And who dares go against the thrust of world history itself?

Yet we needn't give in to such despair, for we are, in fact, dealing with a mirage of inevitability. From a distance, deindustrialization and labor-union decline can look like the inevitable end point of ironclad historical laws. But when we inspect these developments more closely, we can see them for what they are: the result of choices made by a narrow elite in favor of its own interests—political choices, to be precise, that can be reversed by political action.

Neoliberals tell us that every time an industrial firm closes up shop in the United States and shifts jobs overseas, it's because the developing-world destination has some inherent advantage for producing the goods in question. But there is nothing "natural" about low wages and brutal labor laws in places like China and Vietnam, just as there is nothing "natural" about a global trade regime that encourages firms to shift production out of the United States and into such locations.

Washington under Republican and Democratic administrations pressed for such a trade regime. The result was that when COVID landed on our shores, Americans found that we couldn't manufacture simple things like masks and other personal protective equipment; that we overwhelmingly relied on China for the basic components for many drugs; and that our globalized supply chains were stretched so thin that they snapped under the press of the emergency.

What the pandemic also taught us, however, is that these trends can be reversed. In the heat of the crisis, the then president, Donald Trump, inked deals with manufacturers aimed at returning pharmaceutical production to the homeland, and ordered federal agencies to "buy American" when it came to essential drugs and medical supplies.[6] To be sure, these initiatives were often ad hoc and undisciplined—a challenge for any administration dealing with a pandemic and not made easier by a White House as chaotic as Trump's.

I still remember how, while serving as op-ed editor of the *New York Post* around that time, I received a submission from a senator from a deep-red state calling on the Trump administration to go even further on reshoring drug production. I told the senator's communications director that I would happily run the piece, provided he would add a few lines suggesting that decoupling and reshoring be broadened out to other industries as well. The response (in effect): *Erm, we aren't quite ready to go there. We'll take this piece elsewhere.*

Still, beginning in the spring and summer of 2020, talk of "decoupling" American manufacturing and supply chains from China was normalized across partisan lines. More recently, in the wake of China's own prolonged lockdowns that crippled the Middle Kingdom's economy, it has become common to hear CEOs fret that "globalization" is slowing down or even reversing. The establishment has adopted the critique of globalization mounted by left activists a generation ago.[7]

The end point of world history, it seems, is no more certain to be the borderless capitalism championed by Davos elites than it was the global dictatorship of the proletariat dreamed of by Marxists in the nineteenth century.

The Once and Future Union

Let's grant for argument's sake that the share of U.S. workers employed in manufacturing might never return to earlier levels. It doesn't follow that we must give up entirely on the return of work-

ers' countervailing power to the economic stage. For while globalization has certainly been a factor in the decline of private-economy
trade unionism, the extent of its role is frequently overstated, especially by those who want to keep workers unable to exert countervailing power.

We opened this book with the story of Christian Smalls, the Amazon warehouse worker who was fired for leading a small protest
against unhygienic conditions at the retailer's JFK8 facility on Staten
Island. After losing his job, Smalls set about organizing his former
co-workers who were still on the inside, and thus was born the independent Amazon Labor Union. In April 2022, almost exactly two
years after Smalls's termination, a majority of workers at JFK8 voted
"yes" to having the ALU represent them in collective bargaining.

The success of the ALU is part of a broader ferment of union action sweeping the U.S. labor market, what the historian Gabriel Winant has described as a "strike wave": "an unexpected revival in
working-class militancy in its classic form."[8] Baristas at dozens of
Starbucks locations are at various stages of organizing new unions.
There is a formidable movement to organize flight attendants at
Delta, the only major air carrier without such a union. Hospital
nurses and orderlies, journalists, musicians and film technicians,
John Deere and Kellogg's factory hands, and West Coast dockwork-
ers are among many other groups that have pitched intense battles
to unionize or to win better contracts with the help of existing
unions.

Yet, as Winant notes, the current strike wave is still nowhere near
as potent as labor militancy was in the decades before the New Deal.
And while workers are rising up across a wide range of geographic
regions and industries, the inflow of employees into unions remains
a trickle compared with unionism's halcyon days from the 1940s to
the 1960s. This, even though polling shows that unions are today
more popular than they have been in more than half a century.[9]

Understanding the decline of unions is essential to reversing it.

The answer offered by many status quo–friendly pundits, liberal and conservative, is to shrug and blame "globalization." In this telling, the opening up of developing-world labor markets to American corporations was bound to undermine private-economy unions at home—a tragic situation not made better by the labor organizations insisting on the old bargains in the teeth of macroeconomic change.

But what if that's wrong? Or at least incomplete?

One alternative explanation is that America's private unions declined because this nation's corporate employers and their political allies became very good at waging class war. Put another way: Unions have lost power not primarily because of globalization and deindustrialization but because of union-busting employers deploying the same sort of unchallenged private coercion that characterizes many other areas of our economy.

Christian Smalls's story—that of a small group of organizers making it partway through the gauntlet that is U.S. labor law—is all too rare. As the Economic Policy Institute's Lawrence Mishel and his co-authors conclude in a 2020 white paper, the reason private-economy unions are in the doldrums is that "corporations took advantage of the weak labor-law regime in the United States to thwart union organizing and robust bargaining."[10]

Big business's counterstrike began with the 1947 Taft-Hartley Act, passed by Congress over President Harry Truman's veto, which created a "free-speech" right for employers to campaign against unionization in the workplace. In framing the issue as a matter of bosses' and workers' symmetrical right to "free speech," the law ignored the preexisting power asymmetry between the parties, making Taft-Hartley an early throwback to the pre–New Deal era. In the coming decades, employers would use the provision to full effect.[11]

In Taft-Hartley's aftermath, the National Labor Relations Board ruled that bosses could frighten workers at captive-audience meetings by telling them that unionization would mean job losses and factory closures, as long as they didn't make concrete threats of re-

prisal or offers of new benefits. The board also ruled that labor organizations don't have a right to respond to captive-audience anti-union
meetings held by employers.[12]

The Supreme Court has also played a decisive role in weakening
countervailing power. In the years following Taft-Hartley's enactment, for example, the high court held that employers could deny
union organizers access to the workplace parking lot unless there is
no other means to communicate with workers; that they could bar
union representatives from attending captive-audience meetings;
and even that they could silence employees who wish to speak up at
these meetings. Then, in 1974, the court held that employers could
reject unions recognized on the basis of a majority "card check" and
instead insist on the slower, more cumbersome NLRB election process, with lots more time built in for delays and anti-union tactics.[13]

The sum effect of these changes was that by the 1990s nine of ten
employers were using captive-audience meetings to discourage collective bargaining and a majority had threatened shutdowns.[14] When
employers still overstep these already-pro-company parameters,
penalties are "scant," note Mishel and his co-authors. "No fines are
levied, no employer goes to jail, and any costs incurred are negligi-
ble."[15] A new election is sometimes ordered in case of repeated violations, as happened in the case of an Amazon warehouse in Alabama,
but the coercion will have already worked its effects, instilling fear in
workers and chilling "yes" votes.

The pivotal shifts came in the 1970s. That's when the share of
workers voting in, and then winning, union elections and contracts
declined precipitously. The pivot coincided with the rise of automation and intense global pressure on U.S. manufacturers. But, Mishel
and his co-authors argue, correlation truly isn't causation in this
case. They have the empirical data to prove it.

To get a union, workers have to jump over three hurdles. First,
they have to gather enough signatures to show that there is sufficient
interest in an election. Second, they have to win that election by ma-

jority vote. Finally, they have to hammer out a contract with the employer within a year of their ballot-box victory. As of this writing, for example, the Amazon Labor Union has passed the first and second hurdles, having garnered enough signatures to get an election and then winning it.

As Mishel and his co-authors show, however, the share of employed Americans clearing each of those hurdles diminished, especially in the 1970s and 1980s. The share of workers participating in union elections fell by 90 percent between the 1950s and the early years of the twenty-first century. Election victories have also become rarer since the immediate postwar decades. Unions won four out of five elections in the 1940s. By the mid-1970s, the victory rate was down to less than half; by the 1990s, it was 40 percent. Finally, victorious unions have struggled mightily to win contracts since the 1970s. In the 1950s, 86 percent of newly formed unions got a first contract within a year; 56 percent did in the 1990s.[16]

What happened? It certainly wasn't the case that unions' "collectivist" New Deal ethos clashed with the civil rights movement's "individualist" sensibility, as some liberals claim. It's true that unions, to their shame, once barred the way to women and African Americans. But once the Civil Rights Act forced unions to open the gates, African Americans and women emerged at the forefront of union organizing. Indeed, black women were the only demographic that enhanced its representation in the otherwise-dismal 1970s; a union-busting consultant even warned managers in 1979 that "blacks tend to be more prone to unionization than whites."[17]

But what about the Asia-and-robots explanation? It, too, falls short. Globalization and automation have undoubtedly threatened manufacturing employment in the United States and other developed nations. Hold on a second, say Mishel and his colleagues. Since the mid-1970s, union coverage—the share of workers who are either union members or otherwise covered by a collective-bargaining agreement—has lessened for manufacturing industries. Yet "the decline was far from unique." Manufacturing union coverage collapsed by 74 percent from 1977 to 2019; in nonmanufacturing, it fell by a comparable 60 percent.[18]

Statistical analysis leads Mishel and colleagues to conclude that "the erosion of the manufacturing share of employment from 1979 to 2019, a decline from 30.2 percent to 12.6 percent, is responsible for a decline of private-sector union coverage of 3.3 percent, or about a fifth of the overall 15.8 percentage point decline in the private nonagricultural sector." Globalization and automation, the forces that displaced domestic manufacturing and slashed the industrial share of the U.S. labor market, are important factors behind union misery, but they aren't "dominant."[19]

In a simulation conducted by the authors, in which they transposed 2019's deindustrialized conditions to 1979's economy, union coverage changed by only 2.5 percentage points. Bottom line: "The shift out of manufacturing employment has had an impact that accounts for less than a fifth of the overall decline of private-sector union coverage between 1979 and 2019."[20] That is to say, saving manufacturing wouldn't have necessarily saved the union in the face of the anti-union distortion of American labor law, especially since the 1970s.

If globalization and automation aren't chiefly to blame, and if the risible scapegoating of the civil rights movement for undermining the New Deal is just that, the best and simplest explanation is class politics. Mishel and his co-authors decry the "policy drift" of U.S. labor law, away from encouraging collective bargaining toward granting employers every possible advantage and barely rapping them on the knuckles when they violate the few pro-worker safeguards still in place.

In the almost ninety years since the passage of the NLRA, lawmakers, courts, and GOP-dominated labor boards have effectively nullified large chunks of the original Wagner Act. Many employees who want union representation currently go without it. This runs contrary to another popular canard used to defend the status quo:

that American workers just don't want unions anymore. On the contrary, scholars have found that the desire to be represented has steadily *increased* among nonunionized workers since the 1970s, with one study indicating that 48 percent of the nonunionized labor force in 2017 would vote to join a union if given the choice—a figure that "translates into an under-representation [by] unions of approximately 58 million workers."[21]

Insofar as deindustrialization has decimated union density and coverage, it has been the result of political decisions, not inevitable world-historical "forces." And insofar as bosses have mastered union busting, that, too, is ultimately a matter of politics. When it comes to ordering our market economies, not everything is up for grabs, but many things are. We need only recognize that "the market" isn't some mystical, self-directing being but a human institution subject, as all human affairs are, to political choice.

Conclusion: A New Consensus

Private tyranny won't be repealed by the market itself. It can't be brought to heel by more "ethical" consumer choices, as a certain kind of liberal would have it, nor by some "revolutionary" new technology of the kind touted by more public-minded Silicon Valley types. The "fair trade" boutique is too small and pricey to serve an economy of national and global scale, while innovation doesn't address the class structure (indeed, technologies hatched in the Bay Area often widen material inequalities without actually producing anything of real productive value).

As we have gone to great pains to show, private tyranny is a *political* crisis that therefore requires a *political* solution. Similar trends came to a head in the 1930s, impelling a generation of Western leaders, including many conservatives, to rethink whether large businesses should be handed the unrestrained power they enjoyed. Those leaders left behind a political map for building a better economy and a more authentically free society. They guided us, above all, to workers' countervailing power: the indispensable lever for improving the lot of the asset-less and for stabilizing economies otherwise prone to turbulence and speculative chaos.

The supreme challenge today is to forge a similar left-right consensus in favor of tackling the coercion inherent to markets.

Among progressives, this requires abandoning what Sahra Wagenknecht, a former leader of Germany's Left Party, has called "lifestyle leftism." Instead of prioritizing issues of class and political economy, Wagenknecht worries, this form of progressivism obsesses over "questions regarding lifestyle, consumption habits, and moral attitudes."[22] In this sense, it might even be described as a kind of neo-Victorian ideology, with progressive HR managers playing the role of missionaries and social workers sent to inculcate better habits and manners among the poor.

The fundamental goal of lifestyle leftism isn't to reform the class structure but to suffuse it with cultural sensitivity. Not to discipline the workings of capital, but to regulate how people use language in the workplace. Not to limit the executive suite's power to coerce us, but to populate it with a more diverse cast of characters—to replace the old boss with a spunky #GirlBoss. We saw this in the case of the REI diversity officer who began her anti-union tirade with a nod to the victims of colonialism, and in Amazon's loud championing of Black Lives Matter even as the firm sought to silence a protesting black employee. Another glaring example came courtesy of Carolyn B. Maloney, a progressive lawmaker from New York. In response to a *New York Times* story about corporate CEOs making as much as $211 million amid the pandemic, Maloney asked, "Where are the women?"[23] Lifestyle leftism of this kind is a boon to big business. Thanks to it, the left has won many symbolic victories over questions of culture and identity, while private tyranny has gathered strength on the material plane.

As unhelpful as lifestyle leftism is, building a new consensus against private tyranny on the right is an even more uphill battle. Despite the populist ferment stirred by Donald Trump in 2016, the movement as a whole either continues to deny or play down the existence of coercion in the marketplace or dismisses the possibility that politics can do anything good about it.

To be sure, conservative defenders of the system are often the first to lament its cultural ramifications: the loss of social contact and communion between economic winners and losers, who now inhabit not just starkly different physical geographies but even starkly different mental spaces; a decline in civic and religious engagement, particularly among the poor and working classes; low rates of marriage and family formation; and so on.

Yet many of the same conservatives ardently refuse to link these cultural developments to the shape of our political-economic order. Instead, they pretend that cultural and material conditions have little to do with each other—as if cultural norms, practices, and beliefs don't rest on a material substrate that includes law, politics, and economics. It doesn't help that many of these right-wing politicians and pundits are in one way or another on the payroll of economic elites, giving them an incentive to keep their blinders on. In this way, the system's apologists replicate one of its chief characteristics: the erosion of authentic political debate by the compensatory power at the disposal of the asset rich.

Whatever the motive, the result is a downright ludicrous politics centered on preaching timeless virtues while denying what political theory going back to the Greeks has taught, and what every good parent or teacher knows: that cultivating virtue requires tangible, structural supports. A child will struggle to master honesty if his parents routinely model dishonesty; a body politic will likewise spurn the virtues if subjected to merciless economic exploitation.

It's true that more populist conservatives these days are prepared to defend right-wing cultural values against "woke capital." But few if any dare question the coercive power of capital itself. Dig into the policy platforms of tub-thumping GOP populists, and you will likely find effusions of unreserved praise for capitalism. This, even as they also complain about Big Tech censorship, a textbook example of market-based coercion, and even as they claim that their party is now the true representative of the "multiracial working class."

Such rhetoric notwithstanding, the working-class, populist conservatism heralded by Trump's election in 2016 has so far proved illusory. It is largely a cultural phenomenon, with Republican lawmakers, for example, loudly griping about businesses that discriminate against conservative employees and customers—without lifting a finger to alter the fundamental balance of power between corporations and the rest of us.

In this sense, right-wing neo-populism mirrors the lifestyle leftism that prevails among some progressives. Indeed, the two camps are locked in a bizarre sort of symbiotic embrace. Lifestyle leftists celebrate, and conservatives complain, when big brands update their logos in line with progressive cultural causes du jour. Both sides are rewarded with clicks and retweets. But the biggest winner of all is corporate America, which has learned that a little progressive signaling is all it takes to garner brownie points from the culturally dominant left; learned, too, that the right can be relied upon to protect its material interests behind closed doors, notwithstanding all the conservative harrumphing about the "woke neo-Marxism" supposedly sweeping the Fortune 500.

If there is hope to be found, I have come to believe, it lies mostly in ordinary workers, citizen-activists, and the labor organizers and lawyers who rally to their cause. Think of Christian Smalls making trouble on behalf of his fellow warehouse workers at Amazon and, when he was fired, resolving to make still more trouble. Or of Alicia Fleming, who since leaving the food-service industry has taken up work with the group Massachusetts Jobs with Justice, where she promotes reforms intended to combat unstable workplace scheduling in the Bay State.

Or of Ann Lai risking her career to expose the abuses inscribed into Silicon Valley employment contracts. Or Stephen Morris and David Heller taking the fight against arbitration abuse all the way to their respective countries' high courts. Or think of Bruce Miller. After losing his job and home to Eddie Lampert's financial mismanagement at Sears, Miller joined the labor-activist group United for Respect and helped lobby for New Jersey's first-in-the-nation severance law, which requires employers to offer laid-off employees at least a week's worth of pay for every year of service. Think of Kimberly Naranjo, afflicted by cancer, but still fighting—and overcoming—a corporation as large and as powerful as Johnson & Johnson.

Pressure from below, as noted, played a decisive role in forging the New Deal. Once more, it's up to the American worker to drag our politicians and corporate leaders into a new consensus. On our shared vigilance depend the broadly shared prosperity and checks against private tyranny without which there can be no land of the free.

Self-Privatization–Complicit Pension Investments

Warburg Pincus (Owned Rural/Metro Corp. from 2011 to 2013)

Retirement System	Year Funds Committed	Fund(s)	Amount Committed	Notes
Florida State Board of Administration	2012	Warburg XI[1]	$200 million	The FSBA oversees the Florida Retirement System, which provides retirement plans for firefighters and other emergency personnel. Rural/Metro operates in the Sunshine State, where it entered into a settlement with the Department of Justice over alleged Medicare overbilling during Warburg's ownership.[2]
Kansas Public Employees Retirement System	2013	Warburg XI[3]	$50 million	The KPERS is the umbrella asset manager for Kansas's three public-employee pensions, including the Kansas Police and Firemen's Retirement System. Rural/Metro operates in the Sunflower State.
Minnesota State Board of Investment	2012	Warburg XI[4]	$200 million	The board manages pensions for Minnesota public employees, including tax-deferred defined-contribution plans for some firefighters. Rural/Metro operates in the state.
Division of Investment (New Jersey)	2012	Warburg XI[5]	$300 million	In 2021, the Garden State's Police and Firemen's Retirement System wrested control over its assets from the Division of Investment, yet that wasn't the case in 2012, when the division signed up for Warburg's eleventh fund. Rural/Metro has limited operations in New Jersey, but recall that we are concerned with aggregate harm to a nationwide *class* of public workers.

Comptroller's Bureau of Asset Management (New York City)	2012	Warburg XI[6]	$35 million	The bureau manages investments for five city-employee pension funds, including that of city firefighters. Rural/Metro has limited operations in Gotham, but again, we are concerned here with aggregate harm to a nationwide *class* of public workers.
Ohio Police & Fire Pension Fund	2012	Warburg XI[7]	$55 million	The fund provides retirement plans for Buckeye State firefighters. Rural/Metro operates extensively in Ohio. Rural/Metro of Southern Ohio, Inc., entered into a settlement with the Department of Justice in the Eastern District of Kentucky over alleged Medicare overbilling during (and after) Warburg's ownership.[8]
South Carolina Retirement System Investment Commission	2012	Warburg XI[9]	$50 million	The commission manages investments for public servants in South Carolina, including firefighters. The $50 million commitment made in the fall of 2012 became the subject of a bitter dispute between the state treasurer, Curtis Loftis Jr., and his fellow commissioners over alleged procedural irregularities, including his inability, as the custodian of public funds, to access a copy of the 500-page contract with Warburg, as well as high fees more generally; eventually, he relented and released the $50 million.[10] Rural/Metro operates in South Carolina.
Washington State Investment Board	2012	Warburg XI[11]	$750 million	The WSIB manages public-employee retirement funds, including for the Law Enforcement Officers' and Fire Fighters' Plans 1 and 2. Rural/Metro operates in Washington State.
State of Wisconsin Investment Board	2012	Warburg XI[12]	$100 million	The SWIB manages investments for the Wisconsin Retirement System, which provides retirement plans for firefighters and other emergency personnel. Rural/Metro operates in the Badger State.
Self-Privatization-Complicit Investment Total for Warburg Pincus: $1.74 billion				

KOHLBERG KRAVIS ROBERTS & CO. (CURRENTLY OWNS GLOBAL MEDICAL RESPONSE, RURAL/METRO CORP.'S PARENT)[13]

Retirement System	Year(s) Funds Committed	Fund(s)	Amount Committed	Notes
Arizona Public Safety Personnel Retirement System	2017–2018	Asian II; Asian III; Revolving Credit Partners II[14]	$210 million	See chapter 6.
Florida State Board of Administration	2014	Accel-KKR Structured Capital Partners II[15]	$25 million	See Rural/Metro table, on page 199.
Public Employee Retirement System of Idaho	2016	Americas XII[16]	$50 million	PERSI manages pension plans for public servants throughout Idaho, including firefighters. Rural/Metro doesn't operate in Idaho, but the aggregate privatization harm to the nationwide *class* of firefighters and other first responders is real, all the same.
Maine Public Employees Retirement System	2013–2019; expired investments omitted	Americas XII; Special Situations II; Real Estate Partners Americas; Real Estate Partners Americas II; Real Estate Partners Europe; Real Estate Partners Europe II; Global Infrastructure II; Global Infrastructure III; Diversified Core Infrastructure[17]	$695 million	The MainePERS manages pension plans for public servants throughout Maine, including firefighters. Rural/Metro doesn't operate in Maine, but as noted repeatedly, we are concerned with aggregate harm to a nationwide *class* of public workers.

New York State Common Retirement Fund	2017	Asian III[18]	$275 million	The fund, overseen by the state comptroller, manages investments for members of the New York State and Local Retirement System, including firefighters. Rural/Metro operates in upstate New York, where the firm has been accused of overbilling, altering medical records to justify higher charges, and forcing patients to pay extra for services that were supposed to be included in its fee.
Ohio Police & Fire Pension Fund	2017	Asian III[19]	$30 million	See Rural/Metro table on page 200.
Oregon Investment Council	2013	Asian; Asian II; Asian III; European Fund III; North America XI; North America XII[20]	$3.1 billion[21]	The council manages investments for the Oregon Public Employees Retirement System, which covers firefighters, among many others. Rural/Metro maintains extensive operations in Oregon, and its Oregon unit was among several implicated in an alleged Medicare false-billing scheme that was resolved in a 2013 settlement with the U.S. Department of Justice.[22]
Sacramento County Employees' Retirement System	2014	Real Estate Partners Americas[23]	$35 million	The SCERS serves multiple classes of public servants in Sacramento County, California, including county firefighters. Rural/Metro operates in California, where in 2015 two ambulance companies subsequently acquired by Rural/Metro were party to an $11.5 million settlement to resolve kickback allegations.[24]

Washington State Investment Board	2013–2022	Asian II; Asian III; Asian IV SCSp; European IV; European V; Americas XII; North America XIII SCSp[25]	$3.4 billion	See Rural/Metro table on page 200.

Self-Privatization-Complicit Investment Total for KKR: $7.82 billion

Acknowledgments

THIS BOOK WAS conceived on election night 2020. The outcome was still murky, but one thing was clear: Republicans had widened their appeal among voters without college degrees and those doing tangible forms of labor. Democrats, meanwhile, had emerged as the party of Wall Street, Hollywood, Silicon Valley, and the professional classes. Reality was more complex, but all the same the right-wing pundit sphere was aflutter with talk of the "multiracial working class."

President Donald Trump had lost his reelection bid, it turned out. But that mattered far less to me than this latest demonstration of an apparent class realignment in American politics. In the days that followed, I crafted a proposal for what was to be a manifesto-cum-book for a new working-class conservatism. My editor, Derek Reed, and his colleagues at Penguin Random House were sold.

But then came time to identify the barriers standing in the way of working- and middle-class flourishing in the twenty-first century. The more reporting and thinking I did, the clearer it became that a book of the type I had in mind would put the cart before the horse. The GOP's new pro-worker posture was largely divorced from the material problem of private economic coercion and the inequalities in power and income it generated.

That some workers were abandoning the Democrats didn't ratify what the GOP had to offer. It wasn't uncommon to hear Republican neo-populists complain about so-called woke capital, only to add something along the lines of "and that's why we must return to the pre–Woodrow Wilson era, when there weren't so many regulations." This made no sense. The surest way to limit big business's ideological influence—whatever the ideology—was to raise up the countervailing power of those subjected to it. And that meant regulations and unions. It meant reasserting the primacy of the common good, precisely what the neo-populists refused to contemplate as most of them collapsed back into the embrace of conventional conservatism.

Some other kind of book was needed, something much more reportorial and historical, something that would give readers a tour of today's political economy as it is experienced by those at the bottom—and then situate these conditions in a broader arc: roughly from Lincoln's speech to the Wisconsin Agricultural Society to the era of socially managed capitalism, and from there to the rise of neoliberalism. Something, in short, like the book you just finished.

It is to Derek's credit as an editor that he trusted my instincts and permitted the project to evolve from its early origins. He then elevated the manuscript with sound structural feedback and meticulous line edits, steering me clear of dead ends and serving as a constant sounding board. Keith Urbahn, Dylan Colligan, Matt Carlini, and the entire team at the Javelin literary agency have my gratitude, once again, for their unmatched enterprise and support.

This book would have been impossible to pull off had not a large and diverse group of sources lent me their ideas and their stories. I owe a large debt of gratitude, foremost, to the workers who agreed to share their firsthand accounts of what were often painful episodes in their lives (not all of which made it into the final book). Gloria Song, Gord Magill, David Heller, and Bruce Miller exemplify courage and solidarity, and I can only pray that I did their cause justice. Thanks to June Jarvis and the United for Respect team for connecting me with Gloria and Bruce, and likewise to David's lawyers at the firm Samfiru Tumarkin, especially Samara Belitzky.

On to the experts. My friend Adrian Vermeule of Harvard Law School helped me view market transactions in a fresh light, pointing me to the work of Robert Hale on coercion in supposedly noncoercive societies and John Dewey's account of liberty as a measure of relative power. Bartolus's premonition of private tyranny has also gained wider appreciation thanks to Adrian's writing at the groundbreaking legal blog *Ius & Iustitium.*

The early chapters on workplace coercion and the employment contract were enriched by the insights of the legal eagles Harmeet Dhillon and Chris Baker. Max Folkenflik, who represented Stephen Morris at the Supreme Court, proved an invaluable resource on arbitration law. Oren Cass and his American Compass colleague Wells King were the guiding spirits behind the chapter on corporate erosion, in Oren's case going so far as to crunch the data on Sears's investment behavior going back to the 1970s and through the downfall (confirming my thesis that Eddie Lampert had acted as a classic Eroder).

Over a single lunch at a Guatemalan joint in Brooklyn, Steve Waldman of Report for America illuminated the dismal state of local journalism for me, apportioning just but not excessive blame to Big Tech and Big Finance (his is a careful, judicious mind). Once I had written up the chapter, he kindly offered detailed feedback and answered my endless queries.

I reached out to David Webber of Boston University School of Law not knowing what exactly I was looking for. He alerted me to the problem of workers' capital being used to privatize their own jobs. It was he who suggested I look into this phenomenon particularly in respect to firefighting and emergency services. David Skeel of the University of Pennsylvania Law School made important corrections to the bankruptcy chapter, saving me not a few embarrassments.

Lawrence Mishel of the Economic Policy Institute is a tireless champion of working Americans, and his influence can be felt throughout this book, as the index attests. The early chapters on workplace coercion and the employment agreement, as well as the final section on the decline of unionism, were shaped by his published scholarship and the interview time he generously granted this oddball pro-labor right-winger. I would be remiss if I failed to commend EPI's broader work, on issues ranging from arbitration and free speech at work to macroeconomics.

David Rolf of the Service Employees International Union put his experience as a veteran organizer at my disposal for an extensive interview that helped guide the final chapters, and I'm grateful to my friend Michael Toscano for putting me in touch with him.

In Harry Scherer, I found the best editorial assistant an author could ask for. Any given day, I would task him with some complex research assignment or a long-shot interview request, and he would invariably revert with good news: "Here's a memo on that [unspeakably obscure] question you had on Arizona firefighters' pensions." Or: "So-and-So will speak with you on Tuesday." Harry, you will go far. Thanks also to Johnny Burtka and the Intercollegiate Studies Institute for funding Harry's time with me.

Michael Lind read and commented on the first draft of the manuscript, reassuring me that I was on the right track while also offering a critical piece of feedback on the structure of the book's conclusion, which I incorporated into later revisions. As the index also attests, Michael has been a significant influence over my thinking. Each of his books is an education, his friendship a profound personal and intellectual blessing. Another friend, the macroeconomist Philip Pilkington, kindly read the manuscript and likewise offered numerous worthwhile pieces of feedback. Needless to say, all outstanding errors and shortcomings are mine alone.

The section on *Super-Cannes* was first delivered as keynote addresses at the Collegium Intermarium in Warsaw and at the 2021 National Conservatism Conference in Orlando. I thank these organizers for inviting me to speak. Bits and pieces of the book also found embryonic expression in my weekly column at *The American Conservative*. Thank you to Emile Doak, Helen Andrews, Micah Meadowcroft, Declan Leary, and the rest of the *TAC* crew for letting me tag along.

Many of the ideas in this book were first developed in the pages of *Compact,* the journal I co-founded with Matthew Schmitz and Edwin Aponte in March 2022. I benefit daily from my friendship with Matthew, my *Compact* business partner, aspiring, often unsuccessfully, to imitate the balance he strikes between courage and prudence. Thanks also to our senior editor, Nina Power, managing editor, Geoff Shullenberger, and editorial assistants, Emily Vermeule and William Pecknold.

To my family—Ting, Max, Fina, my mother, and my in-laws—I love you all so much. Once more, I'm indebted to Ting and her parents, Libo and Feng-Qiao, for lifting so many of the burdens of running a household off my shoulders so that I could hit this book's deadlines. Finally, thanks (as always) to Bret Stephens for opening my path into this business.

New York
Feast of the Nativity of the Blessed Virgin Mary
September 8, 2022

Notes

INTRODUCTION

1. The phrase and its definition are common enough. See, for example, William A. Galston, "Democracy Promotion in a World Growing More Dangerous," *Wall Street Journal,* April 13, 2021, www.wsj.com/articles/democracy-promotion-in-a-world-growing-more-dangerous-11618355267.

2. Task Force on US Strategy to Support Democracy and Counter Authoritarianism, *Reversing the Tide: Towards a New US Strategy to Support Democracy and Counter Authoritarianism* (Washington, D.C.: Freedom House, 2021), 8.

3. See Jodi Kantor, Karen Weise, and Grace Ashford, "Power and Peril: 5 Takeaways on Amazon's Employment Machine," *New York Times,* June 15, 2021, www.nytimes.com/2021/06/15/us/politics/amazon-warehouse-workers.html. On Amazon employees struggling to urinate, see David Streitfeld, "Amazon's Clashes with Labor: Days of Conflict and Control," *New York Times,* April 5, 2021, www.nytimes.com/2021/04/05/technology/amazon-control-bathroom-breaks.html, and Jules Roscoe, "Amazon Drivers Are Still Peeing in Bottles," *Vice,* Nov. 2, 2022, www.vice.com/en/article/z348y9/amazon-drivers-are-still-peeing-in-bottles.

4. Ginia Bellafante, "'We Didn't Sign Up for This': Amazon Workers on the Front Lines," *New York Times,* April 3, 2020, www.nytimes.com/2020/04/03/nyregion/coronavirus-nyc-chris-smalls-amazon.html.

5. Ibid.

6. Ibid.

7. Karen Weise and Coral Murphy Marcos, "Amazon Workers on Staten Island Aim for Union Vote," *New York Times,* Nov. 12, 2021, www.nytimes.com/2021/10/21/technology/amazon-workers-union-staten-island.html.

8. See Tara Law, "Shell Union Workers Had to Choose Between Attending President Trump's Speech or Losing Pay: Reports," *Time,* Aug. 17, 2019, time.com/5654772/shell-union-trump-speech-no-pay.

9. On American Express, see Christopher F. Rufo, "Lie of Credit—American Express Tells Its Workers Capitalism Is Racist," *New York Post,* Aug. 11, 2021, nypost.com/2021/08/11/american-express-tells-its-workers-capitalism-is-racist/; on Disney, see Christopher F. Rufo, "Disney Is Interested in Your Kids," *City Journal,* March 30, 2022, www.city-journal.org/disneys-ideological-capture ("Disney hosted Nadine Smith, the ex-

ecutive director of a pressure group called Equality Florida, who told employees that Governor Ron DeSantis and his press secretary, Christina Pushaw, wanted to 'erase you,' 'criminalize your existence,' and 'take your kids' "); on CVS, see Christopher F. Rufo, "CEO Rakes In Millions but Workers Must Examine Their 'Privilege,'" Fox News, Sept. 23, 2021, www.foxnews.com/opinion/ceo-millions-workers-privilege -christopher-rufo.

10. Darrell M. West, "How Employers Use Technology to Surveil Employees," Brookings Institution, Jan. 5, 2021, www.brookings.edu/blog/techtank/2021/01/05/how -employers-use-technology-to-surveil-employees/.

11. *Rene v. G. F. Fishers Inc.,* 817 F. Supp. 2d 1090 (S.D. Ind. 2011).

12. West, "How Employers Use Technology to Surveil Employees."

13. Ronald Reagan, "The President's News Conference," White House, Aug. 12, 1986, www.reaganfoundation.org/media/128648/newsconference2.pdf.

1. The Rise of Private Tyranny

1. See, for example, "Federalist No. 51," in Alexander Hamilton, John Jay, and James Madison, *The Federalist: A Commentary on the Constitution of the United States,* ed. Robert Scigliano (New York: Modern Library, 2001), 333: "It is of great importance in a republic not only to guard the society against the oppression of its rulers, but to guard one part of the society against the injustice of the other part." On a more cynical reading, the founders—Hamiltonians especially, as defenders of early market society—took steps to limit the threat posed by political democracy to economic domination. See, for example, Christian Parenti, "'Diversity' Is a Ruling-Class Ideology," *Compact,* Jan. 19, 2023, www.compactmag.com/article/diversity-is-a-ruling-class-ideology; see also Charles Sellers, *The Market Revolution: Jacksonian America, 1815–1846* (Oxford: Oxford University Press, 1991), 32.

2. See Aristotle, *Politics,* trans. H. Rackham (Cambridge, Mass.: Harvard University Press, 1944), 205–7.

3. Bartolus of Saxoferrato, "On the Government of a City [*Tractatus de regimine civitatis*]," trans. Jonathan Robinson (emphasis added), individual.utoronto.ca/jwrobinson /translations/bartolus_de-regimine-ciuitatis.pdf.

4. Ibid.

5. On this problem generally, see O. Carter Snead, *What It Means to Be Human: The Case for the Body in Bioethics* (Cambridge, Mass.: Harvard University Press, 2020).

6. John Dewey, *Problems of Men* (New York: Philosophical Library, 1946), 111 (emphasis in original).

7. Ibid., 116.

8. Ibid.

9. Milton Friedman, *Capitalism and Freedom,* 40th anniversary ed. (Chicago: University of Chicago Press, 2002), 13.

10. Ibid.

11. See Karl Polanyi, *The Great Transformation: The Political and Economic Origins of Our Time* (Boston: Beacon Press, 2001). We will return to Polanyi's account of the coercive rise of market society in much greater depth toward the end of the book.

12. See R. A. Radford's classic account, "The Economic Organization of a P.O.W. Camp," *Economica* 12, no. 48 (Nov. 1945): 189–201.

13. Robert L. Hale, "Coercion and Distribution in a Supposedly Non-coercive State," *Political Science Quarterly* 38, no. 3 (1923): 470.

14. Ibid., 471.

15. Ibid., 474.

16. See ibid., 473.

17. Ibid., 477.

18. Ibid.

19. Elizabeth Anderson, *Private Government: How Employers Rule Our Lives (and Why We Don't Talk About It)* (Princeton, N.J.: Princeton University Press, 2017), 41.

20. Ibid., 43.

21. Ibid., 44–45.

2. The Workplace Trap

1. Quoted in Stephanie Wykstra, "The Movement to Make Workers' Schedules More Humane," *Vox*, Nov. 5, 2019, www.vox.com/future-perfect/2019/10/15/20910297/fair -workweek-laws-unpredictable-scheduling-retail-restaurants.

2. Ibid.

3. For Fleming's inability to quit and the inadequacy of her restaurant wages, see Jennifer Berkshire, "Erratic Scheduling Forces Mom to Choose Between Work and Her Son," Economic Policy Institute, Oct. 7, 2021, www.epi.org/unequalpower/worker -stories/erratic-scheduling-forces-mom-to-choose-between-work-and-her-son/.

4. Figures from Bureau of Labor Statistics, "Employment Status of the Civilian Population by Sex and Age," updated Nov. 4, 2022, www.bls.gov/news.release/empsit.to1 .htm; and "Labor Force Statistics from the Current Population Survey," updated Jan. 20, 2022, www.bls.gov/cps/cpsaat18.htm.

5. See Daniel Schneider and Kristen Harknett, "Consequences of Routine Work-Schedule Instability for Worker Health and Well-Being," *American Sociological Review* 84, no. 1 (Feb. 2019): 97.

6. See ibid., citing Greg Duncan and Richard Murnane, *Whither Opportunity: Rising Inequality, Schools, and Children's Life Chances* (New York: Russell Sage Foundation, 2011); and Lawrence Mishel, Elise Gould, and Josh Bivens, "Wage Stagnation in Nine Charts," Economic Policy Institute, Jan. 6, 2015, www.epi.org/publication/charting -wage-stagnation/. See also Drew Desilver, "For Most U.S. Workers, Real Wages Have Barely Budged in Decades," Pew Research Center, Aug. 7, 2018, www.pewresearch .org/fact-tank/2018/08/07/for-most-us-workers-real-wages-have-barely-budged-for -decades/; Juhohn Lee, "Why American Wages Haven't Grown Despite Increases in Productivity," CNBC, July 19, 2022, www.cnbc.com/2022/07/19/heres-how-labor -dynamism-affects-wage-growth-in-america.html.

7. See Ken Jacobs, Ian Perry, and Jenifer MacGillvary, *The High Public Cost of Low Wages: Poverty-Level Wages Cost U.S. Taxpayers $152.8 Billion Each Year in Public Support for Working Families* (Berkeley, Calif.: UC Berkeley Center for Labor Research and Education, 2015), 3, 2.

8. Federal Reserve, *Economic Well-Being of U.S. Households in 2020–May 2021* (Washington, D.C.: Board of Governors of the Federal Reserve System, 2021), 34.

9. Schneider and Harknett, "Consequences of Routine Work-Schedule Instability for Worker Health and Well-Being," 82.

10. Claire Cain Miller, "How Unpredictable Work Hours Turn Families Upside Down," *New York Times*, Oct. 16, 2019, www.nytimes.com/2019/10/16/upshot/unpredictable -job-hours.html.

11. Ibid.

12. See Wykstra, "Movement to Make Workers' Schedules More Humane."

13. For the worker killed by an "autonomous" colleague, see Alec MacGillis, *Fulfillment: Winning and Losing in One-Click America* (New York: Farrar, Straus and Giroux, 2021), 93–97; for workers wearing diapers (in the poultry industry), see Elizabeth Chuck, "Poultry Workers, Denied Bathroom Breaks, Wear Diapers: Oxfam Report," NBCNews.com, May 12, 2016, www.nbcnews.com/business/business-news/poultry -workers-denied-bathroom-breaks-wear-diapers-oxfam-report-n572806; for the phony company clinics, see Ann Rosenthal, *Death by Inequality: How Workers' Lack of Power Harms Their Health and Safety* (Washington, D.C.: Economic Policy Institute, 2021), 13–17, www.epi.org/unequalpower/publications/death-by-inequality-how-workers -lack-of-power-harms-their-health-and-safety/.

14. Abraham Lincoln, "Address to the Wisconsin State Agricultural Society, Milwaukee, Wisconsin," in *Speeches and Writings, 1859–1865,* ed. Don E. Fehrenbacher (New York: Library of America, 1989), 91.

15. Ibid., 96.

16. Abraham Lincoln, "Fragments on the Tariff," in *Speeches and Writings, 1832–1858,* ed. Don E. Fehrenbacher (New York: Library of America, 1989), 153.

17. Richard Hofstadter, *The American Political Tradition and the Men Who Made It* (New York: Vintage, 1989), 136.

18. Lincoln, "Address to the Wisconsin State Agricultural Society," 97–98.

19. Ibid., 98.

20. Joseph Fishkin and William E. Forbath, *The Anti-oligarchy Constitution: Reconstructing the Economic Foundations of American Democracy* (Cambridge, Mass.: Harvard University Press, 2022), 91.

21. See Christopher Lasch, *The Revolt of the Elites and the Betrayal of Democracy* (New York: W. W. Norton, 1996), 58.

22. As Elizabeth Anderson writes, "Lincoln's disparaging judgment of wage laborers is akin to blaming those left standing in a game of musical chairs, while denying that the structure of the game has anything to do with the outcome. Thus, what began as an egalitarian ideal ended as another basis for esteem hierarchy: to raise the businessman on a higher plane than the wage worker." Anderson, *Private Government*, 33.

23. Hofstadter, *American Political Tradition and the Men Who Made It*, 137.

24. Julia B. Isaacs, Isabel B. Sawhill, and Ron Haskins, *Getting Ahead or Losing Ground: Mobility in America* (Washington, D.C.: Brookings Institution, 2008), 38–39.

3. Gagged by the Contract

1. See *Walter Scott Lamb v. Liberty University Inc.*, Defendant's Answer and Counterclaim, Case No. 6:21CV00055 (W.D. Va., 2021), 11, www.wfxrtv.com/wp-content/uploads /sites/20/2021/11/ECF-10-Answer-and-Counterclaim.pdf.

2. Drew Menard, "Gala Celebrates Pres. Falwell and Father's Legacy as They Join Business Hall of Fame," Liberty.edu, Nov. 6, 2018, www.liberty.edu/news/2018/11/06 /gala-celebrates-pres-falwell-and-fathers-legacy-as-they-join-business-hall-of-fame/.

3. Standing for Freedom Center, "Our Purpose & Beliefs," accessed Feb. 11, 2022, www .standingforfreedom.com/our-purpose-beliefs/.

4. See Santina Leuci and Doug Lantz, "Former Pool Attendant Details Alleged Relationship with Becki and Jerry Falwell Jr.," ABC News, Aug. 28, 2020, abcnews.go.com/US /pool-attendant-details-alleged-relationship-becki-jerry-falwell/story?id=72649159.

5. Office of Communications and Public Engagement, "Executive Trustees: 'You Can Call Him President Prevo,'" Liberty.edu, Feb. 5, 2021, www.liberty.edu/news/2021 /02/05/executive-trustees-you-can-call-him-president-prevo/.

6. *Walter Scott Lamb v. Liberty University Inc.*, Plaintiff's Complaint, Case No. 6:21CV00055 (W.D. Va., 2021), 6, static.politico.com/fb/f7/9c719910470fb59713485767298d/liberty -lawsuit.pdf.

7. See Hannah Dreyfus, "'The Liberty Way': How Liberty University Discourages and Dismisses Students' Reports of Sexual Assaults," ProPublica, Oct. 24, 2021, www .propublica.org/article/the-liberty-way-how-liberty-university-discourages-and -dismisses-students-reports-of-sexual-assaults.

8. Quoted in Michael Stratford and Brandon Ambrosino, "Liberty U President Says on Tape That 'Getting People Elected' Is His Goal," *Politico*, Oct. 27, 2021, www.politico .com/news/2021/10/27/liberty-university-jerry-prevo-influence-517303.

9. See *Lamb*, at 7–8.

10. Quoted in Michael Gryboski, "Liberty University Files Restraining Order Against 'Whistleblower' Suing for Wrongful Firing," *Christian Post*, Nov. 9, 2021, www .christianpost.com/news/liberty-university-files-restraining-order-against-title-ix -whistleblower-wrongful-firing.html.

11. Rachel Mahoney, "After Tense Hearing, Liberty University to Recover Files from Ex–Comms Executive," *News and Advance*, Dec. 17, 2021, newsadvance.com/news /local/crime-and-courts/after-tense-hearing-liberty-university-to-recover-files-from -ex-comms-executive/article_97b6a44a-5f84-11ec-aadd-27364ad46a71.html.

12. Stephanie Clifford, "Ann Lai Filed a Lawsuit to Tell This Story," *Elle*, Jan. 27, 2022, www.elle.com/culture/a38883820/silicon-valley-tech-lawsuit-ann-lai-2022.

13. Ibid.

14. Ibid.

15. Ibid.

16. Quoted in ibid.

17. Quoted in *Ann Lai v. Binary Capital et al.*, Case No. 17-CIV-02882 (Super. Ct. Cal. 2018), 5, bakerlp.com/wp-content/uploads/2018/12/Lai-Binary_Second-Amended -Complaint.pdf.

18. Quoted in ibid. at 21.

19. "What We Believe," Liberty.edu, accessed Feb. 15, 2022, www.liberty.edu/residential/what-we-believe.

20. Jared Polites, "Justin Caldbeck: How This Binary Capital Co-founder and Former Duke Basketball Player Is Trying to Change the World for Good," Thrive, July 8, 2020, thriveglobal.com/stories/justin-caldbeck-how-this-binary-capital-co-founder-and-former-duke-basketball-player-is-trying-to-change-the-world-for-good.

21. Tiffani R. Alexander, "Q&A with the EiC: Walmart Executive VP & GC Karen Roberts on Growth and Change," *ACCDocket*, Jan. 22, 2018, www.accdocket.com/qa-eic-walmart-executive-vp-gc-karen-roberts-growth-and-change.

22. Lawrence Mishel, "The Legal 'Freedom of Contract' Framework Is Flawed Because It Ignores the Persistent Absence of Full Employment," Economic Policy Institute, Feb. 3, 2022, www.epi.org/unequalpower/publications/legal-freedom-of-contract-framework-is-flawed.

23. *Payne v. Western Atlantic and Railroad,* 81 Tenn. 507, 518–19 (Tenn. 1884), casetext.com/case/payne-v-railroad-company.

24. Ibid. at 519.

25. Ibid. at 518.

26. See *Lochner v. New York,* 198 U.S. 45 (1905), supreme.justia.com/cases/federal/us/198/45/#tab-opinion-1921257.

27. *Adair v. United States,* 208 U.S. 161, 174–75, 175 (1908), scholar.google.com/scholar_case?case=3072585965506695672.

28. See, in order, *Hammer v. Dagenhart,* 247 U.S. 251 (1918); *Bailey v. Drexel Furniture Co.,* 259 U.S. 20 (1922); and *Railroad Retirement Board v. Alton Railroad Co.,* 295 U.S. 330 (1935).

29. *West Coast Hotel Company v. Parrish,* 300 U.S. 379, 399 (1937).

30. See, for example, Raymond Holger, "How Noncompete Clauses Clash with US Labor Laws," *Observer,* Aug. 31, 2017, observer.com/2017/08/how-noncompete-clauses-clash-with-us-labor-laws-jimmy-johns-pullman-strike-civil-rights-act/.

31. See White House Council of Economic Advisers, "The State of Our Unions," Sept. 5, 2022, www.whitehouse.gov/cea/written-materials/2022/09/05/the-state-of-our-unions.

32. Samuel Bagenstos, "Lochner Lives On," Economic Policy Institute, Oct. 7, 2020, www.epi.org/unequalpower/publications/lochner-undermines-constitution-law-workplace-protections/.

33. More recently, the Federal Trade Commission under Chairwoman Lina Khan has proposed to ban noncompete agreements, to predictable howls of protest from pro-business organs. See, for example, Andrea Hsu, "Millions of Workers Are Subject to Noncompete Agreements. They Could Soon Be Banned," NPR, Jan. 5, 2023, www.npr.org/2023/01/05/1147138052/workers-noncompete-agreements-ftc-lina-khan-ban.

34. Mishel, "Legal 'Freedom of Contract' Framework Is Flawed Because It Ignores the Persistent Absence of Full Employment."

35. Charlotte Garden, "Was It Something I Said? Legal Protections for Employee Speech," Economic Policy Institute, May 5, 2022, www.epi.org/unequalpower/publications/free-speech-in-the-workplace, citing Nicole B. Porter, "The Perfect Compromise: Bridging the Gap Between At-Will Employment and Just Cause," *Nebraska Law Re-*

view 87, no. 1 (2008): 62–121 and Richard S. Pincus and Steven L. Gillman, "The Common Law Contract and Tort Rights of Union Employees: What Effect After the Demise of the At Will Doctrine," *Chicago-Kent Law Review* 59, no. 4 (1983): 1007–39.

36. Elizabeth Anderson comments, "It is an odd kind of countervailing power that workers supposedly have to check their bosses' power, when they typically suffer more from imposing it." Anderson, *Private Government*, 5.

37. Mishel, "Legal 'Freedom of Contract' Framework Is Flawed Because It Ignores the Persistent Absence of Full Employment."

38. Ibid.

4. The Bosses' Court

1. *Uber Technologies Inc. v. Heller*, 2020 SCC 16 (emphasis added), decisions.scc-csc.ca/scc -csc/scc-csc/en/item/18406/index.do.

2. See *Stephen Morris v. Ernst & Young, LLP*, Class Action Complaint, Case No. 4:12-cv-04964-JSW (S.D.N.Y., 2012), 10.

3. Ibid., 11.

4. Brief of Respondents in *Ernst & Young v. Stephen Morris and Kelly McDaniel*, Case No. 16-300 (U.S., 2017), 5.

5. See ibid.

6. See ibid. at 1.

7. *Epic Systems Corp. v. Lewis*, 584 U.S. ___ (2018), 6, www.supremecourt.gov/opinions /17pdf/16-285_q8l1.pdf.

8. Katherine V. W. Stone and Alexander J. S. Colvin, *The Arbitration Epidemic: Mandatory Arbitration Deprives Workers and Consumers of Their Rights* (Washington, D.C.: Economic Policy Institute, 2015), 7.

9. See Alexander Colvin, "The Growing Use of Mandatory Arbitration: Access to the Courts Is Now Barred for More Than 60 Million American Workers," Economic Policy Institute, Sept. 27, 2017, www.epi.org/publication/the-growing-use-of-mandatory -arbitration/.

10. Stone and Colvin, *Arbitration Epidemic*, 19.

11. Ibid., on the damages differential; and 19–21 on why other factors can't account for it.

12. Ibid., 22, on lack of employee access to counsel; and 23 for repeat-player statistics, citing Alexander Colvin and Mark D. Gough, "Individual Employment Rights Arbitration in the United States: Actors and Outcomes," *ILR Review* 68, no. 5 (2015): 1033–34.

13. See Edward Powell, "Arbitration and the Law in England in the Late Middle Ages: The Alexander Prize Essay," *Transactions of the Royal Historical Society* 33 (1983): 54–56; see also generally, Douglas Hurt Yarn, "Commercial Arbitration in Olde England (602–1698)," *Dispute Resolution Journal* 50, no. 1 (1995): 68–73.

14. See Yarn, "Commercial Arbitration in Olde England," 68.

15. For the legislative history of the 1925 Federal Arbitration Act that follows, and how the U.S. Supreme Court lost the thread of that history in recent decades, I rely heavily on Margaret L. Moses's irreproachably thorough scholarship. See her "Statutory

Misconstruction: How the Supreme Court Created a Federal Arbitration Law Never Enacted by Congress," *Florida State University Law Review* 34 (2006): 101, 107; see also Stone and Colvin, *Arbitration Epidemic*, 7.

16. Moses, "Statutory Misconstruction," 105, quoting U.S. Congress, Joint Committee of the Subcommittees on the Judiciary, *Arbitration of Interstate Commercial Disputes: Hearing on S. 1005 and H.R. 646*, 68th Cong., 1924, 14 (henceforth cited as Joint Hearings).

17. Ibid., 106, 107, quoting U.S. Congress, Subcommittee of the Senate Committee on the Judiciary, *Sales and Contracts to Sell in Interstate and Foreign Commerce, and Federal Commercial Arbitration: Hearing on S. 4213 and S. 4214*, 67th Cong., 1923, 9, 10.

18. See ibid., 105.

19. Federal Arbitration Act, 9 U.S. Code §1 (2000).

20. Moses, "Statutory Misconstruction," 105 (emphasis added).

21. Ibid., quoting Joint Hearings, 37.

22. Justice Fortas, writing for the majority, claimed that "it is clear beyond dispute that the federal arbitration statute is based upon and confined to the incontestable federal foundations of 'control over interstate commerce and over admiralty.'" The internal quotations refer to a piece of the legislative history. Yet as Justice Black countered in a forceful dissent, there was overwhelming evidence that the act was "designed to provide merely a procedural remedy which would not interfere with state substantive law." See *Prima Paint Corp. v. Flood & Conklin Manufacturing Co.*, 388 U.S. 395 (1967), 405 (for Fortas's holding that the FAA rests on Congress's power to regulate interstate commerce), 411 (for Black's repudiation of the majority's expansive reading), supreme .justia.com/cases/federal/us/388/395/; see also Moses's account of the legislative history, which clarifies that Cohen's allusion to Congress's power to regulate interstate commerce was a mere "fall-back" position and that for Cohen and company Congress's power to direct "inferior courts" sufficed. Moses, "Statutory Misconstruction," 110, 121.

23. See Moses, "Statutory Misconstruction," 116–22.

24. The "liberal federal policy" was first discussed by the high court in *Prima Paint*, 388 U.S., but it was in the majority opinion in *Moses H. Cone Memorial Hospital v. Mercury Construction Corp.*, 460 U.S. 1 (1983), 24, supreme.justia.com/cases/federal/us/460 /1/, ironically authored by Justice William Brennan, the liberal stalwart, that it won a definite endorsement. Brennan's declaration was subsequently taken up by the conservative revolutionaries to create an entirely new FAA. It is necessary to note here, moreover, that the Reagan-nominated justice Sandra Day O'Connor and the George H. W. Bush–nominated Clarence Thomas resisted at least some of these expansionary moves along the way, by insisting that the FAA was a narrow procedural statute directing federal courts. See, for example, O'Connor's dissent in *Southland Corp. v. Keating*, 465 U.S. 1, 21–36 (1984), supreme.justia.com/cases/federal/us/465/1/; and Thomas's dissent in *Buckeye Check Cashing v. Cardegna*, 546 U.S. 440, 449 (2006), supreme.justia .com/cases/federal/us/546/440/#tab-opinion-1961964.

25. Moses, "Statutory Misconstruction," 123.

26. See *Southland Corp.*, 465 U.S.

27. The antitrust case is *Mitsubishi Motors Corp. v. Soler Chrysler-Plymouth*, 473 U.S. 614 (1985), supreme.justia.com/cases/federal/us/473/614/; the RICO case, *Shearson/American Ex-*

press v. McMahon, 482 U.S. 220 (1987), supreme.justia.com/cases/federal/us/482/220/; the antidiscrimination case, *Gilmer v. Interstate/Johnson Lane Corp.,* 500 U.S. 20 (1991), supreme.justia.com/cases/federal/us/500/20/.

28. Stone and Colvin, *Arbitration Epidemic,* 8.

29. For the decision striking down the Montana law, see *Doctor's Associates Inc. v. Casarotto,* 516 U.S. 681 (1996), supreme.justia.com/cases/federal/us/517/681/; for the high court's insistence that arbitration clauses are separable even from illegal or unconscionable contracts, see *Buckeye Check Cashing,* 546 U.S., and *Rent-A-Center West v. Jackson,* 561 U.S. 63 (2010), www.supremecourt.gov/opinions/09pdf/09-497.pdf.

30. See *Circuit City Stores v. Adams,* 532 U.S. 105 (2001), supreme.justia.com/cases/federal/us/532/105/.

31. *AT&T Mobility LLC v. Concepcion,* 563 U.S. 333, 334 (2011), supreme.justia.com/cases/federal/us/563/333/.

32. *Mitsubishi Motors Corp.,* 473 U.S. at 637.

33. *American Express Co. v. Italian Colors Restaurant,* 570 U.S. 228 (2013), www.supremecourt.gov/opinions/boundvolumes/570bv.pdf.

34. *Epic Systems Corp. v. Lewis,* 584 U.S. ___ (2018), 3–4.

35. Gorsuch also rapped the knuckles of the National Labor Relations Board, the agency empowered by Congress to administer the National Labor Relations Act, for suggesting that the NLRA grants workers a right to bring class actions notwithstanding individual-arbitration clauses tucked into their employment agreements. This, Gorsuch said, was "the first time in 77 years since the NLRA's adoption" that the agency had "asserted that the NLRA effectively nullifies the Arbitration Act." Ibid. at 4. Again, this could only be described as a lie issued from the highest bench: The labor board had been forced to reassert the NLRA's protection of collective action in such cases only in response to the court's own relatively recent upending of the meaning of the FAA. And as if his FAA revisionism weren't bad enough, Gorsuch also read the NLRA's protection of "concerted activities" to exclude workers banding together to pursue class-action litigation or class arbitration; see ibid. at 11–14. This was an inexplicable narrowing of a broad statute, eviscerated by Justice Ruth Bader Ginsburg in her dissent (discussed below).

36. Ibid. at 6.

37. See ibid. at 11–13.

38. Justice Ginsburg's dissent in *Epic Systems Corp.,* 584 U.S. at 4, quoting Senator George Norris, speaking on S. 935, 72nd Cong., *Congressional Record,* 75, pt. 4: 4504.

39. Ibid. at 19, 20, 21 (internal quotation marks omitted).

40. Ibid. at 20, 21.

41. Ibid. at 23, 26–27, citing Annette Bernhardt et al., *Broken Laws, Unprotected Workers: Violations of Employment and Labor Laws in America's Cities* (New York: National Employment Law Project, 2009), 6.

42. See, for example, Antonin Scalia, *On Faith: Lessons from an American Believer,* ed. Christopher J. Scalia and Edward Whelan (New York: Crown Forum, 2019).

43. Catholic Church, "The Proliferation of Sin," in *Catechism of the Catholic Church,* Nov. 4, 2003, citing Deut. 24:14–15, James 5:4, www.vatican.va/archive/ENG0015/__P6D.HTM#$21Y.

5. THE CORPORATE ERODER

1. See Suzanne Kapner, "How Sears Lost the American Shopper," *Wall Street Journal*, March 15, 2019, www.wsj.com/articles/how-sears-lost-the-american-shopper-11552647601.

2. Sears Archives, "Sears History—Early 1900s," SearsArchives.com, March 21, 2012, www.searsarchives.com/history/history1900s.htm (internal quotation marks omitted).

3. See Shoshana Delventhal, "Who Killed Sears? Fifty Years on the Road to Ruin," *Investopedia*, Sept. 26, 2020, www.investopedia.com/news/downfall-of-sears/.

4. See William D. Cohan, "'They Could Have Made a Different Decision': Inside the Strange Odyssey of Hedge-Fund King Eddie Lampert," *Vanity Fair*, April 2018, www.vanityfair.com/news/2018/03/the-strange-odyssey-of-hedge-fund-king-eddie-lampert-sears-kmart. Jim Baker et al. put the number of lost jobs at 260,000. See their advocacy study *Private Equity* (Oakland: United for Respect, 2019), 22; see also Kapner, "How Sears Lost the American Shopper."

5. See Delventhal, "Who Killed Sears?"

6. See ibid. on the logistics hub; for Sears's antiracist retailing, see "The Collapse of an American Retail Giant," *Economist*, Oct. 20, 2018, www.economist.com/business/2018/10/20/the-collapse-of-an-american-retail-giant; for the Ten Commandments anecdote, see Michael Lind, *Land of Promise: An Economic History of the United States* (New York: Harper, 2013), 164, citing David Lewis Cohn, *The Good Old Days: A History of American Morals and Manners as Seen Through the Sears, Roebuck Catalogs* (New York: Simon & Schuster, 1940).

7. Delventhal, "Who Killed Sears?"

8. See "Donald M. Nelson, Chief of the U.S. Treasury Procurement, Will Have Charge of Streamlining Procurement Methods Under the Defense Program as Ordered by President Roosevelt," June 29, 1940, Prints and Photographs Division, Library of Congress, www.loc.gov/item/2016877799/; Lind, *Land of Promise*, 310.

9. The virtuous cycle got going in large part thanks to New Deal legislation, not least the National Labor Relations Act, briefly discussed in chapters 3 and 4 and covered more extensively later in this book. The NLRA boosted American workers' bargaining power, which, in turn, secured higher wages that enhanced demand for consumer goods, a boon to enterprise. See Judith Stein, *Pivotal Decade: How the United States Traded Factories for Finance in the Seventies* (New Haven, Conn.: Yale University Press, 2010), 4.

10. Quoted in Kapner, "How Sears Lost the American Shopper."

11. Quoted in ibid.

12. Quoted in ibid.

13. See Stephanie Strom, "Sears Eliminating Its Catalogues and 50,000 Jobs," *New York Times*, Jan. 26, 1993, www.nytimes.com/1993/01/26/business/sears-eliminating-its-catalogues-and-50000-jobs.html.

14. Quoted in Kapner, "How Sears Lost the American Shopper."

15. See Delventhal, "Who Killed Sears?"

16. See Kapner, "How Sears Lost the American Shopper," and Delventhal, "Who Killed Sears?"

17. Oren Cass, "We're Just Speculating Here . . . : The Rise of Wall Street and the Fall of American Investment," *American Compass*, March 25, 2021, americancompass.org /essays/speculating-wall-street-investment/, citing Senator Marco Rubio, *American Investment in the 21st Century: Project for Strong Labor Markets and National Development* (Washington, D.C.: U.S. Senate, 2019), 26.

18. See Oren Cass, *The Corporate Erosion of Capitalism: A Firm-Level Analysis of Declining Business Investment, 1971–2017* (Washington, D.C.: American Compass, 2021), 1; see also Cass, "We're Just Speculating Here."

19. Cass, "We're Just Speculating Here."

20. Ibid.

21. See Cass, *Corporate Erosion of Capitalism*, 2.

22. Ibid.

23. Ibid., 6.

24. See ibid.

25. See William Lazonick, *Stock Buybacks: From Retain-and-Reinvest to Downsize-and-Distribute* (Washington, D.C.: Brookings Institution, 2015), 19.

26. Wells King, "Coin-Flip Capitalism: A Primer," *American Compass*, May 20, 2020, americancompass.org/essays/coin-flip-capitalism-a-primer/.

27. Quoted in Chris Flood, "Private Equity Barons Grow Rich on $230bn of Performance Fees," *Financial Times*, June 14, 2020, www.ft.com/content/803cff77-42f7-4859 -aff1-afa5c149023c. We explore why hedge funds and private equity often aren't good investments on their own terms, let alone from a public-policy standpoint, in chapter 6.

28. See King, "Coin-Flip Capitalism," citing Brian Ayash and Mahdi Rastad, "Leveraged Buyouts and Financial Distress" (working paper, SSRN, July 22, 2019), papers.ssrn.com /sol3/papers.cfm?abstract_id=3423290.

29. King, "Coin-Flip Capitalism."

30. See American Compass, *A Guide to Private Equity* (Washington, D.C.: American Compass, 2021), 2, 3, 4.

31. King, "Coin-Flip Capitalism."

32. Quoted in Kapner, "How Sears Lost the American Shopper."

33. See Paul Takahashi, "Sears to Shutter Store in High-Performing Memorial City Mall," *Houston Chronicle*, Aug. 23, 2018, www.houstonchronicle.com/business/article /Sears-to-shutter-store-in-high-performing-13178725.php.

34. Quoted in "How Sears Lost Its Mojo," *Wall Street Journal*, Oct. 12, 2018, www.wsj .com/articles/how-sears-lost-its-mojo-1539385808.

35. Quoted in Kapner, "How Sears Lost the American Shopper."

36. Quoted in ibid.

37. Quoted in ibid.

38. See ibid.

39. See Michal Rozworski and Leigh Phillips, "Failing to Plan: How Ayn Rand Destroyed Sears," *Verso Blog*, July 18, 2019, www.versobooks.com/blogs/4385-failing-to-plan -how-ayn-rand-destroyed-sears.

40. See ibid.; see also Kapner, "How Sears Lost the American Shopper," and Delventhal, "Who Killed Sears?"

41. Rozworski and Phillips, "Failing to Plan."

42. Quoted in Hayley Peterson, "Sears Workers Reveal Why the Company Is Bleeding Cash," *Business Insider*, Aug. 27, 2016, www.businessinsider.com/sears-workers-reveal -bad-workplace-2016-8.

43. Quoted in Kapner, "How Sears Lost the American Shopper."

44. Baker et al., *Private Equity*, 22.

45. "Edward and Kinga Lampert," *Inside Philanthropy*, accessed June 5, 2022, www .insidephilanthropy.com/wall-street-donors/edward-lampert.html.

46. "Edward Lampert," Superyachtfan.com, accessed June 6, 2022, www.superyachtfan .com/yacht/fountainhead/owner/.

47. "Carrying the Torch of Freedom," *Reason*, June 2020, reason.com/2020/06/01 /carrying-the-torch-of-freedom-2/.

6. Privatizing Emergency

1. Quoted in Surprise, Arizona, "City Facts & History," accessed June 25, 2022, www .surpriseaz.gov/177/City-Facts-History.

2. See David Lohr, "Arizona Firefighters Charge Family Nearly $20,000 After Home Burns Down," *Huffington Post*, Nov. 11, 2013, www.huffpost.com/entry/justin-purcell -fire_n_4242734; see also Charlene Sakoda, "Home Burns Then Fire Department Charges Residents Nearly $20,000," Yahoo, Nov. 6, 2013, sports.yahoo.com/blogs /oddnews/home-burns-then-fire-department-charges-residents-nearly—20-000 -204449952.html.

3. Quoted in Lohr, "Arizona Firefighters Charge Family Nearly $20,000 After Home Burns Down."

4. On the bankruptcy filing, see, for example, "U.S. Ambulance Operator Rural/Metro Files for Bankruptcy," Reuters, Aug. 4, 2013, www.reuters.com/article/us-ruralmetro -bankruptcy/u-s-ambulance-operator-rural-metro-files-for-bankruptcy-idUSBRE97402 J20130805; for Warburg Pincus's current assets under management, see the firm's home page, accessed Jan. 8, 2023, warburgpincus.com/.

5. Quoted in Lohr, "Arizona Firefighters Charge Family Nearly $20,000 After Home Burns Down."

6. Quoted in Sakoda, "Home Burns Then Fire Department Charges Residents Nearly $20,000."

7. Quoted in Lohr, "Arizona Firefighters Charge Family Nearly $20,000 After Home Burns Down."

8. See ibid.

9. For a brief history of American firefighting, see, for example, Alexis C. Madrigal, "Kim Kardashian's Private Firefighters Expose America's Fault Lines," *Atlantic*, Nov. 14, 2018, www.theatlantic.com/technology/archive/2018/11/kim-kardashian -kanye-west-history-private-firefighting/575887/; and Craig Collins, "The Heritage and Evolution of America's Volunteer Fire Service," in *A Proud Tradition: 275 Years of the American Volunteer Fire Service*, ed. Chuck Oldham et al. (Tampa: National Volunteer Fire Council/Faircount Media Group, 2012), 10–19.

10. For a brief history of ambulance services, see Olivia Webb, "Private Equity Chases

Ambulances," *American Prospect,* Oct. 3, 2019, prospect.org/health/private-equity
-chases-ambulances-emergency-medical-transport/; see also Hiroyuki Nakao, Isao
Ukai, and Joji Kotani, "A Review of the History of the Origin of Triage from a Disaster Medicine Perspective," *Acute Medicine and Surgery* 4, no. 4 (Oct. 2017): 379–84.

11. Webb, "Private Equity Chases Ambulances."

12. See, for example, Ron Shinkman, "Warburg Pincus Acquires Ambulance Operator
Rural/Metro," *Fierce Pharma,* April 5, 2011, www.fiercehealthcare.com/finance/warburg
-pincus-acquires-ambulance-operator-rural-metro.

13. Rural/Metro Corporation, "Warburg Pincus Completes Acquisition of Rural/Metro
Corporation," filed with Securities and Exchange Commission, June 30, 2011, www
.sec.gov/Archives/edgar/data/906326/000110465911037631/a11-16101_1ex99d1.htm.

14. See Dan Levine and Martha Graybow, "Dial 911-FOR-PROFIT—Just Don't Tell a
Firehouse," Reuters, April 15, 2015, www.reuters.com/article/uk-ambulance/dial-911
-for-profit-just-dont-tell-a-firehouse-idUSLNE73E05O20110415.

15. On Tilton's raunchy Christmas cards, see Michelle Celarier, "Lynn Tilton Regrets
Sending Steamy Christmas Card to Clients," *New York Post,* July 16, 2015, nypost.com
/2015/07/16/lynn-tilton-regrets-sending-steamy-christmas-card-to-clients; her stated
preference for stripping men rather than assets is quoted in Danielle Ivory, Ben Protess, and Kitty Bennett, "When You Dial 911 and Wall Street Answers," *New York
Times,* June 25, 2016, www.nytimes.com/2016/06/26/business/dealbook/when-you
-dial-911-and-wall-street-answers.html.

16. See Ivory, Protess, and Bennett, "When You Dial 911 and Wall Street Answers."

17. Ibid.

18. Ibid.

19. Quoted in ibid.

20. Donald Cohen and Allen Mikaelian, *The Privatization of Everything: How the Plunder
of Public Goods Transformed America and How We Can Fight Back* (New York: New
Press, 2021), 175.

21. Ibid.

22. Quoted in Ivory, Protess, and Bennett, "When You Dial 911 and Wall Street Answers"
(emphasis added).

23. See ibid.; see also Webb, "Private Equity Chases Ambulances," on the case of a Boston woman who fell into a subway gap but begged bystanders not to call an ambulance, because "do you know how much an ambulance costs?"

24. See Ivory, Protess, and Bennett, "When You Dial 911 and Wall Street Answers."

25. Quoted in ibid.

26. Ibid. Some of these lapses occurred after the bankruptcy and after Warburg Pincus
lost its stake in Rural/Metro—to another private equity fund, the Los Angeles–based
Oaktree Capital Management.

27. Ibid.

28. Quoted in "Investigation Underway at Rural/Metro Ambulance into Missing Morphine," WDRB, April 2, 2014, www.wdrb.com/news/investigation-underway-at-rural
-metro-ambulance-into-missing-morphine/article_2b14fd39-f7de-5005-a516-97a97
b063736.html.

29. Quoted in Ivory, Protess, and Bennett, "When You Dial 911 and Wall Street Answers."

30. See ibid.

31. Quoted in ibid.

32. See Karla Walter, Divya Vijay, and Malkie Wall, *Federal Contractors Are Violating Workers' Rights and Harming the U.S. Government* (Washington, D.C.: Center for American Progress, 2022), 2, 15, finding that of forty-nine large federal contractors with repeat violations of health and safety rules, fourteen, or a third, "had significant performance problems" on their U.S. government contracts. One of the fourteen firms was none other than Rural/Metro, which faced a $1.1 million back-pay penalty in June 2011. Walter, Vijay, and Wall rely on a 2013 report from the U.S. Senate's Committee on Health, Education, Labor, and Pensions, which found that large federal contractors were slapped with fifty-eight, or more than a quarter, of the two hundred biggest health-and-safety and back-pay penalties issued over the previous half decade. See U.S. Senate, Health, Education, Labor, and Pensions Committee, Majority Staff, *Acting Responsibly? Federal Contractors Frequently Put Workers' Lives and Livelihoods at Risk,* 113th Cong., 2013, 8, www.help.senate.gov/imo/media/doc/Labor%20Law%20Violations%20by%20Contractors%20Report.pdf/.

33. U.S. Attorney's Office, District of Arizona, "Rural/Metro to Pay $2.8 Million to Resolve False Claims Allegations," Department of Justice, Dec. 26, 2013, www.justice.gov/usao-az/pr/attachment2013-099ruralmetrosettlement-agreement-pdf.

34. U.S. Attorney's Office, Middle District of Florida, "Rural/Metro Corporation Agrees to Pay $650,000 to Settle Civil False Claims Relating to Ambulance Services," Department of Justice, March 24, 2021, www.justice.gov/usao-mdfl/pr/ruralmetro-corporation-agrees-pay-650000-settle-civil-false-claims-relating-ambulance#:~:text=Orlando%2C%20FL%20%E2%80%93%20Acting%20United%20States,to%20Medicare%20for%20ambulance%20transports.

35. U.S. Attorney's Office, Eastern District of Kentucky, "Rural Metro of Southern Ohio, Inc. Agrees to Pay $275,116 to Resolve Allegations of False Claims to Medicare," Department of Justice, July 10, 2019, www.justice.gov/usao-edky/pr/rural-metro-southern-ohio-inc-agrees-pay-275116-resolve-allegations-false-claims#:~:text=LEXINGTON%2C%20Ky.,government%2C%20agreeing%20to%20pay%20%24275%2C116.22.

36. Quoted in Ivory, Protess, and Bennett, "When You Dial 911 and Wall Street Answers."

37. James Politi and Francesco Guerrera, "How US Public Funds Fuel Private Equity," *Financial Times,* Aug. 28, 2006, www.ft.com/content/210bc9ca-36c2-11db-89d6-0000779e2340.

38. See, for example, David Webber, *The Rise of the Working-Class Shareholder: Labor's Last Best Weapon* (Cambridge, Mass.: Harvard University Press, 2018), 200.

39. David Webber, "The Use and Abuse of Labor's Capital," *Harvard Law School Forum on Corporate Governance,* April 7, 2014, corpgov.law.harvard.edu/2014/04/07/the-use-and-abuse-of-labors-capital/.

40. For simplicity's sake, we are eliding the interval during which Rural/Metro was controlled by Oaktree Capital.

41. The Surprise Fire-Medical Department had invested more than $11 million in the Arizona Public Safety Personnel Retirement System by 2020, with $1.3 million contributed in the fiscal year that ended in June 2021. Staff of PSPRS, *Annual Comprehensive Financial Report for the Fiscal Year Ended June 30, 2021 for Public Safety Personnel Retirement System,*

Elected Officials' Retirement Plan, Corrections Officer Retirement Plan (Administrative Offices of the Courts) (Phoenix: Public Safety Personnel Retirement System, 2021), 127. For PSPRS's investments in KKR funds, see, for example, Rob Kozlowski, "Arizona Public Safety Allocates to 6 Managers," *Pensions & Investments*, Aug. 4, 2017, www.pionline .com / article / 20170404 / ONLINE / 170409958 / arizona-public-safety-allocates-to -6-managers ("The pension fund . . . committed up to $40 million directly and up to $20 million for co-investments to KKR Asian Fund III, a buyout fund managed by KKR & Co. The pension fund previously committed up to $25 million to KKR Asian Fund II"). See also Rob Kozlowski, "Arizona Public Safety Goes with Direct Lending Fund," *Pensions & Investments*, Dec. 11, 2017, www.pionline.com / article / 20171211 / ONLINE / 171219939 / arizona-public-safety-goes-with-direct-lending-fund ("Arizona Public Safety Personnel Retirement System, Phoenix, committed $75 million to KKR Revolving Credit Partners II, a direct lending fund managed by KKR & Co."); and Johnny Madrid, "Arizona PSPRS Ropes Off $1bn for Private Credit Over 2018–19," *Private Debt Investor*, May 30, 2018, www.privatedebtinvestor.com / arizona-pspr-ropes-off-1bn-private-credit -2018-19/ ("The remaining $125 million committed last year went to special situation funds: KKR's KKR Revolving Credit Partners II").

42. See Center for Retirement Research at Boston College, "National Data," Public Plans Data, updated April 1, 2022, publicplansdata.org / quick-facts / national /.

43. See Martin Z. Braun, "Aramark Fights Unions over Pension Benefits," Bloomberg, Nov. 23, 2012, www.concordmonitor.com / Archive / 2012 / 11 / pension-cmnw-112212; see also Webber, *Rise of the Working-Class Shareholder*, 181–82.

44. Daniel Rasmussen, "Private Equity: Overvalued and Overrated?," *American Affairs* 2, no. 1 (Spring 2018): 11.

45. See Amy Whyte, "The Faulty Metric at the Center of Private Equity's Value Proposition," *Institutional Investor*, Sept. 11, 2019, www.institutionalinvestor.com / article / b1h3qtbcslyjyr / The-Faulty-Metric-at-the-Center-of-Private-Equity-s-Value -Proposition.

46. Rasmussen, "Private Equity," 12.

47. See Webber, *Rise of the Working-Class Shareholder*, 186.

48. See ibid., 187.

49. On recent recessions' negative effects on the national funding ratio, see Center for Retirement Research, "National Data"; see also "Pew Study Finds Shortfall in States' Retirement Systems," Pew Trusts, April 25, 2011, www.pewtrusts.org / en / about / news -room / press-releases-and-statements / 0001 / 01 / 01 / pew-study-finds-shortfall-in-states -retirement-systems. On stabilization and recent improvement, see Center for Retirement Research, "National Data."

50. The Center for Retirement Research at Boston College found in a 2021 study that the layoffs that swept public agencies as a result of the pandemic "caused funded ratios and required contribution amounts to be only slightly worse than they would have been if payrolls had grown as expected." Meanwhile, "the required contribution *rate* increased more noticeably due to the lower payroll base." Had COVID not ravaged public payrolls, "the total employer contribution rate would have been 19.8 percent rather than 22.0 percent." All this led the researchers to conclude that the COVID layoffs "may have negatively impacted public pension finances." Jean-Pierre Aubry

and Kevin Wandrei, "2021 Update: Public Plan Funding Improves as Workforce Declines," *State and Local Pension Plans* 78 (June 2021): 4, 3, 1.

7. Parched for Truth

1. See Will Wright, " 'Set the Buckets Out.' A Family of 7 Prays for Rain as a Mountain
   Water System Crumbles," *Lexington Herald-Leader,* May 5, 2019, www.kentucky.com
   /news/local/watchdog/article221411045.html.
2. Ibid.
3. Ibid.
4. On the loss of treated water to leaky pipes, see ibid.; on the wider failures of the red-
   state model, see Aaron M. Renn, "Red-State Blues," *Compact,* May 9, 2022, compactmag
   .com/article/red-state-blues.
5. Steven Waldman, *The Information Needs of Communities: The Changing Media Landscape
   in a Broadband Age* (Washington, D.C.: Federal Communications Commission, 2011), 5,
   transition.fcc.gov/osp/inc-report/The_Information_Needs_of_Communities.pdf.
6. Ibid., 38, citing Mark G. Contreras, presentation at the Aspen Institute Forum on
   Communications and Society, Aug. 16, 2010, 5, www.yumpu.com/en/document/read
   /39522149/mark-g-contreras-mark-g-contreras-knightcomm.
7. See Steven Waldman, "How to Stop Hedge Funds from Wrecking Local News," *Los
   Angeles Times,* June 8, 2021, www.latimes.com/opinion/story/2021-06-08/newspapers
   -hedge-funds-journalism-business-models.
8. Ibid.
9. See Feven Merid, "McClatchy to Decline Future Report for America Participation,
   Following Hedge-Fund Critiques," *Columbia Journalism Review,* Nov. 5, 2021, www.cjr
   .org/local_news/mcclatchy-report-for-america-hedge-funds.php.
10. Historian of the United States Postal Service, "Postage Rates for Periodicals: A Nar-
    rative History," U.S. Postal Service, June 2010, about.usps.com/who/profile/history
    /periodicals-postage-history.htm#_ftn1.
11. Waldman, *Information Needs of Communities,* 34, citing Paul Starr, *The Creation of the
    Media: Political Origins of Mass Communication* (New York: Basic Books, 2004), 89–90.
12. See Lasch, *Revolt of the Elites and the Betrayal of Democracy,* 161–75.
13. See Waldman, *Information Needs of Communities,* 35; for the number of cities, see Eli
    M. Noam, *Media Ownership and Concentration in America* (Oxford: Oxford University
    Press, 2009), 141.
14. Waldman, *Information Needs of Communities,* 36.
15. Ibid., 42.
16. Ibid., 37.
17. Quoted in ibid., 38.
18. Ibid., 39, for the Waldman quotation and the 2000 and 2005 figures.
19. For the *Star Tribune,* see "How Star Tribune Increased Digital Subscription Volume by
    35%," Optimizely, accessed Dec. 7, 2022, www.optimizely.com/insights/star-tribune/.
    For the *Globe,* see Don Seiffert, "Boston Globe Shows Growth in Digital Subscrip-
    tions," *Boston Business Journal,* May 12, 2022, www.bizjournals.com/boston/news/2022

/05/12/boston-globe-shows-growth-in-digital-subscriptions.html. In addition to the *Star Tribune* and *The Boston Globe,* the *Los Angeles Times, The Seattle Times,* and *The Philadelphia Inquirer* are typically recognized for successful leadership on local digital subscription. Notably, all five are controlled by either local families, civic leaders, or nonprofit foundations. See Brier Dudley, "Study: Private Equity Firms Buying Newspapers Cut Local News," *Seattle Times,* Feb. 18, 2022, www.seattletimes.com/opinion /study-private-equity-firms-buying-newspapers-cut-local-news/.

20. For a detailed account of these developments, see U.S. Congress, House Subcommittee on Antitrust, Commercial, and Administrative Law, Committee on the Judiciary, *Investigation of Competition in Digital Markets: Majority Staff Report and Recommendations,* 116th Cong., 2020, 57–73, judiciary.house.gov/uploadedfiles/competition_in _digital_markets.pdf?utm_campaign=4493-519/.

21. Ibid., 63.

22. See Evan Horowitz, "Even Fishing and Coal Mining Are Not Losing Jobs as Fast as the Newspaper Industry," *Boston Globe,* July 3, 2018, www.bostonglobe.com/business /2018/07/03/even-fishermen-and-coal-miners-are-faring-better-than-newspaper -employees/snK506ritw8UxvD51O336L/story.html.

23. Penny Abernathy, "The State of Local News: The 2022 Report," Northwestern University Medill Local News Initiative, June 29, 2022, localnewsinitiative.northwestern .edu/research/state-of-local-news/report/.

24. Waldman, *Information Needs of Communities,* 41.

25. Lloyd Grove, "The Gordon Gekko of Newspapers: A Vulture Capitalist Kneecapping Journalists," *Daily Beast,* April 19, 2018, www.thedailybeast.com/the-gordon-gekko -of-newspapers-a-vulture-capitalist-kneecapping-journalists.

26. Jon Wertheim, "Local Newsrooms Strained by Budget-Slashing Financial Firms," CBS News, Feb. 27, 2022, www.cbsnews.com/news/local-news-financial-firms-60-minutes -video-2022-02-27/.

27. "Editorial: As Vultures Circle, the Denver Post Must Be Saved," *Denver Post,* April 6, 2018, www.denverpost.com/2018/04/06/as-vultures-circle-the-denver-post-must-be -saved/.

28. Rick Edmonds, "Alden Buyouts Have Eliminated More Than 10% of Tribune Publishing Newsroom Staffing in Just Six Weeks," Poynter, July 1, 2021, www.poynter.org /locally/2021/alden-buyouts-have-eliminated-more-than-10-of-tribune-publishing -newsroom-staffing-in-just-six-weeks/.

29. Jonathan O'Connell and Emma Brown, "A Hedge Fund's 'Mercenary' Strategy: Buy Newspapers, Slash Jobs, Sell the Buildings," *Washington Post,* Feb. 11, 2019, www .washingtonpost.com/business/economy/a-hedge-funds-mercenary-strategy-buy -newspapers-slash-jobs-sell-the-buildings/2019/02/11/f2c0c78a-1f59-11e9-8e21-59a09 ff1e2a1_story.html.

30. Michael Ewens, Arpit Gupta, and Sabrina T. Howell, "Local Journalism Under Private Equity Ownership" (working paper no. 29743, National Bureau of Economic Research, Feb. 2022), abstract, www.nber.org/system/files/working_papers/w29743 /w29743.pdf.

31. Ibid., 3 (for declines in local coverage and staffing), 21–23 ("Instead of local news . . .").

32. Ibid., 25 (documenting decline in civic engagement), 32 ("unambiguously negative").

33. The researchers studied the following counties: Treasure County, Montana; Fremont County, Idaho; McPherson County, Nebraska; Colfax County, New Mexico; Cochran County, Texas; Bethel Census Area, Alaska; Orleans County, New York; Union County, Pennsylvania; Putnam County, West Virginia; and Kenton County, Kentucky. See "Life in a News Desert," *Columbia Journalism Review* (Winter 2019), www.cjr.org/special_report/life-in-a-news-desert.php.

34. "The share of articles in a newspaper concerning local governance, which includes words such as 'city council,' 'zoning,' and 'state legislature,' declines following private equity buyouts by 3.6 percentage points. . . . Instead of local news, private equity firms may produce more national news content, which can be syndicated across many different papers. Indeed, we observe an increase in the share of articles on national politics (which includes words such as 'Obama,' 'Bush,' and 'White House') of 1.3 percentage points." Ewens, Gupta, and Howell, "Local Journalism Under Private Equity Ownership," 3. (Overall, these authors take a much more sanguine view of private equity ownership than many scholars and journalists, yet on this point their findings are consistent with the concerns of more Wall Street–critical observers).

35. Philip Napoli et al., *Assessing Local Journalism: News Deserts, Journalism Divides, and the Determinants of the Robustness of Local News* (Durham, N.C.: DeWitt Wallace Center for Media and Democracy, 2018), 3 (for core findings), 8 (for definition of critical information needs), dewitt.sanford.duke.edu/wp-content/uploads/sites/3/2018/08/Assessing-Local-Journalism_100-Communities.pdf.

36. See Waldman, *Information Needs of Communities,* 46.

37. Quoted in ibid.

38. See Pengjie Gao, Chang Lee, and Dermot Murphy, *Financing Dies in Darkness? The Impact of Newspaper Closures on Public Finances* (Washington, D.C.: Brookings Institution, 2018), 4–5, www.brookings.edu/wp-content/uploads/2018/09/WP44.pdf; see also Kriston Capps, "The Hidden Cost of Losing Your City's Newspaper," Bloomberg, May 30, 2018, www.bloomberg.com/news/articles/2018-05-30/when-local-newspapers-close-city-financing-costs-rise.

39. See Filipe R. Campante and Quoc-Anh Do, "Isolated Capital Cities, Accountability, and Corruption: Evidence from US States," *American Economic Review* 108, no. 8 (2014): 2456–57, 2471–72.

40. Jonas Heese, Gerardo Pérez-Cavazos, and Caspar David Peter, "When the Local Newspaper Leaves Town: The Effects of Local Newspaper Closures on Corporate Misconduct" (working paper, SSRN, Aug. 9, 2021), papers.ssrn.com/sol3/papers.cfm?abstract_id=3889039. The researchers came by their findings after comparing the locations of corporate citations and penalties issued by some four dozen federal agencies with the national newspaper terrain.

41. Jessica Bruder, "Is the Death of Newspapers the End of Good Citizenship?," *Christian Science Monitor,* Nov. 11, 2012, www.csmonitor.com/USA/Society/2012/1111/Is-the-death-of-newspapers-the-end-of-good-citizenship.

42. Sophie Yeo, "Why the Decline of Newspapers Is Bad for the Environment," *Pacific Standard,* Nov. 20, 2018, psmag.com/environment/why-the-decline-of-newspapers-is-bad-for-the-environment.

43. Michael Barthel et al., "Civic Engagement Strongly Tied to Local News Habits," Pew Research Center, Nov. 3, 2016, www.pewresearch.org/journalism/2016/11/03/civic-engagement-strongly-tied-to-local-news-habits/.

44. Daniel J. Moskowitz, "Local News, Information, and the Nationalization of U.S. Elections," *American Political Science Review* 115, no. 1 (2021): 114–29; see also "Can TV News Keep Politics Local?," Niskanen Center, June 2, 2021, www.niskanencenter.org/can-tv-news-keep-politics-local/.

45. See Barthel et al., "Civic Engagement Strongly Tied to Local News Habits."

8. "Broke" Billionaires

1. U.S. Congress, Senate, Committee on the Judiciary, "Written Testimony of Kimberly A. Naranjo," *Abusing Chapter 11: Corporate Efforts to Side-Step Accountability Through Bankruptcy*, 117th Cong., 2nd sess., 2022, www.whitehouse.senate.gov/imo/media/doc/Naranjo%20Testimony.pdf.

2. Ibid.

3. Ibid.

4. Ibid.

5. Ibid.

6. See Tucker Higgins, "Supreme Court Rejects Johnson & Johnson's Appeal of $2 Billion Penalty in Baby Powder Cancer Case," CNBC, June 1, 2021, www.cnbc.com/2021/06/01/supreme-court-rejects-johnson-johnsons-appeal-of-2-billion-baby-powder-penalty.html.

7. Quoted in Jamie Smyth, "J&J Can Proceed with Controversial Bankruptcy Strategy, Judge Rules," *Financial Times*, Feb. 25, 2022, www.ft.com/content/4bff8f60-8fdd-4e52-aaaf-5ada92d4311d.

8. U.S. Congress, "Written Testimony of Kimberly A. Naranjo."

9. "Breakdown" comes courtesy of Adam J. Levitin, *"Purdue's Poison Pill: The Breakdown of Chapter 11's Checks and Balances," Texas Law Review* 100, no. 6 (2022): 1079–155. "Lawlessness" is Lynn M. LoPucki's characterization in "Chapter 11's Descent into Lawlessness," *American Bankruptcy Law Journal* 96 (2022), available as a working paper at SSRN, papers.ssrn.com/sol3/papers.cfm?abstract_id=3946577.

10. See Bankruptcy, 11 U.S. Code §1101 et seq. (1978).

11. For a thorough but accessible overview of the Chapter 11 process, see U.S. Courts, "Chapter 11—Bankruptcy Basics," accessed July 15, 2022, www.uscourts.gov/services-forms/bankruptcy/bankruptcy-basics/chapter-11-bankruptcy-basics.

12. Levitin, *"Purdue's* Poison Pill," 1079.

13. Michael A. Francus, "Texas Two-Stepping Out of Bankruptcy" (working paper, SSRN, Jan. 30, 2022), 2, papers.ssrn.com/sol3/papers.cfm?abstract_id=4021502.

14. Ibid., 3.

15. Ibid., 7.

16. Ibid.

17. LTL Management LLC, "Equitable Resolution of All Current and Future Talc Claims," accessed July 15, 2022, ltlmanagementinformation.com/.

18. Francus, "Texas Two-Stepping Out of Bankruptcy," 4.

19. For the 1999 to 2020 figures, see Centers for Disease Control and Prevention, "Understanding the Epidemic," June 1, 2021, www.cdc.gov/opioids/basics/epidemic.html. For the 2021 figure, see Centers for Disease Control and Prevention, "Drug Overdose Deaths in the U.S. Top 100,000 Annually," Nov. 17, 2021, www.cdc.gov/nchs/pressroom/nchs_press_releases/2021/20211117.htm. For the economic-costs estimate, see Pew Charitable Trusts, "The High Price of the Opioid Crisis, 2021," Aug. 27, 2021, www.pewtrusts.org/en/research-and-analysis/data-visualizations/2021/the-high-price-of-the-opioid-crisis-2021.

20. Levitin, *"Purdue*'s Poison Pill," 1102, 1103.

21. On the Sacklers' personal fortune, see Katie Warren and Taylor Nicole Rogers, "The Family Behind Oxycontin Pocketed $10.7 Billion from Purdue Pharma. Meet the Sacklers, Who Built Their $13 Billion Fortune off the Controversial Opioid," *Business Insider,* March 23, 2020, www.businessinsider.com/who-are-the-sacklers-wealth-philanthropy-oxycontin-photos-2019-1. The settlement language releasing the Sacklers is from Notice of Filing of Term Sheet with Ad Hoc Committee, *In re* Purdue Pharma, L.P., Case No. 19-23649 (Bankr. S.D.N.Y. 2019), 5, quoted in Levitin, *"Purdue*'s Poison Pill," 1105.

22. Levitin, *"Purdue*'s Poison Pill," 1105–6.

23. Ibid., 1110.

24. See ibid., 1112–13.

25. Definition of "poison pill," see ibid., 1114; states' hostility to public-benefit transformation, 1115; poison pill at Purdue's behest, 1115–16.

26. On how the poison pill ensured the third-party release, see ibid., 1117; on the $6 billion contribution from the Sacklers, see Geoff Mulvihill, "Appeals Court to Consider Paving Way for Purdue Pharma Deal Out of Bankruptcy," PBS, April 29, 2022, www.pbs.org/newshour/nation/appeals-court-to-consider-paving-way-for-purdue-pharma-deal-out-of-bankruptcy; on the Sacklers' refusal to admit wrongdoing, see Brian Mann, "Purdue Pharma, Sacklers Reach $6 Billion Deal with State Attorneys General," NPR, March 3, 2022, www.npr.org/2022/03/03/1084163626/purdue-sacklers-oxycontin-settlement; on the Sacklers' remaining billionaires, see Angel Au-Yeung, "Despite Years of Litigation, the Sackler Family Behind OxyContin Is Still Worth Billions," *Forbes,* Dec. 17, 2020, www.forbes.com/sites/angelauyeung/2020/12/17/despite-years-of-litigation-the-sackler-family-behind-oxycontin-is-still-worth-billions/?sh=643ee9155047. See also Jeremy Hill, et al., "Sacklers to Exit from Complex Purdue Bankruptcy with Billions," Bloomberg, Sept. 1, 2021, www.bloomberg.com/news/features/2021-09-01/sackler-family-exits-bankruptcy-trial-over-purdue-pharma-s-oxycontin ("One expert witness engaged by the State of Washington estimated in a report submitted to the court that the Sackler fortune could increase to $14.6 billion by the time the last installment has been paid").

27. For an exhaustive and highly persuasive argument for why they should be illegal, see Ralph Brubaker, "Bankruptcy Injunctions and Complex Litigation: A Critical Reappraisal of Non-debtor Releases in Chapter 11 Reorganization," *University of Illinois Law Review* 1997, no. 4 (1997): 959–1080. For a more favorable treatment specifically defending the practice in the Purdue context, see Betsy L. Feldman, "Bankruptcy Can Establish True Peace: The Importance of Non-consensual Third-Party Releases in Purdue Pharma's Chapter 11 Case," *Norton Journal of Bankruptcy Law*

and Practice 30, no. 4 (Aug. 2021), www.youngconaway.com/content/uploads/2021
/11/Bankruptcy-Can-Establish-True-Peace-The-Importance-of-Non-Consensual
-Third-Party-Releases-in-Purdue-1.pdf.

28. On forum shopping generally, see Samir Parikh, "Modern Forum Shopping in Bankruptcy," *Connecticut Law Review* 46, no. 1 (2013): 159–226; on J&J's choice of North
Carolina, see Francus, "Texas Two-Stepping Out of Bankruptcy," 9.

29. Levitin, *"Purdue's* Poison Pill," 1128.

30. Ibid., 1129.

31. Ibid., citing Lynn LoPucki and UCLA School of Law, UCLA-LoPucki Bankruptcy
Research Database, Oct. 31, 2021, lopucki.law.ucla.edu/.

32. See David Skeel, "The Populist Backlash in Chapter 11," Brookings Institution,
Jan. 12, 2022, www.brookings.edu/research/the-populist-backlash-in-chapter-11/.

33. Levitin, *"Purdue's* Poison Pill," 1129.

34. See James Nani, "N.Y. Mega Bankruptcies to Get Random Judges After Purdue
Furor," Bloomberg, Nov. 22, 2021, news.bloomberglaw.com/bankruptcy-law/new
-york-chapter-11-mega-cases-to-be-assigned-random-judges.

35. Levitin, *"Purdue's* Poison Pill," 1130.

36. Ibid., 1136–37.

37. See ibid., 1138–39.

38. See ibid., 1141–42.

39. Ibid., 1132.

40. Ibid., 1133 (emphasis added).

41. Ibid., 1134.

42. Ibid., 1146.

43. Quoted in Nani, "N.Y. Mega Bankruptcies to Get Random Judges After Purdue
Furor."

44. See U.S. Congress, "Written Testimony of Kimberly A. Naranjo."

45. See Jamie Smyth, "Talc Ruling a Blow to J&J and the 'Texas Two-Step' Bankruptcy
Jig," *Financial Times*, Feb. 6, 2023, www.ft.com/content/e8eb2715-54cd-4dd0-8ca7
-cc342ef49973.

9. An Unspeakable Problem

1. Paul Ryan, "Saving the American Idea: Rejecting Fear, Envy, and the Politics of Division," Heritage Foundation, Nov. 15, 2011, www.heritage.org/political-process/report
/saving-the-american-idea-rejecting-fear-envy-and-the-politics-division.

2. Dickinson and Madison quoted in Hofstadter, *American Political Tradition and the Men
Who Made It*, 17–18; Jefferson quoted in Sellers, *Market Revolution*, 36.

3. Lasch, *Revolt of the Elites and the Betrayal of Democracy*, 57–58.

4. Quoted in Hofstadter, *American Political Tradition and the Men Who Made It*, 236–37.

5. Lasch, *Revolt of the Elites and the Betrayal of Democracy*, 52.

6. See ibid., 76–79.

7. For an astute and amusing reflection on the invisible-hand systems as (poor) substi-
tutes for the theological concept of divine providence, see Adrian Vermeule, "Liberalism and the Invisible Hand," *American Affairs* 3, no. 1 (Spring 2019): 172–97.

8. Adam Smith, *The Wealth of Nations, Books I–III* (London: Penguin Classics, 1999), 117.

9. Karl Polanyi, *The Great Transformation: The Political and Economic Origins of Our Time* (Boston: Beacon Press, 2001), 147, 258.

10. Ibid., 37.

11. Ibid.

12. On Britain's use of tariffs, export bounties, and the like, see ibid., 143; on Britain's efforts to restrict knowledge and technology transfers, see Lind, *Land of Promise*, 25, 40.

13. See, for example, Shashi Tharoor, "Viewpoint: Britain Must Pay Reparations to India," BBC News, July 22, 2015, www.bbc.com/news/world-asia-india-33618621. Tharoor makes an especially strident polemical argument that includes the oft-repeated myth that the British cut off the thumbs of Bengali weavers to kill off India's once-prized fabric industry. Nevertheless, his basic account of how Britain used coercive measures to turn India into a resource pool and captive market is sound—indeed, a scholarly commonplace.

14. Polanyi, *Great Transformation*, 172.

15. See ibid., 48.

16. John Kenneth Galbraith, *American Capitalism: The Concept of Countervailing Power* (Cambridge, Mass.: Riverside Press, 1952), 13.

17. F. A. Hayek, *The Road to Serfdom: Texts and Documents—the Definitive Edition*, ed. Bruce Caldwell (Chicago: University of Chicago Press, 2007), 86.

18. Friedman, *Capitalism and Freedom*, 14–15.

19. See Lind, *Land of Promise*, 217, citing Walter Adams and James W. Brock, *The Bigness Complex: Industry, Labor, and the Government in the American Economy* (New York: Pantheon Books, 1986), 25–27.

20. See Youssef Cassis, *Big Business: The European Experience in the Twentieth Century* (Oxford: Oxford University Press, 1999), 9–31.

21. See Galbraith, *American Capitalism*, 41, citing National Resources Planning Board, *The Structure of the American Economy. Part I. Basic Characteristics* (Washington, D.C.: U.S. Government Printing Office, 1939).

22. See Galbraith, *American Capitalism*, 44–45 (on the coinage of "oligopoly"), 49 (on its price effect).

23. See ibid., 98; see also Lind, *Land of Promise*, 192–94, on how Thomas Edison served more as a manager and organizer of a research-and-development *system* than the lone-genius progenitor of most of the inventions associated with his name.

24. See Lind, *Land of Promise*, 154.

25. Galbraith, *American Capitalism*, 53.

26. In 1941, James Burnham, an ex-Trotskyist who later became a *National Review* stalwart, argued that the managers had ousted the exhausted and out-of-touch capitalists from the commanding heights of politics and economics. Many developments since then have cast doubt on his theory, revealing the enduring power of the bourgeoisie. See James Burnham, *The Managerial Revolution: What Is Happening in the World* (London: Lume Books, 2021). Burnham, in turn, relied upon a highly influential 1932 study by Adolf Berle and Gardiner Means that showed the extent of the corporatization (and thus managerialization) of American capitalism. See Adolf A.

Berle Jr. and Gardiner C. Means, *The Modern Corporation and Private Property* (New York: Macmillan, 1932).

27. Quoted in Alex N. Press, "REI Wants You to Know They Are Busting a Union on Indigenous Land," *Jacobin*, Feb. 10, 2022, jacobin.com/2022/02/rei-union-busting -podcast-land-acknowledgment-liberals.

28. See Vivek Chibber, *The Class Matrix: Social Theory After the Cultural Turn* (Cambridge, Mass.: Harvard University Press, 2022), 23.

29. For an example of the former, see Michael Novak, *The Spirit of Democratic Capitalism* (Lanham, Md.: Madison Books, 1991); for an example of the latter, see Ernesto Laclau and Chantal Mouffe, *Hegemony and Socialist Strategy: Towards a Radical Democratic Politics* (London: Verso Books, 2014).

30. Chibber, *Class Matrix*, 33.

31. Pope Leo XIII, *Rerum novarum* (Encyclical on Capital and Labor), May 15, 1891, www .vatican.va/content/leo-xiii/en/encyclicals/documents/hf_l-xiii_enc_15051891 _rerum-novarum.html.

32. Karl Marx and Friedrich Engels, *The Communist Manifesto* (London: Penguin Classics, 2002), 233.

33. Ibid.

10. There *Was* an Alternative

1. Tony Judt, *Postwar: A History of Europe Since 1945* (New York: Penguin Press, 2005), 363.

2. "There is no alternative" was, of course, Margaret Thatcher's slogan-cum-argument for neoliberal "reform," first articulated in a 1980 speech. See her "Speech to Conservative Women's Conference: May 21, 1980," Margaret Thatcher Foundation, www .margaretthatcher.org/document/104368.

3. The left-wing blogger Mark Fisher used "capitalist realism" to describe the ideological effort to frame any alternative to neoliberal capitalism as hopelessly romantic. See his *Capitalist Realism: Is There No Alternative?* (Winchester, U.K.: Zero Books, 2009), 8.

4. Judt, *Postwar*, 363.

5. For the New Deal's roots in the Wilson and Hoover administrations (not to mention Churchillian political economy), see Lind, *Land of Promise*, 257–59, 289–90.

6. Chantal Mouffe, *For a Left Populism* (London: Verso Books, 2018), 11. Mouffe rejects— incorrectly, in my view—that it is in their position as economic actors (that is, as workers) that people are most likely to form an *effective* "subject of collective action."

7. Smith, *Wealth of Nations, Books I–III*, 169.

8. Chibber, *Class Matrix*, 55.

9. Ibid., 59.

10. Ibid., 89.

11. Galbraith, *American Capitalism*, 121.

12. For this typology of power—compensatory, conditioned, and condign—see John Kenneth Galbraith, *The Anatomy of Power* (Boston: Houghton Mifflin, 1983).

13. For a glimpse of such brutality in just one industry, railroads, see Ryan Zickgraf,

"Crushing Rail Strikes Is an American Tradition," *Compact*, Dec. 12, 2022, www
.compactmag.com / article / crushing-rail-strikes-is-an-american-tradition.

14. Lind, *Land of Promise*, 353.

15. Ibid., 262 (emphasis added).

16. See Marriner Stoddard Eccles, *Beckoning Frontiers* (New York: Alfred A. Knopf, 1951),
    112, quoted in ibid., 274.

17. See Galbraith, *American Capitalism*, 20–21.

18. Ibid., 21.

19. Ibid., 118.

20. See ibid., 125.

21. See ibid., 121–22.

22. Ibid., 133.

23. Ibid.

24. Ibid., 142.

25. See Chibber, *Class Matrix*, 143.

26. See Lind, *Land of Promise*, 353.

27. Among contemporary economic writers, few have done as much to champion the
    virtues of this tripartite arrangement as Michael Lind. See ibid., 352–53. See also Mi-
    chael Lind, *The New Class War: Saving Democracy from the Managerial Elite* (New York:
    Portfolio, 2020), 136–37.

28. Galbraith, *American Capitalism*, 155.

29. For the concept of political exchange, see Chibber, *Class Matrix*, 108–9. For social
    democracy as a form of "class compromise," see David Harvey, *A Brief History of
    Neoliberalism* (Oxford: Oxford University Press, 2005), 10.

30. F. A. Hayek might well have pioneered that febrile mode of laissez-faire argument,
    according to which all solidaristic and planned economies lead back invariably to
    Stalinism and/or Nazism. See his *Road to Serfdom*, 58–63.

31. Stein, *Pivotal Decade*, 2.

32. Lind, *Land of Promise*, 362.

11. The Neoliberal Counterpunch

1. For "corporate puritanism," see J. G. Ballard, *Super-Cannes: A Novel* (New York: Picador, 2000), 169. With remarkable prescience, Ballard predicted the rise of social distancing: One of the villains tells Paul that as part of her new job at Eden-Olympia,
   his wife "is running a new computer model, tracing the spread of nasal viruses across
   Eden-Olympia. She has a hunch that if people moved their chairs a further eighteen
   inches apart they'd stop the infectious vectors in their tracks." Ibid., 98.

2. Ibid., 343.

3. For the quotation, ibid., 254, 256. For Amazon's childless adult playground-cum-
   office, with its six thousand or so pet dogs, see MacGillis, *Fulfillment*, 31–33.

4. Ballard, *Super-Cannes*, 38.

5. Ibid., 94.

6. Ibid., 79.

7. Harvey, *Brief History of Neoliberalism*, 74.

8. Ibid., 2.

9. See Chris Bell, "'Design Crimes': How a Bench Launched a Homelessness Debate," BBC, May 14, 2018, www.bbc.com/news/blogs-trending-44107320.

10. Hayek, *Road to Serfdom*, 17.

11. Ibid., 68, 69.

12. Ibid., 83.

13. Ibid., 78, 77.

14. Ibid., 86–87.

15. See ibid., 85.

16. Ibid., 86.

17. "Neoliberalism activates the state" is from Wendy Brown, *Undoing the Demos: Neoliberalism's Stealth Revolution* (New York: Zone Books, 2015), 62; "regulate society by the market" is from Michel Foucault, *The Birth of Biopolitics: Lectures at the Collège de France, 1978–1979* (New York: Picador, 2008), 145, quoted in ibid.

18. F. A. Hayek, *The Constitution of Liberty: The Definitive Edition* (Chicago: University of Chicago Press, 2011), 57.

19. Franklin D. Roosevelt, "December 29, 1940: Fireside Chat 16: On the 'Arsenal of Democracy,'" University of Virginia Miller Center, accessed Aug. 10, 2022, millercenter .org/the-presidency/presidential-speeches/december-29-1940-fireside-chat-16 -arsenal-democracy.

20. Mont Pelerin Society, "Statement of Aims," April 1, 1947, www.montpelerin.org /event/429dba23-fc64-4838-aea3-b84701022a4/websitePage:6950c74b-5d9b-41cc-8da1 -3e1991c14ac5.

21. For an amusing roundup of 1950s statements about "liberty versus socialism" that strikingly recall the hyperventilation of today's free-market politicians and media organs, see Galbraith, *American Capitalism*, 3–4.

22. See Stein, *Pivotal Decade*, 33: "The American market was the huge carrot that solidified Cold War alliances"; see also Lind, *Land of Promise*, 369: "During the Cold War and after it, the United States subordinated its preference for a liberal global trading system to the imperatives of keeping its European and Asian allies within the American-led alliance, even if it meant sacrificing the interests of particular American industries. The United States made one-way trade concessions in order to secure the cooperation of other countries needed as allies."

23. Harvey, *Brief History of Neoliberalism*, 12.

24. See the Economic Policy Institute's Productivity-Pay Tracker. EPI, "The Productivity–Pay Gap," updated Oct. 2022, www.epi.org/productivity-pay-gap/.

25. See Harvey, *Brief History of Neoliberalism*, 87–119.

26. Another fine overview of the many downsides of neoliberalism can be found in Robert Kuttner, "Neoliberalism: Political Success, Economic Failure," *American Prospect*, June 24, 2019, prospect.org/economy/neoliberalism-political-success-economic -failure/.

27. See Jodi Kantor and Arya Sundaram, "The Rise of the Worker Productivity Score," *New York Times*, Aug. 14, 2022, www.nytimes.com/interactive/2022/08/14/business /worker-productivity-tracking.html.

28. Brown, *Undoing the Demos*, 30.

29. For an overview of common-good politics in the classical and Christian tradition, see Sohrab Ahmari, *The Unbroken Thread: Discovering the Wisdom of Tradition in an Age of Chaos* (New York: Convergent, 2021), 123–42.

30. A. G. Sertillanges, O.P., *The Foundations of Thomistic Philosophy*, trans. Godfrey Anstruther, O.P. (Providence: Cluny, 2020), 101.

31. See Brown, *Undoing the Demos*, 93–97.

32. See Harvey, *Brief History of Neoliberalism*, 75 ("It is hard to argue that increased flexibility is all bad, particularly in the face of highly restrictive and sclerotic union practices").

33. Hayek, *Road to Serfdom*, 161.

34. Margaret Thatcher, "Interview for *Woman's Own* ('No Such Thing as Society')," Margaret Thatcher Foundation, www.margaretthatcher.org/document/106689.

35. Brown, *Undoing the Demos*, 33, 34.

36. "Let's All Go to the Yard Sale," *Economist*, Sept. 25, 2003, www.economist.com/middle-east-and-africa/2003/09/25/lets-all-go-to-the-yard-sale.

37. Harvey, *Brief History of Neoliberalism*, 7; for an enraging account of the Bremer Orders' deleterious effects on Iraqi agriculture, see Brown, *Undoing the Demos*, 143–50.

38. See *Citizens United v. Federal Election Commission*, 558 U.S. 310 (2010), www.law.cornell.edu/supct/html/08-205.ZO.html.

39. Brown, *Undoing the Demos*, 155, 161.

40. Ballard, *Super-Cannes*, 356.

12. In Defense of Politics

1. Mutatis mutandis, this picture also holds true for much of the rest of the world, a consequence of the neoliberal model's undying impulse to replicate itself everywhere. What began in the Anglo-American sphere in the 1970s didn't stay in the Anglo-American sphere. In the post-Communist world, the same neoliberal model was imposed via "shock therapy" in the immediate aftermath of the Cold War. In western and northern Europe, the older social democratic and Christian-democratic traditions held strong for a bit longer but began finally to give way in the 1990s and first decade of the twenty-first century. In the Global South, the model has often been imposed coercively, from above, as a condition of Western financing and development assistance—if not through the force of Western bombs in the case of Iraq, as we saw in chapter 11.

2. See chap. 3, n. 33.

3. On resignation as the prevailing response among workers to the system today, see Chibber, *Class Matrix*, 106–10.

4. See Ellen E. Schultz, *The Retirement Heist: How Companies Plunder and Profit from the Nest Eggs of American Workers* (New York: Portfolio, 2012).

5. Limited immigration was another helpful factor. Political-exchange capitalism in the United States coincided with a tightening of immigration restrictions following the flood of newcomers in the early twentieth century, when Ellis Island processed more than a million would-be Americans each year. Employers, and the political system as a whole, feel less pressure to make concessions to the asset-less when there is a great

deal of slack in labor markets and a large reserve army of precarious newcomers willing to toil for lower wages. This is why, until relatively recently, America's major labor unions were hostile to the open borders beloved of the *Journal* editorial page, the Cato Institute, and the like. Other supportive factors typically identified by scholars include the proximity of workers living in industrialized urban cores, which allowed them to develop a shared "lifeworld" and to join hands not just as fellow wage laborers but as neighbors and friends, industrial brothers and sisters. Somewhat paradoxically, the sociologist Vivek Chibber adds the relative *disenfranchisement* of workers in an earlier era as a boon to developing countervailing power: Exclusion from the political process, he argues, kindled a righteous anger among the asset-less. That anger, in turn, impelled them to band together not just at the factory but in the democratic public square, to defend their shared material interests. See Chibber, *Class Matrix*, 162–63. Today, almost all of these other preconditions look as unfavorable as the manufacturing question: The Immigration Act of 1965 flung open the gates once more, and since then the United States has accepted more newcomers than any other country. A whole host of factors—most notably urban deindustrialization, suburban sprawl, and the changing nature of labor, away from stable factory work and toward itinerant "gig" work—have conspired to eliminate the American city as a hothouse of proletarian solidarity and militancy. Finally, while workers are no longer formally disenfranchised or excluded from the political process, neoliberalism's tendency toward depoliticization (see chapter 11) has sapped the vitality of all democratic politics, leading the asset-less to conclude that no matter which party or politician they pull for, the neoliberal policy mix is here to stay. Who can blame them?

6. On onshoring pharmaceutical manufacturing, see, for example, "Trump Signs Deal with Company in Effort [to] Shift Drug Manufacturing to U.S.—NYT," Reuters, May 19, 2020, www.reuters.com/article/health-coronavirus-usa-phlow/trump-signs -deal-with-company-in-effort-shift-drug-manufacturing-to-u-s-nyt-idUSL4N2D11E8; on the "buy American" order, see David Lim, "Trump Signs 'Buy American' Executive Order for Essential Drugs," *Politico*, Aug. 6, 2020, www.politico.com/news/2020 /08/06/trump-sign-buy-american-drugs-order-392247.

7. See, for example, Jonathan Moules, "Deglobalisation Tops the Agenda for World Leaders," *Financial Times*, May 23, 2022, www.ft.com/content/7e528bba-e5b6-41f3 -9626-69904618253a; see also Thomas Fazi, "The Deglobalization We Need," *Compact*, Jan. 5, 2023, compactmag.com/article/the-deglobalization-we-need.

8. Gabriel Winant, "Strike Wave," *NLR Sidecar*, Nov. 25, 2021, newleftreview.org/sidecar /posts/strike-wave.

9. See Chris Isidore, "US Unions Are Better Off, but Still a Long Way from Their Former Might," CNN, Sept. 6, 2021, www.cnn.com/2021/09/06/business/unions -strength-labor-day/index.html.

10. Lawrence Mishel, Lynn Rhinehart, and Lane Windham, *Explaining the Erosion of Private-Sector Unions* (Washington, D.C.: Economic Policy Institute, 2020), 5.

11. See ibid., 18.

12. See ibid., 19–20.

13. See ibid.

14. See ibid., 20, citing Kate Bronfenbrenner, *Uneasy Terrain: The Impact of Capital Mobility on Workers, Wages, and Union Organizing,* submission to the U.S. Trade Deficit Review Commission, 2000, ecommons.cornell.edu/bitstream/handle/1813/74284/Bronfenbrenner_24_Uneasy_Terrain_2000.pdf?sequence=1&isAllowed=y.

15. Mishel, Rhinehart, and Windham, *Explaining the Erosion of Private-Sector Unions,* 21.

16. See ibid., 10–14.

17. Quoted in ibid., 24.

18. Ibid., 35.

19. Ibid., 36.

20. Ibid., 39.

21. Thomas A. Kochan and Will Kimball, "Unions, Worker Voice, and Management Practices: Implications for a High-Productivity, High-Wage Economy," *RSF: The Russell Sage Foundation Journal of the Social Sciences* 5, no. 5 (Dec. 2019): 97, quoted in ibid., 44.

22. Quoted in Thomas Fazi, "The Curse of Lifestyle Leftism," *Compact,* June 19, 2022, compactmag.com/article/the-curse-of-lifestyle-leftism.

23. Carolyn B. Maloney, @RepMaloney on Twitter, April 24, 2021, www.twitter.com/RepMaloney/status/1386124259072913408.

Appendix

1. See Christopher Witkowski, "Florida Pledges $700M to Private Equity Including $100M to AXA Secondaries Fund," *Secondaries Investor,* July 9, 2012 ("The system committed $200 million to Warburg Pincus' eleventh fund"), www.secondariesinvestor.com/florida-pledges-700m-private-equity-including-100m-axa-secondaries-fund/.

2. On the Florida settlement, see chap. 6, n. 34.

3. See Sam Sutton, "Kansas Pledges $50M to Warburg," *Private Equity International,* March 18, 2013 ("The Kansas Public Employee Retirement System's board of trustees approved a $50 million commitment to Warburg Pincus Private Equity Fund XI"), www.privateequityinternational.com/kansas-pledges-50m-to-warburg/.

4. See Minnesota State Board of Investment, *Minnesota State Board of Investment Meeting, December 5, 2017: Agenda and Minutes* (St. Paul: Minnesota State Board of Investment, 2017).

5. See Division of Investment, *Investment Reporting Package: August 2012* (Trenton: Division of Investment, 2012), 19.

6. See Comptroller's Bureau of Asset Management, *Monthly Performance Review December 2019: Prepared for the New York City Fire Department Pension Fund* (New York: Office of the New York City Comptroller, 2020), 33.

7. See Sam Sutton, "Ohio Police & Fire Starts New Relationship with Warburg," *Private Equity International,* Jan. 4, 2013 ("The Ohio Police & Fire Pension Fund's board of trustees committed $55 million to Warburg Pincus Private Equity XI at its December meeting"), www.privateequityinternational.com/ohio-police-fire-starts-new-relationship-with-warburg/.

8. On the Ohio/Eastern District of Kentucky settlement, see chap. 6, n. 35.

9. See Christine Williamson, "South Carolina Takes New Look at Partnerships," *Pensions and Investments*, March 4, 2013 ("a $50 million commitment made in September to Warburg Pincus XI"), www.pionline.com/article/20130304/PRINT/303049982/south-carolina-takes-new-look-at-partnerships.

10. See ibid.; see also Christine Williamson, "South Carolina Treasurer Censured by State Retirement Fund Board," *Pensions and Investments*, Feb. 28, 2013, www.pionline.com/article/20130228/ONLINE/130229871/south-carolina-treasurer-censured-by-state-retirement-fund-board.

11. See Hamilton Lane for Washington State Investment Board, *Private Equity Portfolio Overview by Strategy* (Olympia: Washington State Investment Board, 2021), 2–5.

12. See Rob Kozlowski, "Wisconsin Makes Combined $555 Million in Commitments to 8 Funds," *Pensions and Investments*, Aug. 16, 2012 ("Private equity commitments of $100 million each were made to . . . Warburg Pincus Private Equity XI"), www.pionline.com/article/20120816/ONLINE/120819924/wisconsin-makes-combined-555-million-in-commitments-to-8-funds.

13. The table lists only investments in KKR funds that as of this book's publication (in summer 2023) haven't reached the ten-year termination date typical of most private equity, counting forward from the particular retirement system's initial investment date.

14. See chap. 6, n. 41.

15. Barry B. Burr, "Florida State Board Allocates Nearly $1 Billion to Alternatives," *Pensions and Investments*, April 16, 2014 ("[FSBA] committed $25 million each . . . Accel-KKR Structured Capital Partners II"), www.pionline.com/article/20140416/ONLINE/140419885/florida-state-board-allocates-nearly-1-billion-to-alternatives.

16. See John Tozzi, "How Private Equity Keeps States Invested in Medical Billing Practices They've Banned," Bloomberg, July 3, 2018, www.bloomberg.com/news/articles/2018-07-03/how-private-equity-keeps-states-invested-in-medical-billing-practices-they-ve-banned.

17. For Americas XII, see ibid.; for Special Situations II, see Rob Kozlowski, "Maine Public Employees Makes Up to $185 Million in Commitments," *Pensions and Investments*, Dec. 17, 2014 ("The $12.6 billion pension fund committed up to $60 million to KKR Special Situations (Domestic) Fund II, an event-driven and distressed debt fund managed by KKR & Co."), www.pionline.com/article/20141217/ONLINE/141219899/maine-public-employees-makes-up-to-185-million-in-commitments; for Real Estate Partners Americas, see Rob Kozlowski, "MainePERS Commits to Private Equity, Real Estate," *Pensions and Investments*, Nov. 19, 2013 ("the pension fund committed up to $50 million to KKR Real Estate Partners Americas, a real estate fund managed by KKR & Co. that focuses on acquisitions in Europe and the U.S."), www.pionline.com/article/20131119/ONLINE/131119870/mainepers-commits-to-private-equity-real-estate; for Real Estate Partners Americas II, see Jon Peterson, "Maine PERS Invests in KKR's Second Americas Fund," *IPE Real Assets*, March 15, 2016 ("The US pension fund told IPE Real Estate it had committed $50m (€45m) to KKR Real Estate Partners Americas II"), realassets.ipe.com/maine-pers-invests-in-kkrs-second-americas-fund/10012362.article?adredir=1; for Real Estate Partners Europe, see Rob Kozlowski,

"Maine PERS Commits $25 Million to KKR European Real Estate Fund," *Pensions and Investments*, Aug. 9, 2019 ("Maine Public Employees' Retirement System's board approved committing up to $25 million to KKR Real Estate Partners Europe II, said Andrew Sawyer, chief investment officer, in an email"), www.pionline.com/searches -and-hires/maine-pers-commits-25-million-kkr-european-real-estate-fund; for Global Infrastructure II, see Meaghan Offerman, "KKR Closes Second Global Infrastructure Fund at $3.1 Billion Hard Cap," *Pensions and Investments*, July 8, 2015 ("Investors in KKR Global Infrastructure Investors II include the $12.8 billion Maine Public Employees Retirement System, Augusta"); see also Kozlowski, "Maine Public Employees Makes Up to $185 Million in Commitments" ("The pension fund's most recent commitment to a KKR fund was up to $200 million to KKR Global Infrastructure Investors II"); for Global Infrastructure III, see Jon Peterson, "Maine PERS Makes $100M Commitment to KKR Infrastructure Fund," *IPE Real Assets*, April 19, 2022 ("Maine PERS previously backed a KKR infrastructure fund in March 2018 as it made a $100m commitment to the KKR Global Infrastructure Investors III fund"), realassets.ipe .com/news/maine-pers-makes-100m-commitment-to-kkr-infrastructure-fund /10059300.article; for Diversified Core Infrastructure, see Peterson, "Maine PERS Makes $100M Commitment to KKR Infrastructure Fund." Where available, all public news reports were verified against the Maine system's recent annual reports, which reveal (quite typically) that not all commitments are fully funded, while others have expired and/or had matured capital withdrawn. See, for example, MainePERS, *Annual Comprehensive Financial Report: For the Fiscal Year Ended June 30, 2021* (Augusta: State of Maine, 2021), 88–89.

18. See Alicia McElhaney, "New York State Common Retirement Fund Commits to KKR's Asian Fund," *Institutional Investor*, April 27, 2017 ("The Albany, New York–based pension plan disclosed Thursday in its latest monthly transaction report that it committed $275 million to KKR's third Asian private equity fund, possibly increasing its allocation to as much as $300 million"), www.institutionalinvestor.com/article /b1505qpx8dc1q8/new-york-state-common-retirement-fund-commits-to-kkrs-asian -fund.

19. See ibid. ("The Ohio Police & Fire Pension Fund disclosed in February [2017] that it approved a $30 million commitment to the [Asian III] fund.")

20. See Oregon Public Employees Retirement System, *Annual Comprehensive Financial Report: For the Fiscal Year Ended June 30, 2021* (Tigard: State of Oregon, 2021), 93.

21. As of the fourth quarter of 2019, these KKR investments represented the Oregon Investment Council's fourth-largest exposure by firm. See Oregon State Treasury, *Oregon Investment Council, March 11, 2020* (Tigard: State of Oregon, 2020).

22. On the settlement, see chap. 6, n. 33 (the $2.8 million settlement with the Department of Justice in Arizona included alleged false billing by Rural/Metro of Oregon, Inc.).

23. See Jon Peterson, "KKR Raises $1.2Bn for First Real Estate Fund," *IPE Real Assets*, Jan. 14, 2014 ("KKR has attracted $1.2bn (€880m) of third-party institutional capital for its initial real estate commingled fund, KKR Real Estate Partners Americas. . . . Sacramento County Employees Retirement System invested $30m"), realassets.ipe.com /kkr-raises-12bn-for-first-real-estate-fund/59730.article. A quarterly investment report prepared for a 2017 board meeting of SCERS lists the commitment at $35 million,

though it seems that amount was never fully funded. See Townsend for Sacramento County Employees' Retirement System, *Quarterly Investment Performance Report: Real Estate* (Sacramento: Sacramento County Employees' Retirement System, 2017), 16.

24. See U.S. Attorney's Office, Southern District of California, "Five Southern California Ambulance Companies to Pay More Than $11.5 Million to Resolve Kickback Allegations," Department of Justice, May 4, 2015, www.justice.gov/usao-sdca/pr/five -southern-california-ambulance-companies-pay-more-115-million-resolve-kickback.

25. See Hamilton Lane for Washington State Investment Board, *Private Equity Portfolio Overview by Strategy,* 2-1, 2-2, 2-3.

Index

About the Author

SOHRAB AHMARI is a founder and editor of *Compact*. Previously, he spent nearly a decade at News Corp as op-ed editor of the *New York Post* and as a columnist and editor with *The Wall Street Journal*'s opinion pages in New York and London. In addition to those publications, his writing has appeared in *The New York Times, The Washington Post, The New Republic, The Spectator, The Chronicle of Higher Education, The Times Literary Supplement, Commentary, Dissent,* and *The American Conservative,* for which he is a contributing editor.

TWITTER: @SOHRABAHMARI

About the Type

This book was set in Dante, a typeface designed by Giovanni Mardersteig (1892–1977). Conceived as a private type for the Officina Bodoni in Verona, Italy, Dante was originally cut only for hand composition by Charles Malin, the famous Parisian punch cutter, between 1946 and 1952. Its first use was in an edition of Boccaccio's *Trattatello in laude di Dante* that appeared in 1954. The Monotype Corporation's version of Dante followed in 1957. Though modeled on the Aldine type used for Cardinal Pietro Bembo's treatise *De Aetna* in 1495, Dante is a thoroughly modern interpretation of that venerable face.

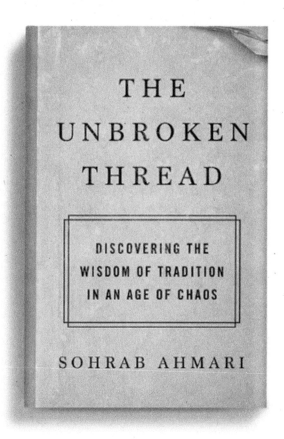